# INTRODUCTION

TO THE

# NEW TESTAMENT

---

*THE COLLECTION OF THE FOUR GOSPELS*

*AND*

*THE GOSPEL OF ST. MATTHEW*

# INTRODUCTION

TO THE

# NEW TESTAMENT

By F. GODET, D.D.

PROFESSOR IN THE FACULTY OF THE INDEPENDENT CHURCH OF NEUCHATEL

---

*THE COLLECTION OF THE FOUR GOSPELS*

*AND*

*THE GOSPEL OF ST. MATTHEW*

Authorised Translation from the French

By WILLIAM AFFLECK, B.D.

---

Wipf & Stock

PUBLISHERS

Eugene, Oregon

Wipf and Stock Publishers
199 West 8th Avenue, Suite 3
Eugene, Oregon 97401

Introduction to the New Testament
The Collection of the Four Gospels and the Gospel of St. Matthew
By Godet, Frederic
ISBN: 1-59244-613-2
Publication date 3/17/2004
Previously published by T&T Clark, 1800

# PREFACE

THE first and strictly preliminary chapter of this second volume will not deal with the composition of our gospels. I shall confine myself to inquire how and when the group, hitherto closed and inseparable, of these four writings was formed, which we shall have thereafter to study separately.

In the first volume of this work I had not to strike out a new path, for studies pursued during a long series of years had led me to convictions very much in accordance with the views generally admitted on the composition, the date, and the chronological order of the thirteen epistles of St. Paul which I regard as authentic.

It is otherwise with the subject treated in this second volume. I find myself obliged by my convictions here to defend a cause that may appear for the moment lost. The hypothesis of the two sources of our synoptic literature—the writing of Mark, for the narrative parts, and the Logia of Matthew for the teachings of Jesus—after having gained a footing in Germany, where it originated (H. Weisse, B. Weiss, H. Holtzmann, A. Ritschl, etc.), has everywhere found eminent adherents, in England (Sanday), in France (Reuss, Sabatier), in Switzerland (Stockmeyer), so that it appears hopeless to seek to oppose another to it.

And yet no one can claim that this theory has succeeded in solving all the difficulties of the problem, nor even that it does not raise new ones, not easy to explain. This is proved by the great differences existing among those that maintain it. What a distance, for example, between the way in which

Reuss and B. Weiss, B. Weiss and Holtzmann present it, and even the Holtzmann of former years, when he wrote his remarkable work on this question, and the Holtzmann of to-day, who renounces the primitive Mark which he made the keystone of his previous explanation, to adopt the use of Matthew by Luke,—a mode which, with Reuss, he formerly absolutely rejected, and which belongs to quite another system. If these circumstances be weighed, the attempt will not perhaps be found too bold to submit this hypothesis to a new examination, and even, if there be cause, to oppose another one to it.

With this object, we shall begin by investigating the manner in which the *collection* of our canonical gospels was formed (Chap. I.). Properly speaking, this subject doubtless belongs to the history of the Canon. But I have preferred to prepare for the special study of the gospels by the study of this more general subject, which will prevent many repetitions in the sequel. Then we shall study *each of our three synoptics* in particular (Chaps. II., III., and IV.). Thereafter we shall finally enter on the very difficult problem of the *relation in origin* between these three writings (Chap. V.). Indeed, I do not think that it is convenient to follow the opposite course, adopted in their Introductions by de Wette, Weiss, and Holtzmann, who begin with the problem of the *relation* between the three writings, before having studied them each by itself. I quite understand that in many cases the text of the one can only be completely appreciated by comparing it with that of the two others. But this comparison, when it is of importance, is not excluded by the method that we propose to follow; and experience appears to me to prove that the explanation of the differences between the texts is in general so much dominated by the idea that one has formed beforehand of the spirit of these three writings, that the conclusion finally turns in a vicious circle. I believe, then, that to grasp well the relation between the three Synoptics, we must begin by studying them each one by itself, so as to enter into their spirit and their peculiar tendency. Only after this will one possess the indispensable elements for judging without partiality of their *relation in origin*, of which Chap. V. will treat.

I speak here only of the Synoptics. This subject is indeed so vast that I find myself compelled to make of these five chapters the *first division* of the second volume, reserving for a *second division* the Fourth Gospel, the Acts of the Apostles, the extra-canonical Gospels and Acts, and the words of Jesus absent from our gospels, called *Agrapha*.

# CONTENTS

## CHAPTER II

### The Gospel according to St. Matthew

# INTRODUCTION TO THE NEW TESTAMENT

## THE FIRST THREE GOSPELS

### CHAPTER I

#### THE FORMATION OF THE COLLECTION OF THE FOUR CANONICAL GOSPELS

IT is well known that Jesus left no writing. So far as we know, He only wrote once during His public career, and that in dust at once dispersed. On the other hand, He is certainly the man about whom most has been written. The philosophic historian, F. de Rougemont, used to observe that of all the personages of antiquity, Jesus is the only one whose history has been related by four contemporary writers.

What has secured Him this distinction? He had not commanded armies and gained brilliant victories; He had not made, in the domain of science, any of those great discoveries that change the face of society. His activity was exerted in the moral domain. He loved, He served, showed God to the world; He saved. According to the beautiful saying of Ullmann, "He possessed in the state of personal life what was to become through Him the life of mankind"; through this essentially spiritual activity He sent up into the old trunk of the human race a new sap that revived all its branches; and humanity, thanks to its indefectible sense of the good, has raised Him by common consent above all that is called man.

However, the four narratives of which we have just spoken are not the only accounts of the life and the work of Jesus that have been current in the Church. The Fathers mention a great number of other writings which dealt with the same subject, and of which several, also bearing the name of *gospels*, already existed in the second century. Men have even spoken with derision in certain popular journals of hundreds of writings of this kind, of which our four canonical gospels were only, as it were, waifs that have accidentally escaped the great shipwreck of oblivion in which all the others have perished.

What can be said without exaggeration is that we still know the titles of some fifty such works, as well as some fragments more or less extensive of several of them. The two most quoted are that called the *Gospel according to the Hebrews* (**Εὐαγγέλιον καθ' Ἑβραίους**), which was related to our Matthew, but with a pronouncedly legal tendency; it was it that was used by the Judæo-Christian communities of Palestine and of all Syria; then that called the *Gospel according to the Egyptians* (**Εὐαγγέλιον κατ' Αἰγυπτίους**), a writing attributing to Jesus strange words conformable to the ascetic tendencies of the people whose name it bears. Others sought, whether by means of oral tradition or by arbitrary inventions, to fill the gaps left in the history of Jesus by our canonical gospels. Such were the *Protevangelium of James*, going back to the history of Mary and of her parents, where there was related in detail her miraculous birth and her purely official marriage to Joseph, all with the object of establishing her perpetual virginity, and making the *brothers of Jesus* the sons of Joseph by a former marriage. This writing was like a *preface* to the accounts of the birth of Jesus in our Gospels of Matthew and Luke, particularly the latter, which it rejoined at the mention of the edict of Augustus (Luke ii. 1); this purely fictitious narrative was prolonged to the murder of the children of Bethlehem (Matt. ii. 16 and foll.), with which it connected the murder of Zacharias, the father of John the Baptist. Then that called the *Gospel of the*

*Infancy*, attributed to the Apostle Thomas: this was an accumulation of imaginary miracles, absolutely grotesque and even immoral in marvel, wrought by the child Jesus between five and twelve years of age; a species of *complement* to the silence kept by the wise sobriety of our gospel accounts on this epoch of the life of the Saviour, which was to remain the secret of God. The *Acts of Pilate*, a writing which, while using our four gospels quite at length, went over the account of the Passion with additions and modifications the object of which was to make of the Roman magistrate a true believer, and to charge the Jewish people with the sole responsibility for the crime. The *Gospel of Nicodemus*, a book in which the *Acts of Pilate* have been introduced as a first part; to the account of the Passion, the principal subject of the book, is attached the mention of the Resurrection and the Ascension, then the account of the descent of Jesus into hell, put into the mouth of the two sons of old Simeon who had received the infant Jesus in the temple, and whom the narrator makes a high priest. Being raised again, they come to relate on the earth the marvels that were wrought in the place of the dead on the arrival of Jesus. This is a *conclusion* of the gospel history, as the *Protevangelium* was to be a preface to it. There has recently been discovered in the tomb of an Egyptian priest the fragment of a gospel called that *of Peter*, where this apostle is supposed himself to relate the Passion and the Resurrection. This is an evident compilation from our four gospels (with a tint of gnosticism), surcharged with certain grotesque details, and tending to aggravate the quality of the Jews, while exculpating Pilate. We see that all these writings rest at bottom, as preambles, complements, or supplements, on the account in our four gospels, without which they could only be as detached leaves hovering in the air. They affect to be well informed of the facts, taking care to indicate the very names of the personages; thus: Joachim and Anne, father and mother of Mary; Dismas and Gestas, the two robbers beside the crucified Jesus, the former the penitent, the second the mocker; Longinus, the soldier who gives the spear-thrust; Procula, the wife of Pilate; Carinus and Leucius, the two sons of Simeon, etc., evidently so many fictitious names.

There must still be mentioned the numerous gospels composed by heretical and gnostic writers under false apostolic names, such as Philip, Matthias, Andrew, Judas Iscariot, etc. Finally, others were published by party chiefs, like those of Cerinthus, Basilides, Marcion (an altered Luke), and the so-called *Gospel of Truth* of the gnostic Valentine. The greatest number of these writings are of the second century, the *Protevangelium* and the *Acts of Pilate* before 150; for they were probably known to Justin.

Here arises a question not without importance. How is it that, from the midst of this confused mass, this species of *diluvium* which we find spread over the soil of the Church in the whole course of the second century, there has been detached, towards the middle of that same century, a group, perfectly distinct and inseparably connected, into which no analogous writing has ever penetrated? In other words, how has this line of demarcation been drawn between our four canonical gospels and all the other writings, known or unknown, of the same kind, which has not given way for a moment down to this hour?

Was it the Church that made this assortment and formed this sacred group by free choice, with the object of opposing it, as an offensive and defensive weapon of war, to the multiplied attacks then directed against her teaching by gnosticism and Montanism? Or must we set aside the supposition of a calm and deliberate choice on the part of the Church, and attribute the privileged position granted to our four gospels to the use that had been made of them from an earlier period in the public readings of the different churches, a use that would be explained in its turn by the remembrance that was preserved of their apostolic origin, in virtue of the delivery that the authors of these books had made of them to the churches for whom they had composed them? These two modes of view have been recently defended in a celebrated discussion between two of the most eminent critics of our time, Ad. Harnack and Th. Zahn.[1]

That is a question of fact that cannot be settled by theoretical considerations. The surest way seems to me to be to begin by consulting *the testimonies* that we still possess of the writers nearest the epoch when the facts in question occurred.

## I

I well know the kind of disdain with which the *reports of the Fathers* on such questions are at present treated. It is none the less true that Irenæus, Clement of Alexandria, and the Fathers that followed them, were not light men desiring to assert themselves, but that they had really received from predecessors, who appeared to them worthy of confidence, what they have transmitted to us. The two, in particular, whom I have just mentioned, and whose testimonies on the matter in hand I am about to report, were, no one will deny, learned men whose life showed their serious character. Without doubt they only wrote towards the end of the second century,—Irenæus about 185, Clement some years later,—and their testimony is thus separated by a whole century from the facts that they report. How many links there would seem to be between those facts and their statements! But, as regards Irenæus, these links are not so numerous as appears at the first glance. In reality they reduce themselves to a single one, Polycarp, the teacher of Irenæus, on the one hand, and on the other the disciple and friend of the Apostle John. For Clement the links are no doubt more numerous, but are not destitute of solidity. Clement affirms that he holds the traditions he records, of the series "of the presbyters that succeeded each other from the beginning (τῶν ἀνέκαθεν πρεσβυτέρων)." The tradition of such men is doubtless not infallible, but ought not to be lightly treated.

[1] Th. Zahn, *Forschungen zur Gesch. des N. T. Kanons* (1881–1893); *Gesch. des N. T. Kanons* (1888–1892). A. Harnack, *Das N. T. um das Jahr* 200 (1889).

The following is the account of Irenæus of the origin of our four canonical gospels (*Hær.* iii. 1. 1), an account from which we can make an inference about the place and epoch when, in the opinion of this Father, these four writings were united:—

Matthew published his gospel writing among the Hebrews in their own language, while Peter and Paul were preaching the gospel at Rome, and founding the Church. After their departure (ἔξοδος, *issue*, doubtless in Peter's case, death; in Paul's, departure from Rome upon his acquittal), Mark, the disciple and secretary of Peter, having committed to writing the things proclaimed by Peter, transmitted them to us. Then Luke, the companion of Paul, recorded in a work the gospel preached by him. Afterwards John, the disciple of the Lord, who had leaned his head on His breast, himself also published the gospel while he dwelt at Ephesus in Asia.

This report, brief, sober, and precise, which affords no room for any legendary amplification, ought to be carefully pondered. It has been severely criticised, and even disdainfully set aside by some, particularly by Reuss (*Hist. Evang.* p. 91), who gives it as an example "of the hypotheses in the air, or the unfounded combinations by which later writers have sought to supply the lack of positive information." Is this singularly haughty judgment of the modern critic regarding the report of the pious and learned bishop of Lyons justified by the facts? The reasons of Reuss are these—"What can we say of this pretended information of Irenæus, declaring that Matthew wrote his gospel at the epoch when Peter and Paul together founded the church of Rome, when we for our part know that neither Peter nor Paul founded the church of Rome, and, above all, that they did not found it together!" To this we reply — 1st, That Irenæus cannot for a single moment have believed that Paul had been the founder of the church of Rome. He knew the Epistle to the Romans, and quotes it frequently, even five times in a single page, and discusses its expressions. Now, in this letter, written to a church assuredly already existing when he wrote to it, Paul twice expressly declares (i. 13 and xv. 22) that he has not yet visited Rome, and is careful to excuse himself. On reading these lines, would a child of ten be dull enough to imagine that Paul could have been the founder of that church, with which he had not yet become personally acquainted? One must necessarily apply the expression in the account of Irenæus, which seems to affirm this, to a time in the life of the apostle following the composition of the Epistle to the Romans (in 59), and even Paul's first arrival at Rome (in 62). Irenæus, then, in speaking of the founding of the Church, meant thereby the immense increase that Christianity underwent in the city of Rome during the captivity of that apostle (from the spring of 62 to the spring of 64). Paul has himself described the powerful effect of his labours at this epoch, in the first chapter of the Epistle to the Philippians. 2nd, It is equally impossible that Irenæus should have attributed to Peter, in any measure whatever, the foundation of the church of Rome. For that it would be necessary that, according to him, this apostle should have sojourned at Rome before the year 59, the date when Paul addressed to that church the Epistle to the Romans. But there is nothing in the work of Irenæus implying adhesion on his part to the legend according to which Peter had visited Rome under the Emperor Claudius in 42. Neither the Acts nor the Epistles of Paul addressed to Rome or from Rome allow the admission of a sojourn of Peter in that city before the time when Paul departed from it after his liberation (spring of year 64). Irenæus knew those writings as well as we, and cannot have judged of them otherwise. The sojourn of Peter at Rome, to which this Father alludes, can only then be that which closely followed the liberation of Paul, and which ended in his martyrdom in July of the year 64. 3rd, But, it will be said, with all that we only reach two successive sojourns, and not a *simultaneous* sojourn of the two apostles at Rome, such as the word *together* indicates. The answer is not difficult; this word, that constitutes the strongest charge which Reuss brings against Irenæus, belongs not at all to the latter, but has been added to the text of Irenæus by Reuss himself. This critic has here committed, involuntarily without a doubt, an inaccuracy, the cause of which is perhaps the recollection of an analogous saying of Dionysius of Corinth about Peter and Paul, where the word ὁμόσε, *together*, is really found. Irenæus guarded himself from committing such an error. It is curious enough to see all the severity of the judge falling upon a fault for which he himself is alone responsible. 4th, Reuss has made another addition to the text he criticises. Irenæus wrote: "When they were founding the Church"; Reuss makes him say, "The church *of Rome*." This addition at the first glance appears just. I believe, however, that it surpasses the thought of Irenæus, and that by this word the *Church* he here meant the Church in general. The apostolic age altogether was in the eyes of the Christians of the second century the era of the foundations. If Irenæus had thought specially of the church of Rome, he would have said: "And that *there* (ἐκεῖ) they were founding the Church," or else, "And that they were founding *this* Church." In the view of Irenæus, so long as the gospel had not been preached at Rome, the universal capital, the Church was not truly founded; it only was so, decisively, by the establishment of Christianity at Rome, first by Paul, then by Peter.

Thus the blunders charged by Reuss against Irenæus disappear, and one is tempted to smile while reading this expression of self-satisfaction: "We for *our* part know," with which the critic opposes his modern science to the alleged ignorance of the old Church Father.

The explanation we have given of the words of Irenæus, as referring to the latest time of the activity of the two apostles, of which their work at Rome was the culmination, agrees very naturally with the first words of this Father's account of the Gospel of Mark: *After their departure* (*Μετὰ δὲ τὴν τούτων ἔξοδον*), that is to say, as regards Peter, by his martyrdom; as regards Paul, by his removal from Rome.

It is important to remark that by these words Irenæus places the composition of Mark's writing after the death of Peter, and thus expressly denies any participation by the apostle in that act. The account of this Father is thus entirely exempt from the tendency manifested in the subsequent traditions to place this writing under the guarantee and authority of the apostle.

One may observe an analogous difference between the statement of Irenæus on the composition of Luke and the assertions of some of his successors. With the latter there prevails the tendency to identify what Paul calls *his gospel*, in an entirely spiritual sense, with the writing of Luke; while, according to Irenæus, the oral gospel teaching of Paul was quite simply recorded in Luke's writing. Here, again, one observes the perfect sobriety of the primitive tradition formulated by this Father.

The account by Irenæus of the fourth gospel has given rise to more numerous and graver objections. According to this Father, and a host of other concordant accounts, the Apostle John ended his life and composed his gospel in Asia Minor. But certain facts are alleged that seem to contradict this very generally diffused tradition. Thus, first, Jülicher (*Einl. in d. N. T.* § 31) alleges that Muratori's Fragment is against it; for mention is made in that document of a society of condisciples (*condiscipuli*) in the midst of which the apostle had written his gospel; but these condisciples could only be the other apostles, and the apostles dwelt at Jerusalem, not at Ephesus. The nullity of this argument is easy to demonstrate. It results from chap. xxi. of the Acts, that from the year 59 the apostles had quitted Jerusalem, since Paul, who in 51 had conferred with them, no longer meets with a single one of them on his arrival there in 59, and only confers with James, and the elders over whom James presides. If, then, the condisciples, who were found with John when he wrote his gospel, were the apostles, and the apostles residing at Jerusalem, this act must have taken place before the year 59. But who will attempt to place the composition of John before the year 59? Not Jülicher, who dates it from 100 to 125. The condisciples, of whom the Fragment speaks, who could not be sought at Jerusalem, are, on the other hand, very easily found in Asia Minor.

There was there the evangelist (or apostle) Philip; also, according to the Fragment itself, the Apostle Andrew, and, by the account of Papias, two personal disciples of Jesus, Aristion and the presbyter John, who might well be called *condisciples* of the apostle. In fine, Irenæus (*Hær.* ii. 22. 5) speaks of the presbyters "who have known in Asia not only John, but also *other apostles.*" Irenæus related again (comp. Eus. *H. E.* v. 24. 16) that Anicetus, the bishop of Rome, when Polycarp visited him in that capital, was not able to convince the latter, who "had celebrated Easter with John, the disciple of the Lord, and *the other apostles.*" This, it seems to me, suffices to prove that the author of the Fragment of Muratori could without improbability speak of *condisciples* of John in Asia Minor. If, in the Fragment, Ephesus is not named as the place of composition, it is because that was unnecessary, the fact being universally notorious not only in the East, but even in the West, as is proved by the details of the meeting of Anicetus and Polycarp at Rome.

A second fact that Jülicher, after Keim, Holtzmann, and others, opposes to the sojourn of John in Asia, is the assertion attributed to Papias by the Greek monk, George Hamartôlos (ninth century), in his Chronicle: that John, as well as his brother James, was killed by Jews; which can only, it is said, have taken place at Jerusalem. According to this, John would have lived in Palestine till his death, and his sojourn in Asia Minor would be a mere fable. To judge this question safely, one must peruse the whole passage of the Greek monk. It was published for the first time in 1862, by Nolte, in the *Theol. Quartalschrift.* This is it *in extenso*: "After Domitian, Nerva reigned during a year; having recalled John from the isle, he freed him, permitting him to dwell at Ephesus (ἀπέλυσεν οἰκεῖν ἐν Ἐφέσῳ). John, alone of the twelve apostles, was still alive. Having composed his gospel, he was judged worthy of martyrdom; for Papias, the bishop of Hierapolis, who was witness of the fact (αὐτόπτης τούτου γενόμενος), says, in the second book of his Expositions of the Lord's Discourses, that he was killed by Jews (ὅτι ὑπὸ Ἰουδαίων ἀνῃρέθη), thus fulfilling, like his brother, the prophecy that Christ had spoken about him. . . . For the Lord had said to them: 'You shall drink the cup that I drink, . . . and shall be baptized with the baptism wherewith I am baptized' (Matt. xx. 22, 23; Mark x. 38, 39). And in effect, it is impossible that God should lie, and so the learned Origen, in his exposition of Matthew, also affirms that John underwent martyrdom, stating that he had learned it of the successors of the apostles. In fine, Eusebius says, in his *Church History*: 'Thomas occupied Parthia; John, Asia; and having lived there, died at Ephesus.'"

The opponents of the sojourn of John in Asia have been eager to find in this passage a proof in favour of their view. Keim in particular has uttered this triumphant cry: "A testimony recently discovered that puts an end to all illusions!" In fact, if John was put to death by Jews, how could that murder have taken place elsewhere than in Palestine? We must therefore erase from history the tradition of the sojourn and death of John in Asia Minor. But is it forgotten that there were also Jews in Asia Minor, that at Ephesus they had formerly put forward their fellow-countryman, Alexander, in the disturbance raised against Paul, to accuse him before the assembly of the people (Acts xix. 33); that they were *Jews of Asia* who put Paul's life in danger at Jerusalem (Acts xxi. 27)? Is the active part forgotten that the Jews of *Smyrna* played in the martyrdom of Polycarp, and that they were the most eager to collect faggots, and did their utmost to prevent the body of the martyr from being given to his friends (Eus. *H. E.* iv. 15. 41)? There would thus be no impossibility in the Apostle John having also suffered death at the hands of the numerous Jews inhabiting Asia Minor. However, the authenticity of this alleged notice of Papias was, the moment it appeared, generally called in question. It was supposed that Hamartôlos had had in his hands a false or interpolated Papias, or that he had applied to John what was only true of his brother James (Acts xii. 2). For the tradition of Asia

Minor was unanimous in affirming his long life, and peaceable and natural death, at Ephesus, in accordance with the expression of Jerome affirming that John died *overcome by age* (*senio confectus*). However, a new discovery, recently made, hardly leaves room to doubt the correctness of the quotation of Papias by Hamartôlos. C. D. de Boor lately published, in the *Texte und Untersuchungen* of Gebhardt and Harnack (1888), a passage of a History of Christianity, written in 430, by a presbyter of Asia Minor, Philip of Sidé, a passage which contains this same quotation from Papias. He says: "Papias relates, in the second book of his Explanation of the Logia, that John, the theologian, and James, his brother, were put to death by Jews (ὑπὸ Ἰουδαίων ἀνῃρέθησαν)." After this twofold quotation one can hardly call in question that the fact mentioned was found in the work of Papias, and one wonders whether it is possible to set aside purely and simply a testimony so ancient. It is no doubt to be observed that, as de Boor himself remarks, in many manuscripts of the Chronicle of Hamartôlos those words: "John was judged worthy of martyrdom," are replaced by these: "And having composed his gospel, he died in peace." But is not this a copier's correction, due to the generally received opinion about the end of the apostle? Admitting, then, that the Greek monk has truly quoted a passage of Papias, that attributed the death of John to the hatred of the Jews, what results from this as regards the place where the deed occurred? Hamartôlos says: John was permitted by the successor of Domitian to quit *the island*; what island? assuredly, the isle of Patmos. He adds, that he was allowed to dwell at *Ephesus*. It was thus the prohibition to inhabit that city that was now revoked. Besides, if Papias, bishop of Hierapolis, had been an eye-witness of the fact, as Hamartôlos says, doubtless after the statement of Papias himself, the fact must have occurred in Asia; and this is so much his opinion that he ends that passage by recalling these words of Eusebius: "Thomas occupied Parthia, and John, Asia; having lived there, he died at Ephesus." What will certainly remain as one of the most incredible effronteries of present criticism is to have been able to essay to derive from this passage the proof that John ended his life in Palestine, and not in Asia Minor. Does not the mention of *the isle,* of the *presence* of Papias, in fine, of the very names of *Ephesus* and *Asia,* suffice to show that it is a question of Asia Minor, not of Palestine? The use made by the above-named critics of the words *by Jews,* to set aside all these indications, belongs to the method, *Hoc volo, sic jubeo.* In general, there can be no question, it seems to me, of a *violent* death of the Apostle John, either in Asia Minor, as Papias must have reported, or at Jerusalem, as the above-named critics would have it. In the first case, it would be impossible that neither Irenæus, nor Polycrates (in his letter to Victor), nor Eusebius, who relates with so much detail the martyrdom of Polycarp, though a much less important man than the Apostle John, should have made any mention of that tragic event. In the second case, one could still less understand how such an event, especially if it happened before the year 64, as Jülicher thinks, should be completely passed over in silence in the Book of the Acts, where the martyrdom of James, the brother of John, is related (chap. xii.); and then in Eusebius, who reproduces with so much detail the account of the death of James, the brother of Jesus, and the martyrdom of Simeon, his cousin, successor of James in the management of the Judæo-Christian Church, who was crucified in the year 107, at the age of 120 years. How should Eusebius, who takes pains to give most precise details of the martyrdom, occurring in Palestine, of these two but secondary personages (*H. E.* ii. 23 and iii. 32), not have given a line to mention the martyrdom of the beloved disciple, if it had really taken place on the same scene? Grimm, in Hilgenfeld's *Zeitschrift,* 1875, No. 2, has rightly made prominent the words addressed by Jesus to John, in which He seems to promise him that he should not die before His coming. However those words may be understood, such a promise, opposed as it is to the immediately preceding announcement of the violent death of Peter, implies the assurance, or even the fact, of the Apostle John's exceptional longevity.

But how, in that case, are we to explain the statement of Papias? That is not so difficult as at the first glance it appears. The book of that Father was an explanation of the *discourses* or *sayings of the Lord.* It was doubtless with this object that he related the frightful death of Judas, in order to explain the malediction pronounced against him; the pardon granted to the adulterous woman, on account of some promise of grace, or even of the declaration of Jesus (John viii. 15); the cup of poison drunk with impunity by Barsabas, in confirmation of Mark xvi. 18; the picture of the vines and clusters of the millennial reign, in explanation of the *new wine* that Jesus promised His disciples to drink with them in the heavenly kingdom. But there was a saying of the Lord which they did not succeed in explaining: the announcement made to the two sons of Zebedee, of a death like that of Jesus (Mark x. 39; Matt. xx. 23). "But," says Hamartôlos, "God cannot lie." There was thus needed a fact fitted to justify the saying of Jesus. In view of that saying, Papias must have been seriously embarrassed, not as regards James, but as regards John. It thus appears to me probable that he eagerly availed himself of some casualty that befell John, caused by Jews, which had hastened the end of the old apostle, in order to see in it the fulfilment of the prophecy of Jesus, which he had so much difficulty in justifying. That is, it seems to me, about the opinion of Hilgenfeld (p. 259 of the number of his journal which we have just quoted). Origen called the exile of John in Patmos a *martyrdom.* Papias uses the same exaggeration. He was perhaps followed in this by the Persian writer, Apraates (fourth century), who reckons as apostle-martyrs, Stephen, Peter, Paul, James, *and John* (Homél. 21).

In whatever manner the life of John ended, the critics who deny his final sojourn in Asia Minor are bound to explain the unanimous opinion that existed in the churches of that country that it was at Ephesus that John died, in the time of Trajan (98–117), in extreme old age. Keim had sought to explain this very general conviction by a confusion that he attributed to Irenæus. As Papias, in the preface of his book, spoke of a person named John who had been a personal disciple of the Lord, Irenæus had imagined that this John, of whom Polycarp had often spoken to him, was the apostle of the same name. It would thus be to this private Christian, of the same name as the apostle, that we should have to apply all the features related by Irenæus as referring to this latter, who had never appeared in Asia. But how would it be possible to explain a tradition so unanimous in the second century, as that of the presence and activity of the Apostle John in Asia Minor, by the misunderstanding of this Father who wrote in Gaul, about 185, or according to Keim himself, about 190? As far back as 150, say, thirty years at least before Irenæus, how should Justin, who came from Asia Minor and had himself sojourned at Ephesus, have spoken at Rome of the Apocalypse as a writing composed by the Apostle John,[1] if he had not there heard that the apostle had lived in the midst of the churches of Asia, and presided over their progress (comp. Apoc. i.–iii.). In 180 the anti-Montanist writer, Apollonius, a man versed in the affairs of the province of Asia, wrote that John raised a dead man *at Ephesus.* He cannot have learned that from Irenæus, who wrote in Gaul from five to ten years later. The touching narrative is known about the young man saved by John from a life of brigandage. Clement of Alexandria, who has preserved it for us in his treatise, *Quis dives salvus?* c. 42, begins it in these terms: "Hear what is related, a true history and not a tale. When, after the death of the tyrant, John had returned from Patmos to Ephesus, he visited the surrounding regions to establish bishops and organise the churches." This narrative of Clement has no point of attachment in Irenæus. Clement had received

[1] *Dial.* c. 81: "A man named John, one of the apostles of the Christ, in the revelation that was granted him, predicted that." . . .

it at Alexandria, like the others he reports, by the testimony of the old presbyters. Among them was Pantænus, his master and predecessor in the management of the catechetical school of that city, who consequently admitted in Egypt, as well as Irenæus in Gaul, the final sojourn of John in Asia Minor.

Jülicher must have regarded Keim's explanation as very inadmissible, as he has tried to substitute for it another, if possible, still more precarious. According to him, the confusion of the apostle with the presbyter John had been the deed not of Irenæus, but of Polycarp. He thus sets forth this mode of view (*Einleit.* § 31): "We have knowledge of one John, surnamed *the presbyter*, a disciple of the Lord and an eye-witness, who lived in Asia Minor and attained an extraordinarily advanced age, so that Papias and Polycarp were yet able to communicate with him. As the title and the circumstances of the life of this John are remarkably like those of the apostle, as church tradition describes him to us, the suspicion naturally arises that the son of Zebedee was substituted by a change of rôle for his namesake, and that entirely *bonâ fide*." But, with the exception of his longevity, what do we know of the life of this John, except it be that he had the title of *presbyter* ("elder"), and that he passed for having been a personal disciple of the Lord, which is very different from having been one of the Twelve? Besides, he is nowhere spoken of but in the well-known passage of Papias, and does not appear to have played any leading part. When Polycrates, the eighth bishop of Ephesus, who had had as predecessors seven of his relations, in his official letter written in the name of the churches of Asia (Eus. iii. 31) to Victor, bishop of Rome, speaks of the *great stars* (μεγάλα στοιχεῖα) that have rendered illustrious the church of Asia, and there repose, awaiting the resurrection, namely, Philip, one of the Twelve, interred at Hierapolis, and moreover John, who rested his head on the Saviour's breast, who was in Asia like a supreme priest bearing the tiara (of holiness and authority), and who was witness and doctor (in his gospel and his epistle), could so glorious a memorial possibly refer to a mere disciple of Jesus whom Papias places on equality with Aristion, a man so far from remarkable that Polycrates does not even name him among the secondary personages thereafter mentioned by him, namely, Polycarp of Smyrna, Thraséas of Eumenia, Sagaris of Laodicea, Papirius and Melito of Sardis?

Does not it offend all the laws of probability to admit the confounding of a mere disciple with the Apostle John? Jerome relates that the brethren carried the old apostle into the assemblies of the church to hear his last exhortations; and the old man who had thus let himself be honoured as the Apostle John had only in reality been that obscure namesake, who carefully kept silence on his real condition! Irenæus relates (Eus. iii. 28 and iv. 14), after the narrative of Polycarp and *other persons* (οἱ ἀκηκοότες αὐτοῦ), that John, repairing one day to the bath at Ephesus, learned that Cerinthus was in the house, and that he at once retired, crying that he feared the house might fall. Without meaning to guarantee the authenticity of this saying attributed to the apostle, one must suppose that some fact is at the bottom of such an account as this. But it cannot have been that those who accompanied the pretended apostle should not have conversed with him, and that in addressing him they had not let him see for whom they were taking him; and he would have left them in their error! In any case, it would not be to him that the *bonâ fide* of Jülicher could be applied. Mystification would here be added to misunderstanding. Even if the contempt of Polycrates, who, as Jülicher acknowledges, personally communicated with this other John, had been able to resist a relation ever so little prolonged with this strange Sosia, there was one there who must necessarily have dispelled this confusion. This was Philip, dwelling at Hierapolis, where Papias was bishop. Whether by this Philip, of whom Papias and Polycrates speak, we are to understand the apostle of that name, the colleague of John, or Philip the deacon and evangelist, a respected member of the primitive community of Jerusalem (Acts vi. 5 and xxi. 8), he behoved personally to know the true John, and to dispel very quickly the error into which he saw Polycrates fall, and with him *all the churches of Asia* (αἱ κατὰ τὴν Ἀσίαν ἐκκλησίαι πᾶσαι), who testified of the relation that Polycarp had sustained "with John and other apostles" (Eus. iv. 14).

But what is stronger is that Papias, whose account has been employed to imply this confusion, himself furnishes the means to establish its falsity. To prove this it is necessary here to reproduce the much-discussed passage of that Father, preserved to us by Eusebius (iii. 39). Papias, then, was explaining, in the preface of his book, the means he made use of to compose it, and to give a sound explanation of the discourses of the Lord. These means were of three kinds.

1st, The things he himself had formerly heard from the mouth of the elders (παρὰ τῶν πρεσβυτέρων)—

> I shall not omit to join to my explanations (συγκατατάξαι ταῖς ἑρμηνείαις) all the things that formerly I surely learned from the mouth of the elders, and which I have exactly retained.

These elders could not be, in the thought of Papias, the official elders of the churches of Asia, for those Christians, simple believers, had not been eye-witnesses of the facts of the ministry of Jesus that he wished to add to his explanations to illustrate them. The elders designate in general, in the usage of the Fathers, the eminent Christians of the preceding generation; for Irenæus, they are Polycarp, Papias, etc.; for these last, born about the year 70, they are not only the apostles, but also all the other eye-witnesses of the facts and deeds of Jesus. The sequel will show that, in the thought of Papias, the apostles are certainly comprised in them. Papias, then, here attributes to himself personal relations (παρά) with several of those Christians of the first generation, but places them at a distance pretty remote by the word τότε, *then*, which suggests the time of his youth.[1]

[1] Eusebius wrongly draws from this passage the opposite conclusion, namely, that Papias declares that he had not himself spoken with the apostles. This mistake appears intentional, and we can understand the reason for it.

2nd, The second means indicated by Papias is the information that he occasionally collected from the mouth of those who visited Hierapolis later, and who, having accompanied (*εἰ δέ που καὶ παρακολουθηκώς τις*) the elders (the apostles and the eye-witnesses), had had occasion to converse more frequently than he with them.

> But if at times there came to me one of those who had accompanied the elders, I inquired of the sayings of the elders, of what had been said (τί εἶπεν) by Andrew or Peter or Philip or Thomas or James or John or Matthew, or any other of the disciples of the Lord.

It seems to me evident, despite the different attempts at explanation that have been advanced, that this list is simply intended to enumerate the names of those elders whose sayings Papias sought indirectly to collect, and that the words "what was said" are the explicative paraphrase of *τοὺς λόγους* (*the words*), the object of *ἀνέκρινον* (*I inquired*): "I inquired of the sayings, . . . I mean to say, of what Andrew said," etc. The following names are thus those of those elders whose accounts Papias was seeking to collect, that is to say, of a certain number of the Twelve.

The name of John appears in this list as that of an apostle, as well as those of all the other personages mentioned. If it is joined to that of Matthew, it is doubtless because they are both the authors of a gospel. "Papias," says Eusebius, "clearly thereby designates *the evangelist*."[1]

3rd, The last means that Papias declares he made use of is, according to his expression—

> *And of what* Aristion and John the presbyter *say* (ἃ λέγουσιν).

Several traits distinguish this John from the preceding

[1] The words of Eusebius are as follows: "Whereby it may be seen that he (Papias) twice reckons the name of John, the first time joining it to those of Peter, James, Matthew, and other apostles, thereby clearly indicating the evangelist. As regards *the other* John (τὸν δ' ἕτερον Ἰωάννην), he puts him beyond the number of the apostles, placing Aristion before him and calling him presbyter."

one—first, his union with Aristion, who was not one of the Twelve, but only an old disciple of Jesus;[1] then the expression "*what they say,*" a verb in the present evidently opposed to the verb in the past, εἶπεν, *said*, that Papias has just employed in speaking of Andrew or Peter, etc.; in fine, the epithet *disciple of the Lord*, which would be idle if it concerned the same man who had just been ranked among the apostles. The opposition of *say* to *said* proves that Aristion and John were living when Papias wrote his preface, while the apostles previously named were no more (John and Philip included). Let us observe that Eusebius here commits a second error in making Papias say that he *himself* communicated with those two still living men. Papias simply says that he also collected their statements by means of brethren who came to visit him. The words "*what they say,*" just like the preceding ones, depend on the verb "*I inquired . . .* (ἀνέκρινον)." The only difference is that, as regards Aristion and the presbyter, he inquired of their words as proceeding from people who are still speaking; while, as regards the apostles whom he has just mentioned, he collected their words as those of people who have ceased to speak.

If anything clearly appears from this passage, it is that in the eyes of Papias, whatever Riggenbach and Zahn may have found to say about it, John the presbyter is a different personage from John the apostle,—as different from him as a companion of Aristion differs from a colleague of Andrew and Peter, or as a dead man differs from a living one. And it is not only Papias who judges in this way; Eusebius is on this point perfectly in agreement with his predecessor, whose words he comments on. It is a singular fact that while our modern critics, Keim, Holtzmann, Jülicher, exert themselves to identify those two Johns of whom Papias spoke, in order to get rid of the presence of the apostle of that name in

[1] The title Πρεσβύτερος, given to this John, denotes for the men of the generation of Papias and Irenæus, *all the believers of the first generation, apostles or not apostles.* Aristion in this sense is *presbyter*, as well as John; only John is more specially so designated, in order to distinguish him from the other John, who was *more and better* than that.

Asia, and at the same time of the authenticity of his gospel, Eusebius, on the contrary, takes great care to distinguish them in order to obtain quite another result, namely, a non-apostolic John, to whose account he might put the Apocalypse, because that book did not please him. After Dionysius of Alexandria, who equally disliked the Apocalypse, two tombs of John were shown at Ephesus, whereby he claimed also to prove that there had lived in that city another John than the apostle of that name. Thus each one identifies or distinguishes according to his particular interest.

To conclude, it appears to me that the true word on this question of the sojourn of John in Asia Minor has been uttered by Weizsaecker (*Apost. Zeitalt.* p. 499), when he said of the presbyter John: "This nail is too weak to hang on it all the Johannic tradition." For my part, I am convinced that when the anti-Johannic fever that reigns meanwhile in the school claiming exclusively the title *critical* shall have subsided, it will be difficult to understand that it was possible to resort to expedients so improbable as those we have just refuted.

Let us add, in fine, that the Dutch professor, Scholten, has proposed another way of explaining the tradition of the sojourn of John in Asia. This error was due, according to him, to the fact that to that apostle was attributed the composition of the Apocalypse, which could only have taken place in Asia. Mangold has justly replied that it was, on the contrary, the certainty of the sojourn of John in Asia that alone could have led the churches of that country to attribute that book to the Apostle John.[1] Holtzmann (*Einl.* p. 435) proposes this alternative: "Either the Apostle John is the author of the Apocalypse, or he never was at Ephesus; for if present in Asia, no other could have taken, in presence of the churches of that country, the position assumed by the author of that writing." But one may without difficulty turn the dilemma and say: Either the John who names himself as the author of the Apocalypse is really the apostle,

[1] Bleek's *Einl.* 3rd ed., edited by Mangold, pp. 167, 168.

and in that case his sojourn in Asia is certain, or else a forger, and in that case he would not have committed the awkward blunder to found his fiction on a fact that had never occurred. This is not the time to examine which of these alternatives is the true one. But in any case one can evidently derive no solid argument from the book of the Apocalypse against the sojourn of John at Ephesus.

There has further been alleged the silence of the Epistles to the Colossians and Ephesians regarding the presence of John at Ephesus. But, if these letters are authentic, they are anterior to that sojourn. The objection is made of the absence of any mention of John in the Epistle of Ignatius to the Ephesians, while he speaks to them of Paul. But Ignatius (chap. xi.) calls the Ephesians Christians who have *always been* (πάντοτε συνῆσαν), or who have *always walked, in harmony* (πάντοτε συνῄνεσαν), with *the apostles* (τοῖς ἀποστόλοις). This plural supposes others than Paul, and if he speaks specially of Paul in the following chapter, it is, as he himself says, because of the analogy presented by the lot of the apostle with his own. "You serve as a place of passage (πάροδός ἐστε) to those who are taken up to God"; that is to say, I am passing through among you on the way to martyrdom, as Paul did (comp. Acts xx. 17, 22–24). Now John did not go on the way of martyrdom.

After this long examination we can therefore revert to the clear and concise account of Irenæus as to a testimony worthy of all respect, and that so much the more that it is confirmed by another which, despite some differences, agrees with his on essential points, that of Clement of Alexandria (Eus. vi. 14. 5–7).

The *account of Clement* evidently proceeds from a different source from that of Irenæus. At Alexandria, Clement had collected the tradition of the old presbyters of that church; moreover, he affirms in the *Stromata* that in the course of his travels he had consulted distinguished members of several churches. The following is the account he gave of the composition of the gospels, as Eusebius mentions it (vi. 14), and which he derives from the *Hypotyposes*, a work written about the year 200. "In the same book," says Eusebius, "Clement sets forth the tradition of the presbyters who succeeded each other from the beginning." This account contains what follows on the order of the gospels—

Those two gospels that contain the genealogies were written before the others. As regards Mark, the thing occurred thus: As Peter was preaching the word at Rome, and animated by the Spirit was setting forth the gospel, his hearers, who were very numerous, prayed Mark, who had accompanied him from a distance and who remembered the things spoken by him, to put them in writing, and after he had composed the gospel, to deliver it to those who asked it of him.[1] And this becoming known to Peter, he neither sought to hinder nor to encourage him. John, the last, having ascertained that the bodily things (τὰ σωματικά) had been published in the gospels, urged by the notables and impelled by the Spirit, composed a spiritual gospel (πνευματικὸν εὐαγγέλιον).

One quite feels that this account is less simple than that of Irenæus; it has doubtless passed through a greater number of mouths. It differs from it especially in two points: (1) Matthew and Luke were composed before Mark, while the order in Irenæus is: Matthew, Mark, Luke; (2) after Clement, Mark had been composed during the life and under the eye of the Apostle Peter, who had not opposed its publication; Irenæus, on the contrary, says clearly: "*After the departure* (the death) of Peter." As regards John, there is complete agreement. Clement, it is true, does not mention Ephesus in this passage as the place of composition, but he does so elsewhere, as in the passage of the *Quis dives salvus?* that we have quoted above: "After the tyrant was dead, John returned from Patmos *to Ephesus*." The two writers equally agree in placing the composition of John after that of the other three. Only Clement here adds this important trait, that John composed, after having taken knowledge of the

[1] It is often translated: "And after he had composed it he delivered it to them." But in this interpretation the sequel no longer has a meaning. It seems to me, then, that we must make the two infinitives ἀναγράψαι and μεταδοῦναι depend on the verb παρακαλέσαι ("they prayed him to edit . . . and to transmit to them").

writings of his predecessors, to complement them on an essential point. Reuss, who previously had keenly opposed this view, now recognises the justice of it. He says himself: "In my previous works I believed I could maintain the independence of the fourth gospel with regard to the synoptic texts; I have had to rank myself with the contrary opinion" (*La Bible, Théologie johannique*, p. 76).

According to Clement, it was not only John who was struck by the lack presented by the Synoptics. The notables of his church, and of the neighbouring churches, requested him to edit the discourses of Jesus that they were accustomed to hear from his mouth, and which they did not find in the Synoptics, and John, under the impulse of the Spirit, feeling that he owed to the whole Church those treasures of which he alone had preserved the deposit, put them in writing. Clement calls these special contents of the fourth gospel *the spiritual things* (τὰ πνευματικά), in opposition to the *corporeal* things (τὰ σωματικά), the external facts of the life of Jesus that the first three had related in detail, and which, for this reason, John thought he could omit. Hence this name, *spiritual gospel*, that he specially gives it. Jülicher (p. 254) thinks he can render this term by *Idealevangelium*, and thus arrives at the conclusion that the author of such a writing might well himself also be only a pneumatic disciple, "an ideal apostle," who invented the beloved disciple to attribute his gospel to him, also doubtless *bonâ fide*. The *Apostle* John had disappeared to give place to the presbyter, and lo! now the presbyter himself is nought but a shadow of a presbyter, and must give place to an ideal author. Can such a method be considered serious? The thought of Clement is entirely simple and very realistic. In his eyes the lofty contents of the words of Jesus in the fourth gospel, while pneumatic, are not less *real* than all the other facts of His life that he also recounts, and to which these discourses are always in close relation. Clement did not for a moment think to relegate what he calls "*the spiritual things*" pronounced by Christ into the nebulous region of the ideal.

## II

But some one will perhaps ask whether, between the time of the composition of the Synoptics and the last ten years of the first century, there is *a sufficient interval* to allow the three Synoptics to come from the East to the West as far as Asia Minor, as if they had made an appointment at Ephesus to meet under the eyes of John and receive there from him at once their copestone and their final consecration. This question causes us to ascend higher, to the publication and dissemination of our gospels. We ought not to think that these writings were published and diffused by the ordinary processes of the book trade. They were not originally entrusted to a bookseller to be offered to purchasers. Their authors composed them in view and, as is positively said of two of them, at the request of the churches they were labouring to edify. These writings being finished, they delivered them to the rulers of those churches that they knew, that knew them personally, and who had to provide for their being read in the assemblies for worship. Irenæus designates this delivering, with reference to Mark, by the term *παραδέδωκε*, and Clement by *μεταδοῦναι*. In reference to John, Irenæus uses the term *ἐξέδωκε*, which merely indicates the fact of the publication without specifying the manner of it. But it results from the last two verses of that gospel (xxi. 24, 25), and from the expression, *that ye may believe*, where the author interrupts his narrative to address the Church (xix. 35), that its publication also took place by the delivery of the writing into the hands of those who had requested it of him, and who had to provide for its being communicated to the assembly of the Church. A like expression is not found in the accounts about Matthew, but it is clear that the author, writing *among the Judæo-Christians* and *in the language of the Fathers*, did so that his work might be read among them, not only individually, but in common, in the assemblies for worship, as that still took place later at Berœa (now Aleppo) in the time of Jerome. As regards Luke, he no doubt forms an exception in this respect.

The author, not exercising his ministry in a special church, and dedicating his book to a friend of high rank, and probably rich enough to publish it at his own expense, it is possible that that writing followed a course more conformable to the ordinary way.

One may naturally presume that at this advanced epoch the oral narration by which the Church had long been nourished had lost much of its primitive freshness, and even perhaps of its primitive purity. The spiritual nourishment of the churches now required something firmer and more living, and in proportion as the time approached when the last witnesses of the history would disappear, who were also the authors of the primitive tradition, the need must have always been the more keenly felt of preserving unaltered their personal accounts, which could only be done by the public reading, in the assemblies of the Church, of those narratives recorded by themselves or by their assistants. Reuss has alleged that a regular reading of the writings of the apostles only began half a century after the destruction of Jerusalem, and after their death, thus about 120.[1] I believe that the need of gospel readings, added to those of the Old Testament, which, according to Reuss himself, had taken place from the beginning, must have made itself felt much sooner. When Matthew says (xxiv. 15), in speaking of the command of Jesus to the Judæo-Christian Church to flee from Palestine at a given time: "Let him that readeth pay attention (*ὁ ἀναγινώσκων νοείτω*)," it is doubtless possible that it refers to a reader reading privately; but how many readers could personally possess such a work? Each community had much rather a common copy, and therefore it appears to me more natural to see in this term, *he who readeth*, the public reader, whom the author exhorts to underline this important notice by his mode of accentuating it in reading it to the assembly. The same is the case with the parallel, Mark xiii. 14. As we have just seen, John also directly addresses the Church as such. He even goes as far as to interrupt his account with

[1] *Histoire du Canon*, p. 19.

this end, evidently expecting that what he writes will be read and read again by those he thus addresses. But there is another passage, more decisive if possible, namely, Apoc. i. 3: "Blessed is he that readeth (ὁ ἀναγινώσκων) and those who hear (οἱ ἀκούοντες) the words of this prophecy." The opposition between the singular, *he that reads*, and the plural, *those that hear*, only allows us to think of a public reading; and those two verbs in the present naturally apply to a repeated and periodic reading. Thus, then, Reuss, who dates the Apocalypse from the year 68, is found in manifest contradiction with his own affirmation that I have just quoted. For my part, placing the composition of the Apocalypse in the time of Domitian, at the end of the first century, I believe we can conclude from this word that at that time, towards the end of the life of John, there was already a public reading of those of the apostolic writings that the churches possessed, along with the reading of the Old Testament.

A prompt dissemination of the apostolic writings must have resulted from the always more pressing need of the churches to possess those only assured means of edification. Thus one of the churches of Italy had just learned from one of its members who had visited the church of Rome, that there was read there in the worship a gospel composed by Mark, the companion of Peter, and at once that church put itself in communication with that of Rome to obtain a copy of it. Tertullian, who was still living quite near the time when that communication between the churches took place, has described it in this way, while addressing Marcion, who wished only to admit the Gospel of Luke (*Adv. Marc.* iv. 5): "The same authority of the apostolic churches [that patronises Luke] equally guarantees the other gospels that we possess "per illas et secundum illas," that is to say, *by them and according to them*, which means: by the copies of the original deposited in their archives, copies that they themselves cause to be made for the other churches; and *according to them*, in this sense that they take care that those copies are exactly conformed to the apostolic original.

We have seen that the mode of publication of our gospels, as we have described it above, excludes all suspicion of fraud; the *mode of propagation*, which we have just described, without excluding all possibility of alteration of the text, does not allow us to expect grave changes, affecting the very foundation of the history and the teaching of Jesus.

If one takes account of the incessant and multiplied relations that existed between the churches of the different countries of the East and West, relations testified to by the *History* of Eusebius, and even by the letters of Paul of the Roman captivity (Col. iv. 7, 8 and foll.; Phil. ii. 19 and foll.), one will understand that nothing of importance could take place in one church without the others being soon informed of it; and that in particular, as a result of the pressing need of sure and authentic information on the life of Jesus, which became more and more felt at that epoch, the report of the existence of an apostolic or semi-apostolic writing on that subject must have immediately spread from place to place in all the churches, and have brought frequent requests addressed to the one that was known as the depository of that treasure. Thus the dissemination of our gospels must have promptly been effected.

A little before the end of the first century we find in *Clement of Rome* the use of the two gospels of Matthew and Luke, whose respective texts of the Sermon on the Mount are found mixed in his letter to the church of Corinth (c. 5), doubtless because he quoted from memory. We equally find the use of Matthew, probably also before the end of the first century, about 95, in the so-called Epistle of *Barnabas*, probably composed at Alexandria: "For fear," it is there said (4, 14), "that, *as it is written* (ὡς γέγραπται), there be found among us many called and few chosen." This word of Jesus occurs in Matt. xxii. 14. Volkmar (*Ursprung unserer Evangelien*, pp. 110–112), after the example of some ancients, prefers to see here a quotation of an apocryphal book, the fourth of Esdras, where it is said (viii. 3): "There are many created, but few will be saved (multi sunt creati, pauci autem salvabuntur"). This preference does little honour to the impartiality of the critic. Not only is it not certain that that apocryphal book is anterior to the Epistle of Barnabas, but besides, the opposition between *called and chosen,* which is the essential idea of the passage of Barnabas and of that of Matthew, presents quite another contrast than that of *created* and *saved.* Hilgenfeld, for his part, frankly says, in speaking of this γέγραπται of Barnabas (*Der Kanon,* p. 10): "Here is the first application of the term *Scripture* to a gospel word." It must further be remarked, that it is very difficult not to see in Barn. c. 5. 9 an allusion to Matt. ix. 13. For our part, we only conclude one thing from these quotations, namely, that even about the year 100 the Gospel of Matthew had arrived in Egypt, just as those of Matthew and Luke had arrived at Rome. There is, then, nothing impossible in this, that in the last ten years of the first century they had reached Ephesus as well. It was probably the same with Mark, although we have no written proof of it. The incessant relations between Rome and Ephesus warrant us to think so; and a little after, about 120, we find that writing in the hands of Papias at Hierapolis. Ephesus occupied at that time a central position for the rest of the Church, and that religiously as well as geographically. "After having passed from Jerusalem to Antioch, the centre of gravity of the Church had been transported from Antioch to Ephesus," Thiersch has justly said. This was the result, first of the labour of Paul, then of the sojourn of John, the last of the apostles, who had come to water what Paul had planted. We have seen from a word of the Apocalypse, a book written, according to Irenæus, in the time of Domitian (81–96), that at that epoch there already existed in the assemblies for worship a regular reading, not only of the Old Testament, but also of Christian writings.

There is consequently every reason to think that the three Synoptics were also to be found in the possession of the church of Ephesus, and that they were read in its worship before the end of the first century. It was then that the difference must have become apparent between the popular and more external character of the traditional narrative, preserved in the

Synoptics, and the loftier, more inward and personal character of the narrations of John. This contrast, clearly perceived from the first, according to Clement's account, by the colleagues and ordinary hearers of John, and by John himself, must naturally have called forth on the part of the former the request of which Clement speaks, and which we find later amplified in Muratori's Fragment and in Jerome (*Comment. in Matth.*, Proœm.). Something in the heart of John must have responded to this invitation. "Divinely impelled," as Clement says, he felt the duty of recording before his death the most exalted things that the Lord had uttered on His relation to the Father, to believers, and to the world. Such was the origin, at once natural and divine, of the fourth gospel, by which the *sacred quadriga*, as the Fathers call the gospel collection, was completed. Reaching Ephesus from Palestine, Italy, and Greece (or Syria) during the thirty years that separate the year 70 from the year 100, the Synoptics received from the hand of John in that church, which was then the centre of Christendom, their copestone, and doubtless at the same time their union in a single volume.

What we here say seems to us to follow naturally from the testimonies of Irenæus and Clement, even although neither the one nor the other carries his account so far as to mention the union of the four in a single whole. They have restricted themselves to certain details that they had received by tradition on the composition of these four writings separately. But it seems to me that one is led to think that no long time elapsed between the composition of the fourth gospel and its union in a single whole with the three others. They were the apostolic documents of the event that serves as basis for the existence and preservation of the Church. Why should not men have felt very quickly what was incomplete and partial, not only in each of them, but also in the first three without the fourth? It had been remarked at Ephesus from the first reading of the Synoptics. The mere respect for the truth on the person of Jesus must have morally obliged those who knew and possessed all the four no longer to separate them, but to unite those very different documents, in order to give the Church the fulness of the knowledge of her Christ. There was, besides, a fact that must have directly led to this, namely, that the last of these writings had been composed in direct relation to the three others, and was only comprehensible by that relation, while, besides, it alone threw full light on the person and teaching of Him whose life and words the others recounted in detail. It cannot be ignored, in fact, that the whole Gospel of John, from beginning to end, supposes in its readers the knowledge of the synoptic narrative. Not only does John supply several gaps left by the preceding gospels: thus, the first year of the ministry of Jesus in Judea; His three sojourns at Jerusalem, before that of the Passion; and the miracle, so influential on the final catastrophe, of the resurrection of Lazarus,—but his own account offers several details that are only explained to him who knows the synoptic narrative: thus, the allusion to the election of the Twelve (vi. 70), of which there had been no question before; the designation of Bethany as "the town of Mary and Martha" (xi. 1), although those two women had not yet been named; the omission of the scenes of Gethsemane and of the institution of the Lord's Supper, supposed to be known by the readers; and above all, the very brief résumé of the whole Galilean activity in that single and unique verse (vi. 2): "A great multitude followed Him, because they beheld the signs which He did on them that were sick." There are even found in John express and intentional corrections of certain features of the synoptic account; for instance, when (iii. 24) he rectifies the error committed by Matthew and Mark, who make the public ministry of Jesus begin after the imprisonment of John the Baptist (Matt. iv. 12; Mark i. 14); or when, several times (xiii. 1, xviii. 28, xix. 42), he brings out in the history of the Passion details designed to specify the true day of the death of Christ, obscured in the synoptical account. With such a correlation between John and the other gospels, to continue to diffuse the latter not united to the former would have been, on the part of any one knowing and possessing all the four, a sort of unfaithfulness.

No doubt the three Synoptics continued to be diffused separately in the different regions of the Church, alongside of copies containing the four united. As regards these latter, it seems to me probable, as Zahn has thought, that they had at the beginning as a general title the single word: **τὸ Εὐαγγέλιον**, *the Gospel*; while each of the four writings of which the collection was composed bore at its head, as a special title, the simple words: **Κατὰ Μαθθαῖον, Κατὰ Μάρκον**, etc. We find even now in the most ancient manuscripts the trace of this the oldest form. Thus in ℵ B, in D (at the top of the pages), in F (for Luke and Mark), and in several manuscripts of the ancient Latin translation and of the Vulgate, this abridged title has even become a sort of substantive, as in these expressions: "Here *ends According to Matthew* (Explicit secundum Matthæum.) Here *begins According to John* (Incipit secundum Joannem"; or again in D: "Here begins According to Mark (Incipit secundum Marcum; **Ἄρχεται Κατὰ Μάρκον**)," etc.

All these considerations lead us to suppose that the union of our four gospels in a single volume must have taken place, if not under the eyes and with the participation of John, at least a short time after his departure, and with the certainty of his approval. It is even difficult to believe that that union could have been effected later without discussion and opposition; for the manifold disagreements that the Synoptics present on a host of particular points, and the very striking general difference that prevails between them and the gospel of John, would certainly have placed an obstacle against their union in a single book which, according to an expression of Celsus, "would be transfixed with its own sword!"

One may in certain respects compare the result to which we have been led by the primitive tradition, recorded in the reports of Irenæus and Clement, with the conclusion to which a writer well abreast of all the modern works, and who cannot be charged with an exaggerated respect for tradition, has arrived. Renan (*Vie de Jésus*, 1st ed. p. xxxvii) thus sums up his point of view on the question: "On the whole, I admit as authentic the four canonical gospels. All, according to me, go back to the first century, and they are pretty much by the authors to whom they are attributed." This *pretty much* refers to the opinion according to which the gospels of Matthew and John had been composed by the *disciples* of these two apostles.

## III

We have now to investigate the facts that may enlighten us on *the presence and the use of these four writings*, whether apart or united, from the beginning till towards the middle of the second century, or between the reign of Trajan and the epoch of Justin Martyr.

The first indication we meet with is found in a passage of Eusebius (*H. E.* iii. 37), where he speaks of a powerful missionary work that was done in the time of Trajan, and in which he attributes a part to our gospels. The passage is as follows:—

> The most of the disciples of that time, possessed in their soul by the Divine Word with an ardent love of wisdom, began by fulfilling the command of the Lord in distributing their goods to the poor; then, expatriating themselves, they fulfilled the work of evangelists, without any ambition but to proclaim Christ to those who had not yet heard the word of faith, and to *transmit to them the book of the divine gospels* (τὴν τῶν θείων εὐαγγελίων παραδιδόναι γραφήν).

In a sense this work was the continuation of the apostolic missionary work, which had not ceased in the Church, as may be seen from 3 John 7: "For they went forth for His name, taking nothing of the Gentiles." Those of whom John thus spoke were doubtless the same persons that the Didaché designates by the title *apostles* (xi. 3). If it forbids them to remain more than two days in the same place, it evidently refers not to the place where they shall exercise their mission, but to the churches through which they would have to pass to repair thither. On the other hand, it cannot be ignored that the passage of Eusebius indicates a new and extraordinary fact: "*The most* of the disciples of that time, he says, *possessed in their soul* by an *ardent love* of wisdom (σφοδεροτέρῳ φιλοσοφίας ἔρωτι πληττόμενοι) by the Divine Word." Perhaps two important facts—the death of the last of the apostles and the end of the hundred years that had elapsed since the coming of Jesus Christ—contributed to impart to believers a new impulse for the missionary work to which the Church was called. Similar movements have many times been reproduced in the history of the Church.

We know, in particular, the powerful missionary revival that arose in the Moravian Church in 1728. "As a Christian festival was being celebrated at Herrnhut, in the midst of the singing, the prayers and addresses, the Spirit of Christ possessed all hearts, and communicated to them a powerful impulse to do, with God's help, some act of value." Then began in that Church the missionary work which has not ceased to this hour, and which from the Antilles (1732) passed successively to Greenland, to the North American Indians, to Guiana, to Kaffraria, to Labrador, to the Mosquito Coast, to Australia, and finally, recently to Alaska on Behring Strait.[1] As this missionary work has lasted in this little Church for more than a century and a half, it was the same with the work begun in the time of Trajan, with which Eusebius even connects the mission of Pantænus in India (Arabia?) towards the end of the second century (v. 10). This is how that historian relates (iii. 37) the work of those evangelists: "After having laid in different places the foundations of the faith and settled pastors, to whom they confided the care of the souls that had been gained, they set out anew for other countries and nations, with the grace and co-operation of God, . . . so that at the first audience crowds received with eagerness the worship of the Creator of all things." The style of this passage, it has been said, is that of Eusebius; he has not, then, derived this from one of his sources; but it is not less certain that he has not derived this account from his

[1] See the interesting work, *Les Missions moraves*, by E. A. Senft.

imagination, even though he may have reproduced it in his own manner. He knew a number of writings, of which he quotes fragments, which we no longer have, and it is certainly from one of them that he had derived the knowledge of that great missionary impulse which had taken place from the beginning of the second century. Besides, history sufficiently proves the reality of the fact. When Pliny, governor of Bithynia, thus described to Trajan the state of things in his province, between 109 and 112 (*Epist.* x. 97), that "many people of every age and rank, of both sexes, have already been and will yet be called to account. In fact, the contagion of this superstition (Christianity) has not only spread in the cities, but also in the villages and the country; yet it appears possible to arrest the evil and remedy it. At least, it is certain that *the temples already almost abandoned* begin to be frequented again, that *the solemn sacrifices long neglected* are resumed, and that they again begin to sell here and there (passim) the flesh of the victims, which *were but very seldom finding buyers* (rarissimus emptor),"—it is impossible to ignore the power of the work to which the Church had just been giving herself in the midst of the empire; and we have no reason to believe that this picture is only applicable to Pliny's province. For a little later, after a voyage that Justin had made from Naplous, his native place, to Rome, between 120 and 140, he thus described his impressions (*Dial.* c. 117): "There is absolutely no race of men, either among the barbarians or the Greeks, or any name that is given them, or Scythians, or those that are called Nomads because they live with their flocks in tents, from the midst of whom prayers and thanksgivings do not ascend to the Father and Creator of all in the name of the crucified Jesus." Allowing the possibility of some exaggeration, an immense work of evangelisation had in any case been wrought during the twenty or thirty years that separate Trajan from Justin, and it was not wrought of itself. The evangelists of Eusebius were no phantoms of his imagination; they had wrought well! Saint Paul had traversed the same regions, doubtless, but had confined himself to lighting the torch of the gospel in the capital cities, Antioch, Ephesus, Thessalonica, Corinth, Rome. Vast empty spaces separated those luminous points. It was those intermediate country districts that the evangelists, of whom Eusebius tells us, had evangelised. Another painfully eloquent proof of the efficacy of their work is found in the terrible persecution by which paganism, severely wounded, took its revenge in the second part of that century, under Marcus Aurelius, as in the previous century it had responded by the persecutions of Nero and Domitian to the mighty success of the apostolic preaching.

But the most interesting feature of this account of Eusebius, for the subject we have in hand, are the last words that speak of *the communication of the divine gospels* to those new churches by the missionaries that had founded them. Even now, one of the first cares of the missionaries, when they have learned the language of a heathen people, and by their preaching have founded a church, is to translate into their language the gospel writings, as the best means of maintaining the faith to which they have given birth. We read in Eusebius (v. 10) that the Apostle Bartholomew, on setting out to proclaim the gospel in India, had taken with him the Gospel of Matthew in the Hebrew language, and that when, a century later, the evangelist Pantænus visited the churches that that apostle had founded, he there found that gospel, which no doubt had been copied more than once. If an apostle who could say, "I have seen with my eyes, heard with my ears," had judged such a support useful, it must with greater reason have been so to mere evangelists who only knew by hearsay what they proclaimed. No doubt in the expressions of Eusebius there is a word redolent of the style of his age more than that of a writer of an older time, namely, the epithet *divine* (θειων) applied to the gospels. But that does not hinder him from having derived the fact itself from the writing of one of his predecessors, while relating it in his own way. Before leaving this statement of Eusebius, let us yet remark the contrast between the term in the singular τὴν γραφήν, *the book*, and the plural term τῶν εὐαγγελίων, *of the gospels*, the one of which indicates the unity of the collection and the other the plurality of the writings of which it is composed.

In any case, it is certain that Eusebius would not have expressed himself in this way if, with his great erudition and by his abundant reading, in which we no longer can follow him, he had not been led to the conviction that "the book of the divine gospels," by which he certainly meant our four canonical gospels,[1] had been diffused at the same time as the gospel preaching, by the missionaries whose work he mentions, at the beginning of the second century. This conviction of the learned historian should have some weight in the balance of science. This all the more that we can test the truth of it by a declaration of Justin Martyr, who, after having traversed Asia and Europe from the year 120 to 140, related that he had found everywhere the *Memoirs of the Apostles*—we shall see that by this he meant our gospels—read beside the Old Testament in the worshipping assemblies of all the churches. Who, then, had brought them to them?[2]

For the rest, the writings of the first part of the second century, by means of which we can test the assertion of Eusebius, are not numerous. At that epoch, when men were doing much, they wrote less, and if they quoted our gospels they did not designate them by the names of their authors, but rather said, as we see in Barnabas and Clement of Rome, "It is written," or "Remember the words of Jesus," or "The words that the Lord said in teaching." In these conditions one cannot expect to find, in the few writings that remain to

[1] Eusebius expresses himself thus, *H. E.* iii. 25: "And we must place in the first rank the sacred quadriga of the gospels (τὴν ἁγίαν τῶν εὐαγγελίων τετρακτύν), which is followed by the Book of the Acts of the Apostles."

[2] It is true that Irenæus (*Hær.* iii. 4) mentions that *several* barbarous nations attained to the faith *sine chartâ et atramento* (without paper and ink). But he cites this fact as an exceptional case. The reference is to barbarous tribes into whose unknown languages the gospel could not yet be translated. It was quite otherwise with the civilised populations of the empire, in general speaking Greek, the language of our gospels, and who could thus read them in the original. The very exception instanced by Irenæus proves that the populations of the empire had not been converted without a written gospel.

us, quotations in which the evangelists are mentioned by name. It was only later, when a crowd of heretical writings swarmed in the Church, that they made a point of giving as guarantee the names of the authors of our gospels, as we begin to notice in Papias.

But if the writings of the Fathers dating from that epoch are far from numerous, this gap is in some measure supplied by the writings of the authors of heterodox systems. They employed the exegesis of the gospels, the texts of which they interpreted at their pleasure, to combat the traditional doctrine taught by the Church. This aggressive attitude gave to their works a vigour not possessed in the same degree by the purely defensive work of the ecclesiastical writers. Let us rapidly glance at the writings of both.

On the threshold of the second century is to be placed, if I mistake not, the writing recently discovered and published by the Greek archbishop, Bryennius, the *Didaché of the Twelve Apostles*, *Διδαχὴ τῶν δώδεκα ἀποστόλων*.[1]

Criticism is very hesitating as regards the date of this writing. Hilgenfeld places it pretty late, in the second half of the second century (from 160 to 190). Harnack a little earlier (from 120 to 165), adding, however, this important observation: "That many of the features of this writing, whether as regards form or contents, are better to be understood between 80 and 120 than between 120 and 165." Bryennius himself says, from 120 to 160. The English in general place it much earlier: Lightfoot from 80 to 100; Farrar in the year 100; Schaff from 90 to 100. Zahn also goes back to the year 80. The French occupy the two extremes, or the middle of this list: Paul Sabatier speaks of the middle of the *first* century; Ménégoz, from 80 to 100; Bonet-Maury, from 160 to 190. To me, the most probable date appears to be a little before or after the year 100. The

[1] This shorter title is followed by this other: Διδαχὴ Κυρίου διὰ τῶν δώδεκα ἀποστόλων τοῖς ἔθνεσιν (*Teaching of the Lord by the Twelve Apostles to the Gentiles*).

Didaché has its likeliest place between the epistle of Clemens Romanus and the letters of Ignatius. Indeed, it still leaves the field completely open to the exercise of the free gifts (*prophets* and *teachers*); it speaks, like Clement, of the bishops and deacons elected by the Church, but without the least trace of the monarchical episcopacy of Ignatius. "Choose for yourselves," says the author (xv. 1), "*bishops* and *deacons*"; these, the only functionaries mentioned, recall those that appear in the writings of the end of the apostolic age (comp. Philip. i. 1 and 1 Tim. iii. 1 and 8). The Lord's Supper appears to be still joined with the feast called Agape: *Μετὰ τὸ ἐμπλησθῆναι, οὕτως εὐχαριστήσατε* (x. 1). This word *ἐμπλησθῆναι*, *to be filled*, can hardly be taken in a spiritual sense. Harnack himself says: "Thus still a real repast." But in the time of Pliny, about 109, the two acts of the Agape and of the Lord's Supper, originally united (1 Cor. 11), appear already separated (the worship takes place in the morning, the repast in the evening). It is the same in the time of Justin. In fine, there is no allusion to the gnosticism stigmatised by Ignatius.

Spence, in his important writing, *The Teaching of the Twelve Apostles*, 1885, Excurs. ii., supposes, with some likelihood, it seems to me, that the author of this writing, so esteemed in the primitive Church, might have been the bishop of Jerusalem, Symeon, the cousin of Jesus and successor of James, the first head of the Judæo-Christian Church after the apostles. Eusebius relates the execution of this Symeon, who was crucified in the year 107, at the age of 120 years.

The author was certainly a Judæo-Christian (the order to pray three times a day, to fast two days a week, not to eat meat offered in sacrifice), but at the same time a Judæo-Christian very hostile to pharisaic Judaism, the fasting of which he calls (viii. 1) the fasting *of hypocrites* (comp. Luke xviii. 12). The Jews fasted on Tuesday and Thursday, in memory of the ascent of Moses to Sinai, and of his descent from the mountain. The author will have men fast on Wednesday and Friday, the days of the betrayal and crucifixion of Jesus, and he even calls the latter day *the preparation* (παρασκευή), in the Jewish manner (viii. 1, 2).

If the sub-title found in the manuscript recovered by Bryennius is authentic, the author drew up this treatise as a kind of manual of apostolic instruction, composed for the use of the Judæo-Christian churches, to be employed in the evangelisation of the surrounding heathen. The first six chapters serve to put the latter above all under the discipline of the law, as Moses had done for Israel. The last ten mark out, for the churches formed of those heathen when baptized, the true course to follow in order to remain faithful to the apostolic gospel.

The Gospel of Matthew is the one most usually quoted in this writing; Luke is so also several times. The author does not quote these writings by name; he says in a general way: "As the Lord has ordained in His gospel" (viii. 2), or, "According to the dogma of the gospel" (xi. 3); and the question is whether by this word *the gospel* he means the Christian teaching in general, or a *writing* in which it is contained. The two passages quoted would allow the first sense, although the word δόγμα rather applies to a decision formulated by writing. But other passages appear to me to decide the question in the second sense; thus xv. 3: "Correct each other in peace, as you have it in the gospel" (ὡς ἔχετε ἐν τῷ εὐαγγελίῳ); xv. 4: "Do your prayers and your alms, as you have it in the gospel of our Lord." These words, *as you have it in*, it seems to me, can only refer to a *writing*; it is as if the author were inviting his readers to compare his precepts with the gospel text that they themselves possess. Harnack, in his fine work on the Didaché (*Texte und Unters.*, vol. ii. No. 1, p. 69), expresses himself thus: "What did the author mean by the word *the gospel*? In any case a *written redaction* well known by the churches, as is shown by the expression, *You have in*."[1] The same scholar adds: "Be-

[1] Harnack has the less difficulty in recognising the true meaning of the word *gospel* in this passage as he places the Didaché much later, about the middle of the second century. We have recognised the impossibility of this view. But the clear declaration of Harnack is not the less valuable to us from our point of view.

cause the plural *εὐαγγέλια* is not employed in the Didaché, it cannot be inferred that the author had only before him a single gospel writing." In fact, Harnack himself recognises that in six passages the author blends together, as we find it also in Clement and Polycarp, the texts of Matthew and Luke (p. 77). Mark is not quoted, doubtless because the quotations are always drawn from the teachings of Jesus, and these are chiefly contained in Matthew and Luke. As regards John, Harnack declares (p. 81) "that it is not possible to call in question the conformity of the prayers of the Lord's Supper (chaps. ix. and x.) with the Gospel of John." He quotes (p. 80) twelve words that recall literally the expressions of John, and he shows the agreement of the two writings in their mode of conceiving that sacred action. He recognises that "these prayers proceed from the same spirit from which have been derived John vi. and xvii." And from all this he does not believe he can conclude "that the author of the Didaché knew the Gospel of John." He only wrote "under the influence of a medium in which the Gospel of John was known." What! the author had lived in the medium where that gospel was known, and had not found the means to procure it for himself! To sum up, we learn from the Didaché that, about the year 100, the author of that writing, working, whether in the Hauran, in Syria, or in Egypt, possessed, as well as the churches whom he addressed, a gospel collection containing Matthew and Luke certainly, and probably also John.

The Didaché forms, as Schaff has said, the transition from the apostolic times to the patristic age; but I add: By what a perpendicular fall!

The first writings that place us decidedly in the second century are the *Letters of Ignatius*. We shall not be expected to reopen here the discussion on this collection. The collection of the fifteen letters is now universally condemned. Since the works of Zahn [1] and Lightfoot,[2] the three letters in

[1] *Ignatius von Antiochien*, 1873.

[2] *The Apostolic Fathers* (S. Ignatius; S. Polycarpus, 2nd ed. 1889).

Syriac found by Cureton have lost the favour that they had at first obtained; it is acknowledged that they are only extracts. The collection of seven letters enumerated by Eusebius seems to me, on the other hand, sufficiently guaranteed, as M. Jean Réville has acknowledged in his study published in the *Revue de l'histoire des Religions* in 1890. The entirely exceptional originality of those letters defends them from the suspicion of forgery; the strange fire that pervades them cannot be a painted fire. Phrases can be artificially composed; such a character is not to be invented. You see here arise a personality absolutely unique in history, even in the history of Christendom. The idea of the monarchic episcopate, which is still absent from the epistle of Clement and the Didaché, is strongly accentuated in these letters; probably the progress of the episcopal organisation took place more rapidly in Syria and in Asia Minor than in the other churches. If the functionaries, called in the Apocalypse, i.–iii., *Angels of the churches,* are either the personification of the presbyterial councils of these churches, or even their presidents, as James and Symeon had been of the church of Jerusalem, the Apocalypse appears to be thus the intermediary between the pastoral epistles and the letter of Clement on the one hand, and the letters of Ignatius on the other. At the same time, we should observe that the bishop in Ignatius is still a purely *parochial* functionary, and in no way belongs to the class of *diocesan* bishops of the second half of this century, such as the bishops of Rome, Pothinus of Lyons, or Serapion in Syria.

If the letters of Ignatius are authentic, they should date from 107 to 115, the probable time of his martyrdom. Mention is made in them several times of *the gospel,* in the abstract sense of gospel teaching; thus *Smyrn.* c. 5: "Those whom the prophecies, the law of Moses, and even the gospel have not convinced"; *Philad.* c. 9: "The gospel is the fulfilment of immortality." But there are other passages where this term, it seems to me, can only be applied to gospel *writings*; thus *Smyrn.* c. 7: "It is fitting to be attached to the prophets, but particularly to the gospel, in which the Passion is revealed to us, and where the resurrection is found accomplished (τετελείωται)"; so again, *Philad.* c. 5: "In order that I may attain the heritage in recurring (προσφυγὼν) to the gospel as to the flesh of Jesus, and to the apostles as to the presbyterial council of the Church (ὡς πρεσβυτερίῳ ἐκκλησίας); and we also love the prophets, because they also prophesied in prospect of the gospel." The gospel, called *the flesh of Jesus,* might doubtless denote the oral narration of His life and death, as it has this sense at the end of the passage quoted. But the expression *to recur to* or *take refuge in* (προσφυγεῖν) rather suggests a concrete object to which one returns, or which one grasps again, as when Clement says, c. 47: "Take up (ἀναλάβετε) the epistle of the blessed Paul." As regards the apostles, they can only, in the time of Ignatius, be compared to the presbyterial council of the Church by reason of their writings, which mark out her course for all time; in fine, it is clear that *the prophets* here denote writings, and not persons. It seems to me we must, for these reasons, conclude that by the term *the gospel* Ignatius here meant to denote gospel *writings.*

This conclusion is confirmed by the numerous quotations of gospel passages that we find in his letters. Matthew is the one quoted most frequently, quite as in the Didaché. In the epistle to the *Smyrneans* this gospel is quoted twice; c. 1, the baptism of Jesus: "In order that all righteousness might be fulfilled" (comp. Matt. iii. 15); c. 6, the word of Jesus regarding celibacy (ὁ χωρῶν χωρείτω); comp. Matt. xix. 12.—*Ephes.* c. 17 (the anointing by Mary); comp. Matt. xxvi. 7 and foll., and John xii. 3 (the Church embalmed like the house of the entertainment).—*Trall.* c. 11. 1 (φυτεία πατρός); comp. Matt. xv. 13.—*Polyc.* c. 2 (φρόνιμος ὡς ὁ ὄφις, etc.); comp. Matt. x. 16.

Luke is only once expressly quoted; *Smyrn.* c. 3: "When he came towards Peter and his own, he said to them: Take, touch me, and see that I am not a spirit without a body (δαιμόνιον ἀσώματον)." There is in Luke: "Behold my hands and my feet, that it is I myself: touch me, and see; for a spirit hath not flesh and bones, as ye see me have" (comp. Luke xxiv. 39, 40). Despite the expression *a spirit without body*, which is not found in Luke, and which Jerome says is borrowed from the Gospel of the Hebrews, the general reproduction of the passage of Luke is incontestable. As regards this strange expression, Eusebius, who well knew the Gospel of the Hebrews, as it existed in his own diocese at Cæsarea, in the library of Pamphilus, did not find it there. No more did Origen; for he derived it from quite another writing, the *Preaching of Peter*. Perhaps Jerome had found it in the copy that he had read and copied at Berœa, and which might differ from that of Cæsarea. It is possible also that Ignatius had borrowed it from oral tradition, whence it had passed both into the Preaching of Peter and into the copy at Berœa; comp. Lightfoot, ii. p. 296, note 2. I think I find another trace of the influence of Luke in Ignatius, in the epistle to the *Smyrneans*, c. 1: "Truly nailed to the cross, under Pontius Pilate and *Herod the Tetrarch*." Luke is the only evangelist that expressly attributes a part to Herod, conjointly with Pilate, in the crucifixion of Jesus.

The Gospel of John has certainly imprinted its mark on the letters of Ignatius. Its influence is especially perceptible in the epistle to the *Romans*; c. 7, Ignatius writes: "I do not take pleasure in the joys of this life; I desire *the bread of God*, which is *the flesh of the Christ*, born of the race of David; I desire *for drink his blood*, which is incorruptible love. My love has been crucified, and there is in me a fire not carnal, a *living water* (ὕδωρ ζῶν) speaking (λαλοῦν)[1] in me, saying to me inwardly: 'Come to the Father.'" Five

[1] In place of the reading λαλοῦν ἐν ἐμοί *speaking in me*, I think we must prefer the reading ἀλλόμενον ἐν ἐμοί, *springing up in me*, first because the image of springing up, with water, is more natural than that of speaking, and then by reason of the very frequent use of this expression of springing water in the second century. See in Lightfoot, p. 225, the numerous passages of the Naassenes, the Sethians, and the gnostic Justin, etc. The quotation of John iv. 14, which strikes one at once, even with the generally admitted reading, becomes still more evident if we accept this correction.

times he calls Satan ὁ ἄρχων τοῦ αἰῶνος τούτου, an expression corresponding to the exclusively Johannine term ὁ ἄρχων τοῦ κόσμου τούτου. He designates Jesus (*Magnes.* c. 6) as "He *who was with the Father before the ages* (πρὸ τῶν αἰώνων)," and c. 8, as "*His Son*, who is *His Logos* (αὐτοῦ λόγος)"; *Eph.* c. 7, as being God in man, and by His death the true life (ζωὴ ἡ ἀληθινή); *Philad.* c. 7, we read these words: "The Spirit is not misled; for he knows whence he comes and whither he goes (πόθεν ἔρχεται καὶ ποῦ ὑπάγει), and he judges hidden things (καὶ τὰ κρυπτὰ ἐλέγχει)"; comp. John iii. 8 and 19, 20. One must conclude from all this that Ignatius possessed a gospel collection, embracing, like that of the author of the Didaché, Matthew, Luke, and John. If these two authors are nearly contemporary, as I think, this relation between them is natural. Mark is still lacking in both, but doubtless for the reason I have indicated above.

About the year 125, a little after the time of Ignatius, there appeared at Alexandria a teacher of a lofty spirit, named *Basilides*, who became the head of the first great gnostic school.

Gnosticism was a powerful effort to explain the history of the universe by means of the appearance of Jesus Christ and of His redemption work. Under its three principal forms, that of Basilides, of Marcion, and of Valentinus, it is a striking homage rendered to the supreme grandeur of the Christian cause, in which it sought to show the keystone of the arch of universal evolution.

Basilides had been preceded by several teachers, in particular by Cerinthus, a contemporary of the Apostle John, at Ephesus, who might be called a gnostic before gnosticism. He held that the union of Jesus with the Godhead had only begun after His baptism. Epiphanius (*Hær.* 28. 5) alleges that in his school they only used the Gospel of Matthew, while rejecting its first two chapters. Basilides, according to a passage in the *Disputation of Archelaus and Manes* (third century), had been a preacher in Persia, *non longe post nostrorum apostolorum tempora* (c. 55). The accounts of his system in

Irenæus, Clement, and Hippolytus are not entirely in agreement. He called himself, after Clement (*Strom.* vii. 17), disciple of a certain Glaucias, who had been taught by Peter. According to Hippolytus (*Philos.* vii. 20), he carried back his system to the Apostle Matthias, who had been privately taught it by the Saviour. What we know about his writings is as follows. After Eusebius (*H. E.* iv. 7), he had composed twenty-four books: On the gospel (εἰς τὸ εὐαγγέλιον), which had been refuted by a known writer named Agrippa Castor. What was this writing? Was it the exposition of his system of religious philosophy? So it might be supposed, when we read in Hippolytus (vii. 27) this definition that his school (αὐτοί, *they*) gave of the word gospel: "The knowledge of supraterrestrial things"; but we possess yet two other statements about this work that give us another idea of it. From both it appears, as from the passage of Eusebius, that this work was of a considerable extent. The first is derived from the *Disputation of Archelaus and Manes*, where it is said (c. 55): "We have the *thirteenth book* of the treatises of Basilides, of which this is the beginning." . . . The second explains not only the considerable *extent*, but also the *nature* of this writing. Clement (*Strom.* iv. 12) says in effect: "Basilides, in the *twenty-third* of his *Exegetical treatises* (τῶν ἐξηγητικῶν), says this *in express terms* (αὐταῖς λέξεσι)." We see from the term ἐξηγητικά what was the true nature of the twenty-four books that Agrippa Castor had refuted. It was not an exposition of the gospel in itself, but an exegetical work on the gospel texts. This was already apparent from the expression of Eusebius: *twenty-four books* εἰς τὸ εὐαγγέλιον, which applies to exegetical dissertations, but not to a speculative exposition. After the *Philosophumena* of Hippolytus (vii. 27), Basilides confirmed this principle, that "each thing has its proper moment," by this word of the Saviour: "Mine hour is not yet come" (John ii. 4). According to vii. 22, he also quoted John i. 9: "That was the true light that lighteth every man that cometh into the world." According to vii. 26, he quoted in these words Luke i. 35: "The power of the Highest will overshadow thee (ἐπισκιάσει σοι)." According to Clement (*Strom.* iii. 1), the school of Basilides, in treating the question of marriage, applied to it the expression of Matt. xix. 11 : "All do not receive it (οὐ πάντες χωροῦσι)." Also we ought not to wonder to find in him for the first time the plural *the gospels* (τὰ εὐαγγέλια). According to Hippolytus, the quotation of the saying, John i. 9, was introduced by Basilides himself, with this formula : "This is what is said (τὸ λεγόμενον) in the gospels," a formula that Hippolytus certainly did not of his own accord attribute to Basilides.

It is true that the word φησί, *he says*, by which Hippolytus attributes these biblical quotations to Basilides himself, must, according to some modern critics, be referred, not to the head of the school, but to some one of his later disciples, so that there would be nothing to be inferred from it for the subject we have in hand. But it seems to me that, in advancing this objection, account has not been taken of the very clear difference that Hippolytus makes between the quotations accompanied by this word, *he says*, like those that occur vii. 21, 22, 23, 25, 26, 27, etc., and those he presents as coming from *the entire school*, with the formula *according to* them (κατ' αὐτούς), as that is the case for the account of the birth of Jesus (c. 27), or for the definition of the gospel (*ibid.*), or for the name Abraxas (c. 25), and always while expressly employing the verbs in the plural (φάσκουσι, *they allege*, or λέγουσιν, *they say*). We see, from this very marked distinction, that Hippolytus took account of the difference between the words of the master and those of the disciples. Renan himself has understood this. Thus he says (*L'Église chrétienne*, p. 158 : "The author of the *Philosophumena* doubtless made this analysis of the original works of Basilides." A few years ago Weizsaecker also shared this opinion. He wrote (*Unters.* p. 233) : "One cannot doubt that we have here quotations from a writing of Basilides." If he afterwards changed his opinion (*Jahrb. für deutsche Theol.* 1868, p. 525), it was because he found in the fragments of Basilides, quoted by Hippolytus, quotations from the Epistles to the Ephesians and Colossians. But this argument, of course, falls to the ground if, as I believe, these letters are authentic, and consequently anterior to Basilides. Thus we again find ourselves with this Egyptian gnostic in presence of the same three gospels, Matthew, Luke, and John, the use of which we have ascertained in Ignatius and the Didaché. It is difficult to allow that they were not already united, since they are found thus used together at this same epoch in Egypt and in Syria. Mark is still wanting, but we shall soon show that, as Zahn says, "the Gospel of Mark was already forming the subject of converse in Asia Minor when the personal disciples of the Saviour were still alive."

Nearly at the same time that Basilides was explaining in his manner these three gospels at Alexandria, about 120 to 125, *Papias*, at Hierapolis, in Asia Minor, related in the preface of his book, *Explanations of the Discourses of the Lord*, the origin of the Gospels of Matthew and Mark, probably after the statements of the presbyter John. As Papias had thought he ought to record such memorials for the churches of Phrygia, those two gospels must certainly have been already known, diffused, and read in those countries; for what interest could those details have had if they had not referred to writings already esteemed in those churches? But, it has been asked, Why does not Papias also speak of Luke and John? Is not his silence a proof that he did not yet know these writings, or that, if he knew them, he did not admit them? But what do we know of the work of Papias? Only the few lines of it that Eusebius has preserved for us. There is no proof that he was really silent about these gospels. And even if he was so, Luke had given in his prologue (i. 1–4) all the necessary details on the composition of his work, and Papias might have learned nothing new to add thereto.[1] And, as regards John, Papias wrote in the

[1] Holtzmann finds in the passage of Papias an evident imitation (*augenscheinliche Nachahmung*) of the prologue of Luke (*Einl.* p. 117), but he wrongly quotes, it seems to me, a work of Riggenbach as being to

country where the composition of that gospel was a recent fact, and known to all, so that he had no need to insist on it.

I think I have shown above (p. 20) that if, as he says himself, the two disciples of Jesus, John the presbyter and Aristion, were still living when he wrote, it is impossible to bring down the composition of this passage in his preface lower than 120 to 125. Volkmar, with his usual hardihood, resolutely says (*Urspr.* etc. p. 163), in his list of the writings of the second century: "In 165, the chiliastic writing of Papias." If the *Paschal Chronicle* is right in placing the martyrdom of Papias at Pergamos at the same time as that of Polycarp at Smyrna, the latter now seeming fixed at the year 155, Papias would be found, according to Volkmar's date, to have composed his work ten years after his death.[1] Holtzmann does not come down so far; he is content with 150, which does not appear more compatible with the terms of Papias himself (ἃ λέγουσιν). This is the testimony of Papias on Mark, or rather that of the presbyter John (in any case at least as regards the first lines):

> And this is what the presbyter said: Mark having become the interpreter [or rather the secretary] of Peter (ἑρμηνευτὴς Πέτρου γενόμενος), wrote exactly, but not in their order (ἀκριβῶς, οὐ μέντοι τάξει), the things either said or done by the Christ; for he had not heard the Lord, nor had accompanied Him, but towards the end, as I have said,[2] he had accompanied Peter who gave his teaching according to the need of the moment, and not as composing a collection (σύνταξιν) of the discourses of the Lord, so that Mark lacked nothing in retracing detached facts, as he recalled them. For he was only concerned about one thing, to omit nothing that he had heard, and to alter nothing.

the same effect (*Jahrb. f. d. Theol.* 1868; the latter simply says: "One might try to." . . .—The οἱ πολλοί of Papias are quite different persons from the πολλοί of Luke. The verb παρακολουθεῖν that is found in Papias and Luke is employed in the former in the proper sense, in the latter in the figurative. The two passages have nothing in common, either in their general sense or in the rest of the terms.

[1] This datum of the *Paschal Chronicle* rests on a confusion of the name of Papias with that of another martyr.

[2] These words prove that the end of the paragraph belongs to Papias himself.

Eusebius continues: This is what Papias relates regarding Mark. Concerning Matthew, what he says is as follows:—

Matthew again composed in writing the discourses (τὰ λόγια συνεγράψατο) in the Hebrew language (ἑβραΐδι διαλέκτῳ); and each one translated them as he was able.

We have not here to go into the value of these two testimonies for the explanation of the origin of our first two gospels, but confine ourselves to bringing out their relations to the traditions of Irenæus and Clement.

As to Matthew, there is complete agreement with Irenæus regarding the place of composition and the original language. But Papias adds two interesting details. The one bears on the *contents* of that work; after Papias it contained an account of the *discourses* or divine teachings (τὰ λόγια) of Jesus; we shall see in the following chapter that this restricted sense of the term λόγιον is that which suits it in this title. Then Papias speaks of a certain time that elapsed until the time when that Hebrew or Aramaic writing was translated into Greek, and thus became accessible to the whole Church. In the interval, those who wished to reproduce its contents in Greek did so as best they could, and that in a merely oral manner. These details are foreign to Irenæus as well as to Clement; but this last is in agreement with Papias and Irenæus regarding the original language of Matthew; for we know that he related (Eus. *H. E.* v. 10) that his master Pantænus having repaired to India on a mission, found there "the Gospel of Matthew, written in the language of the Hebrews (Ἑβραίων γράμμασιν)," that had been brought to that country by the Apostle Bartholomew.

As regards Mark, the tradition of the presbyter is much more detailed than that of Irenæus, and more approaches that of Clement. Rome is no longer named in it as the place of composition; but, as Mark is put into a close relation with Peter, and the time of this relation is determined by the word ὕστερον, *in the last place*, it is clear that Papias thinks, like Clement and Irenæus, it was at the end of the apostolic career of Peter, that is to say, in his final sojourn at Rome, a city where, as Clement says, Peter and Mark had arrived πόῤῥωθεν, *from very far*. No more than Irenæus does Papias say a single word tending to put Mark's writing under the inspection and patronage of this apostle. The most salient feature of his report is the contrast he establishes between the *contents* of the two gospels. According to him, the first is a *collection of discourses* (λογίων σύνταξις), the second a gathering of detached facts (ἔνια γράψας), such as the author had occasionally collected from the mouth of Peter, when he related them without sequence, taking account only of the auditors he had each time before him. Despite the exactness with which these detached facts have been related by Mark, they did not properly constitute, according to Papias, a consecutive history (written τάξει, in order).

The judgment of Papias on these two gospels has often been interpreted in France and Germany in a very unfavourable sense, as if Papias had thereby wished to diminish the value of these two writings. The first, he would have meant to say, is only a translation; the other, but a collection of anecdotes thrown down without sequence; or, as Holtzmann says in two words: "There, a foreign tongue; here, lack of order." And the confirmation of this unfavourable judgment has been found in the last words of the passage, where, after having indicated the means of information that he had employed to compose his book, Papias adds: "For I did not think I could derive from books as much benefit as from the living and still existing voice (the oral tradition of the still living witnesses)."

This whole passage of Papias appears to me to have generally been ill-understood, and it may seem bold to seek to rectify such a misconception, of which I find the strongest expression in Reuss (*La Bible, Hist. évang.* p. 13). There are on this point, it seems to me, two questions to be explained. 1st, What was the task in view of which Papias sought to unite the apostolic recollections, whether by consulting his own memory or by trusting to verbal information? And, 2nd, what were the books to which he attached little value for the accomplishment of this task, in comparison of oral tradition? Did he propose to himself, as Reuss thinks, "to complete *by editing anew* the writings already existing, such as the Gospels of Matthew and Mark which he cites by name," or were the materials that he collected destined not to edit the *text* of the discourses of Jesus, but solely to support the explanation that he sought to give of the gospel texts that he had before him? The answer seems to me not doubtful, if one takes account of the title of his book: "*Explanation* of the discourses of the Lord." On the first supposition he would have required to entitle it, not explanation (ἐξήγησις), but collection (σύνταξις) of the Logia. But, above all, he expresses himself in beginning this piece in a way to remove all uncertainty in this respect when he says: "I shall not weary myself (ὀκνήσω) by *joining* (or co-ordinating) to my explanations (συγκατατάξαι ταῖς ἑρμηνείαις) all that formerly I surely learned from the lips of the elders." It was not, then, for the constitution of a new gospel text, but for the enrichment or the confirmation *of the explanations given by himself*, that he was labouring in collecting the materials of his work. It is, then, quite false to speak with Reuss "of a new edition" of the words of Jesus different from that which he possessed in the two gospels of which he spoke. It is no less so, it seems to me, to rank the writings of Matthew and Mark among the books that he found useless to consult, and to which he preferred the information derived from oral tradition. How could he have thus spoken of writings that he himself declared to be composed, the one by an apostle, the other by a writer editing what an apostle said in his presence? Were those, then, whom he interrogated with so much care at Hierapolis to get from their lips what Peter had said, or Matthew, were they surer witnesses of the statements of these two apostles than what, according to his own declaration, *Matthew had written himself*, or what Mark had heard and edited *of the teaching of Peter?* This supposition is so absurd, that, however small the idea one forms with Eusebius of the range of

Papias, one cannot for a moment impute it to him. It is very evident that the books to which Papias preferred the oral apostolic tradition were not those that he had just himself signalised as authentic depositories of that tradition. In speaking of the books of which one must be doubtful, he is thinking much rather of those whose authors some lines before he had characterised as "people who take pleasure *in saying many things*, and who mix with their instruction *strange commandments, which have not been given to the faith by the Lord*"; they were those of whom his predecessor Ignatius wrote (*Trall.* c. 11): "Flee the evil excrescences that produce a poisonous fruit causing death to him who eats of it"! and whom Polycarp signalised to the Philippians (c. 7), saying: "Turn you from the vanity of the multitude (τῶν πολλῶν, the same expression as Papias) and from false doctrines, and return to the word that has been transmitted to us from the beginning" (evidently the apostolic tradition).

But did there already exist a whole literature which it was necessary to distrust? To answer this question, it is enough to see the deluge of profane writings, opposed to the faith, of which the book of the *Philosophumena* speaks; compare, in particular, Books v.–vii. There were the gospels of Cerinthus, of Saturninus, the numberless writings of the Naasenians, the Perates, the Sethians, offering a mixture of the gospel with the particular ideas of the sects from which they proceeded.[1] Consequently it is entirely false to say, as Reuss does, following on the words of Papias relative to the books that he refused to consult: "*Among these last,* Papias quotes by name the Gospels of Matthew and Mark." This assertion is the more erroneous that the passage relating to

[1] Let us quote some passages of Hippolytus on the subject of these numerous heretical writings. V. 14: "It seems to me good here to adduce *one of the books* honoured by them (the Perates)"; c. 15: "*Their other books* contain the same doctrine"; c. 21: "That is what they (the Sethians) say in numberless books (ἐν ἀπείροις συγγράμμασι); c. 7: "These are the essential points (κεφάλαια) *of the numerous discourses* which they (the Naasenians) say have been transmitted to Marianne by James the brother of the Lord."

the books to be rejected occurred in the *preface* of the book of Papias, while his account of Matthew and Mark probably occurred in the body of the writing. This is, in fact, how Eusebius expresses himself (iii. 39): "He transmits *in his own writing* (τῇ ἰδίᾳ γραφῇ) the traditions of the presbyter John, which we will place here, and first that on Mark who wrote the gospel," to which he then joins that on Matthew.

We see with what grave errors Reuss by his great knowledge and powerful intellect has inoculated French theology, and they have produced their effect; for we find them repeated in almost all the critical works,[1] and it is an opinion admitted even by many laymen who occupy themselves with these questions, that, until well on in the second century, value was attached only to the oral tradition, but not at all to the gospels.

Mark had hitherto remained in the shade; it is now brought to light by the writing of Papias. We see that the writing of Mark is treated in this account, proceeding, at least in the first lines, from the mouth of the presbyter John, a personal disciple of Jesus, as keeping step with that of Matthew, as emanating directly, as well as the latter, from an

[1] This is how some of our French critics, vying with each other, reproduce the judgment of the master: M. Nicolas, in his *Etudes critiques sur la Bible* (*Nouveau Testament*, p. 17), says: "Papias wrote five books of commentaries on this work (Matthew) to which he only allows a secondary importance." M. Réville (*Etudes critiques sur l'évangile de saint Matthieu*, p. 337) speaks of "the claim of Papias boldly avowed to find more and better in the oral tradition than in any writing whatever." M. Sabatier (*Encycl. des sc. relig.* "art. Canon") says: "We know that Papias put books much below oral tradition, and that he has spoken with surprising freedom of the Gospels of Matthew and Mark." But Volkmar even surpasses these judgments of the French critics. According to him, this is what Papias meant to say: "The Gospels of Matthew and Mark may be at bottom very apostolic, but one cannot confide in either of the two; neither in the first, because it is a translation, perhaps ill done, no one can tell in what measure; nor in the second, because, despite all the goodwill of its author, it is incomplete" (*Der Urspr. unserer Evangelien*, p. 61). But how could the same man, at the very same time, relate with care after a venerable source the apostolic or semi-apostolic origin of two writings, and himself turn up his nose at them while teaching his readers to do as much? One sees by the preceding quotations what errors Reuss has disseminated, and how they have sprung up!

apostolic source, and as having shared in some sort with him the picture of the ministry of Jesus, Matthew grouping the *teachings*, and Mark reporting a certain number of discourses and *acts*, after the narrative of the chief of the apostles.

The writing of Luke, though cited several times by the author of the Didaché, by Ignatius, and Basilides, appears to have been up to this time less used than Matthew. He is all at once raised by a heretic to the dignity of the first and even only true gospel. Between 138 and 140 there arrived from Pontus, at Rome, the son of the bishop of Sinope, named *Marcion*. In repairing to the West, he had certainly visited the churches of Phrygia, where he had learned that the so-called Epistle to the Ephesians had in reality been addressed to the church of Laodicea. At Rome, adopting the teaching of Cerdo, he established an absolute opposition between the God of the Old Testament, creator of the visible universe, author of the law, an inferior and limited being who only knows justice, and the God of the New Testament, a being superior to the first, the Father of Jesus Christ, who is charity. And as to find access to the Church it was needful to give an apostolic fulcrum to this mode of view, he chose for this end the Gospel of Luke, and adapted it to this use by subjecting it to manipulation, and above all to the curtailments that his system required. This use of the third gospel would certainly not have had any success if Marcion had not found that book received and accredited in the churches where he sought to recruit the members of his own. Weizsäcker has even acknowledged (*Untersuch.* p. 230) that Marcion had in his hands the three other gospels. In fact, Tertullian reminds Marcion (*Adr. Marc.* iv. 4) that, after one of his own letters, he had formerly admitted the other gospels, but that he rejected them at present, having concluded from the Epistle to the Galatians that their authors had Judaised.

At the same time that Marcion was teaching at Rome, another gnostic established there a famous school as well. This was *Valentine*, the author of the third great gnostic system. He remained there till 160, when he retired to

Cyprus. According to him, from the eternal Father, the unfathomable abyss (*βυθός*), there emanated a first pair, or *syzygia* of Aeons (divine forces); this pair was composed of Intellect (*ὁ νοῦς*), which is called also the *only Son* (*ὁ μονογενής*), and of the *Truth* (*ἡ ἀλήθεια*); it produced a second, the *Word* (*ὁ λόγος*), and the *Life* (*ἡ ζωή*); from this second there proceeded, finally, a third, *Man* (*ὁ ἄνθρωπος*), and *the Church* (*ἡ ἐκκλησία*). In the last place, the Intellect and the Truth (the first syzygia) produced the *Christ from Above* (*ὁ ἄνω Χριστός*), and the *Holy Spirit* (*τὸ πνεῦμα ἅγιον*), which completed the number 30, the numeral of the Pleroma or fulness of the divine powers (see Schaff, *History of the Church*, ii. p. 475).

One cannot ignore in these appellations the influence of the prologue of John. The school of Valentine, in fact, made quite special use of that gospel,[1] as well as of that of Luke, by allegorising them. Tertullian exactly opposed Marcion to Valentine, saying that "the first adapted the Scriptures to his system, while the second adapted his system to the Scriptures" (*De præscr.* 38). The school of Valentine continued to use the fourth gospel. Of the two principal disciples of this master, Ptolemy and Heracleon, the first, in his *Letter to Flora*, cited words derived either from Mark or Matthew; then, certainly, one from John i. 3: "All things have been made by the Logos," etc. (after Epiphanius, *Hær.* 33. 3); and that while calling the author of this last book an *apostle.* The second, Heracleon, wrote, probably about 160,[2] the first commentaries on the Gospels of John and Luke, which proves the importance that was attached to these writings in the school of Valentine.

[1] Irenæus says of the school of Valentine (iii. 11. 7): "Hi autem qui a Valentino sunt, eo quod est secundum Joannem plenissime utentes" . . .

[2] Volkmar has placed Heracleon after Irenæus (according to him between 200 and 220), for this reason, that he was not named by this Father. This is an error of fact; Irenæus says (ii. 4): "The Aeons of Ptolemy *and of Heracleon*, and of those that share their opinions." Heracleon, called the *intimate friend of Valentine*, doubtless wrote shortly before or after his departure from Rome, about 160.

We have arrived at the end of the first half of the second century. It is marked by a writing of a certain importance, the *Apology* of the Athenian philosopher Aristides. It was formerly believed, on the faith of Eusebius (iv. 3), that it had been delivered to the Emperor Hadrian (117–138). Recent discoveries point to a date a little more advanced (140–145), in the time of the reign of Antoninus. Aristides demonstrates to the emperor the absurdity of all the forms of pagan idolatry; he brings out as well the imperfect and external character of the Jewish worship, and to these imperfect religions he opposes *the Gospel,* of which he says that it has been recently preached *among them* (the heathen), adding: "that they will themselves experience the power of it, *if they read it.*" In the Greek text of this writing is here found (c. 15) the expression εὐαγγελικὴ ἁγία γραφή. In chap. xvi. he invites his imperial reader to check all that he affirms by means of *the writings* of which he speaks, which will prove to him that he has said nothing to him that he has not himself read there (ταῖς γραφαῖς τῶν Χριστιανῶν ἐγκύψας εὑρήσεις οὐδὲν ἔξω τῆς ἀληθείας με λέγειν); chap. xvii.: he says, moreover, that there is found among the Christians *in other writings,* words "that are too difficult for him to be able to say, or for a man to be able to repeat." Some have had the idea to refer these words to the writings of Aristides himself. But how should he speak thus to the emperor of his own works? Aristides commenced his writing by a résumé of the principal facts of the gospel history: the coming of Jesus from heaven, His birth of a virgin of Israel, His revelation as Son of God in human nature, His preaching of the life-giving word, the choice of the twelve apostles, His crucifixion with the nails with which the Jews pierced Him, His resurrection and His return to heaven by the ascension, the sending of the apostles into the whole world, and the powerful effect produced by their preaching unto this day, namely, the enlightenment of the world. That is evidently the summary of the gospel history, as we would make it after our four gospels. It is thus probable that those writings of the Christians to which Aristides directs the emperor to test the truth of his account, were no other than our gospels combined in one whole. As regards the *other* writings, more difficult to understand, that he mentions besides these, I cannot for my part doubt that thereby he means the epistles, in particular those of Paul, to which Ignatius had already made a clear allusion, and of which second Peter speaks in a pretty similar way (iii. 16).

We can now sum up the result of this rapid course across the first fifty years of the second century, and that as regards each of our gospels.

We have already ascertained at the end of the first century the presence and the use of *Matthew* at Rome (Clement), and in Egypt (Barnabas). After Clement of Alexandria, it had been carried as far as the Indies (Southern Arabia), from the apostolic age, by the Apostle Bartholomew. Then it is clearly quoted in the Didaché, in Ignatius, Papias, etc.

*Mark* is only quoted later, about 120, by Papias, doubtless because men were more occupied with the teachings than the doings of the Lord. The care that Papias takes to relate its origin, proves the interest that was attached to this book, even in Asia Minor, at the time when contemporaries of Jesus were still living.

*Luke* appears to have been used at Rome by Clement from the end of the first century. It is used in Syria by the author of the Didaché, and a little later by Ignatius. The use that Marcion made of it, proves its general propagation in the churches of the first half of the second century.

The Gospel of *John* has left its stamp on several passages of the Didaché, and of the letters of Ignatius. It was probably at Alexandria in the hands of Basilides, and certainly a little later at Rome in those of Valentine.

Alongside these four gospel writings, the existence and use of which we believe we have recognised from the end of the first century and the first half of the second, in the different countries of the Church, from Syria across Egypt and Asia Minor as far as Italy, and that not only with the Fathers, but also with the heads of the great heterodox parties—alongside, I say, of these four gospels, we do not find at the same epoch, among the numerous gospels mentioned pp. 2–4, *a single writing* that could, even remotely, be put on a par with them, whether as to the number of the quotations, or for the extent of the domain in which they appear to have been diffused, or for the public use that was made of them; while the two passages of Justin, quoted pp. 35 and 37, have, on the one hand, proved the immense propagation of Christianity before 150, and, on the other, shown that in the churches visited by this Father the *apostolic Memoirs* (our gospels; see under) were read in the Lord's day worship equally with the writings of the Old Testament.

The best known writing that could be opposed to us would be the so-called Gospel *of the Hebrews*, composed in the Aramaic language, probably a little after the war of Barcochébas, between 135 and 150 (see Zahn, *Gesch. d. Kan.* vol. ii. p. 122). It is chiefly known to us from Jerome, who had found it in the Judæo-Christian community of Berœa (now Aleppo), and had ascertained its great resemblance to our first gospel, so that at the first moment he took it for the apostolic original of the latter. The difference between the Aramaic gospel and the Greek Matthew was, however, so great, that Jerome did not believe it useless to make a Greek and Latin translation of the former. One may conclude from this that the gospel found by him was an adaptation of our Matthew to the ideas and needs of certain Judæo-Christian communities of Syria. One cannot, then, regard it as an independent gospel to be placed in the same rank as our canonical gospels; the more that the domain in which it was received and used was very restricted, not even extending, according to Eusebius, to the whole of the Judæo-Christian churches. Sometimes this writing is said to have been already quoted by Papias and even by Ignatius. These are two errors. Eusebius has merely declared that the narrative of the adulterous woman which Papias quoted was found *also* in the

Gospel of the Hebrews. As regards the term incorporeal spirit (*δαιμόνιον ἀσώματον*, *Smyrn.* c. 3), it is in the last degree doubtful whether Ignatius derived it from the Gospel of the Hebrews (see pp. 43, 44). The first author known to us who has decidedly quoted it is Hegesippus, who sojourned at Rome between 157 and 168. This Father was probably of Jewish origin, and had known this writing in the East. Eusebius says of him (iv. 22) that he "quotes certain things from the Gospel of the Hebrews, and even also from the Syriac, and in the proper Hebrew language." But he does not say that he only admits that gospel. The best known extra-canonical gospel, after that of the Hebrews, was that called *of the Egyptians.* It is quoted very early in the second epistle attributed to Clement of Rome (xii. 12), and the same quotation is found later in Clement of Alexandria. This writing may have been composed about 150. Harnack, in his treatise on the Canon of the New Testament about the year 200, alleges that it was at first *admitted* and *publicly read* in the churches of Egypt. The principal reason he adduces is the title: *According to the Egyptians*;[1] but this title may have been thus formulated quite simply, with the intention of distinguishing it as a special and purely local gospel from the gospels generally admitted, or even from the Gospel according to the Hebrews. This is confirmed even by him who at the end of the second century quotes it most readily, Clement of Alexandria, who while quoting it takes care immediately to remark (*Strom.* iii. 93) that "this writing is not of the number of the four that have been transmitted to us" (*πρῶτον μὲν οὖν ἐν τοῖς παραδεδομένοις ἡμῖν τέτταρσιν εὐαγγελίοις οὐκ ἔχομεν τὸ ῥητόν, ἀλλ' ἐν τῷ κατ' Αἰγυπτίους*). The uncertain and later origin of the last is thus clearly signalised by the very Father who believes he can quote it with reference to a strange word attributed to Jesus. The name given by Clement to this writing

[1] "This title, 'Gospel according to the Egyptians,' shows that this gospel was not employed by heretics, but by the Church of a whole country." Thus Harnack, p. 47.

is positively designated by Epiphanius (*Hær.* 62. 2) as little diffused. He says: "The so-called Gospel of the Egyptians, to which *some* have given this name." The strained form of some words of Jesus reported in this writing, the restricted circle in which it was employed, in fine, the obscurity of its origin, place it very far beneath our canonical gospels. Hilgenfeld dates the composition of it from the period 170 to 180.

A like judgment, and still more certainly, ought to be formed on the value of two writings much more ancient, quoted by Justin, and consequently dating from the first part of the second century. These are, first, the *Acts of Pilate*, to which he refers (*Apol.* i. c. 35 and 48) to confirm some details of the account of the Passion. This writing, to a large extent founded on the Gospel of John, can in no way pretend to apostolic authority; it only dates, according to Harnack (*Chronologie*), at least in its present form, from a time later than Origen, from the middle of the third century; besides, it only refers to a particular moment in the life of Jesus. The other writing is the *Protevangelium* or Gospel of James, which evidently supposes the Gospel of Luke, see pp. 2–3. According to Zahn, this is "a compilation from Matthew and Luke, so far as it is not a free invention."

The *Gospel of Thomas* appears to be also of the first part of the second century. This book must have been composed in Egypt under gnostic influences. It relates the most fantastic anecdotes of the life of the child Jesus, between five and twelve years; it thus pretends to fill a gap left by our canonical gospels, whereby it betrays its own dependent character with reference to them. One might be tempted to attach a little more value to a writing already quoted by Heracleon (about 160), and entitled *Preaching of Peter* (**Κήρυγμα Πέτρου**). It is from this book that the legendary narrative was perhaps drawn of the fire kindled in the Jordan at the baptism of Jesus. It is also supposed that it was in this book the pretended order was mentioned, as given to the apostles, to remain at Jerusalem during twelve years, before proceeding to bear the gospel to the world. This book was strongly anti-Judaic, and severely handled the legal worship. In this respect it belongs to the same group as the Epistle of Barnabas, that to Diognetus, and the Apology of Aristides, which has some passages in common with it. That severe condemnation of the Jewish ceremonies in these writings was as it were the prelude to the heresy of Marcion. In any case a writing with the title *Preaching* of Peter cannot be regarded as a rival of the gospels. There remains the *Gospel of Peter*, placed much too late (about 170), by its gnostic character, for any question about it as capable of being put on a par with the canonical gospels quoted between 100 and 150.

And what shall we say of that host of writings, absolutely without serious value, entitled Gospels of Cerinthus, and of the Twelve Apostles, or of Basilides, and of Andrew, of Apelles, of Barnabas, of Matthias, of Philip, of Eve, or of Judas Iscariot? This pseudepigraphic fabric of falsified or arbitrarily invented gospels produces the effect of an infectious swamp that had invaded the sacred soil. Let us hasten to plant our foot anew on a more solid territory. We find it on reaching the *writings of Justin*, even though these still raise many delicate questions.

## IV

Before entering on a domain so important for our subject, I think I ought to recall two things: 1st, that we do not here treat of the *canonisation* of the gospels, but only of the *formation of the collection* in which these four writings are found united; 2nd, that the question is not of the Canon of the New Testament in general, but solely of the most ancient and most important group of this Canon.

Justin, whose writings are now to occupy us, born in Samaria in the city of Nablous (the ancient Sichem) at an unknown date, was of heathen origin. Impelled by the deep need of knowing God, he studied Greek philosophy in its principal forms, Stoicism, Pythagorism, Platonism, without finding therein the desired satisfaction. Walking, plunged in thought, on the shore of the sea near Ephesus, he met an aged Christian whom he never saw again, and with whom he had a conversation that decided his life. This man directed his attention to the prophecies of the Old Testament, and said to him on leaving him: "Before all things, pray; it is God who gives knowledge" (*Dial.* c. 7, end). He was thus brought to faith in the gospel by the proof from prophecy. From this moment he consecrated all his powers to the defence of the faith of the Christians. About 140 he came to settle at Rome, where at the same time Marcion and Valentine were teaching, and he established there a school of Christian philosophy. Of his numerous works there only remain to us three certainly authentic, the *two Apologies,* the second and smaller of which is properly only a supplement to the first. The first was presented to the Emperor Antoninus, as well as to the Roman Senate and people, probably about 148 to 150. The second, addressed to the Senate, closely followed. The third work is the *Dialogue* with the Jew Trypho or Tarpho, and is the account of a discussion that Justin maintained at Ephesus with that famous rabbi. In the *Apologies* he defends the Christians against the odious imputations that were circulating against them among the heathen. In the *Dialogue* he proves, against the Jews, the truth of Christianity by the prophecies of which the gospel is the fulfilment.

In these three works he quotes as often as eighteen times a group of writings to which he gives the name of *Memoirs of the Apostles* (Ἀπομνημονεύματα τῶν ἀποστόλων); a name which shows the plurality of them. But often also, where the sentiment of the unity of the contents of these writings predominates, he uses the collective term τὸ εὐαγγέλιον, *the gospel.* So *Dial.* c. 100: "It is written *in the gospel,* saying"; and Trypho himself (*Dial.* c. 10) employs this term as designating something that is very familiar to him. He expresses himself thus: "I know that your precepts *in what is called the gospel* (ἐν τῷ λεγομένῳ εὐαγγελίῳ) are great and admirable, so much so that I suspect no one can observe them, for I have taken care to study them (ἐντυχεῖν αὐτοῖς)." And Justin replies to him (c. 18): "Since thou thyself ownest, O Trypho, to have read the things that the Saviour has taught." . . . The words *study* and *read* allow no doubt that it concerns a writing then well known under the name of *Gospel.*

*List of the Traits quoted by Justin as borrowed from the Memoirs of the Apostles.*[1]

1. *Apol.* i. c. 33; vol. i. p. 102: The supernatural birth (Luke i.; Matt. i.).
2. *Apol.* i. c. 66; vol. i. p. 182: The Lord's Supper (Matt. xxvi. and parall. in Luke and Mark).
3. *Apol.* i. c. 67; vol. i. p. 186: Reading of the *Memoirs* in public worship.[2]
4. *Dial.* c. 88; vol. ii. p. 320: The descent of the Holy Spirit on Jesus after the baptism (Matt. iii.; Mark i.; Luke iii.).
5. *Dial.* c. 100; vol. ii. p. 356: Profession of the divinity of Jesus by Peter. The pre-existence of Jesus (Matt. xvi. 16; John i. 1 and fol.).
6. *Dial.* c. 101; vol. ii. p. 362: The mocking of the Jews before the cross (Matt. xxvii. 39–43; Luke xxiii. 35–37, and Mark xv. 29–32).
7. *Dial.* c. 102; vol. ii. p. 364: Silence of Jesus (Matt. xxvi. 63; Mark xiv. 61; Luke xxiii. 9).
8. *Dial.* c. 103; vol. ii. p. 372: The temptation (Matt. iv.; Luke iv.).
9. *Dial.* c. 103; vol. ii. p. 372: The agony of Jesus at Gethesemane (Luke xx.; Matt. xxvi.; Mark xiv.).
10. *Dial.* c. 104; vol. ii. p. 374: Parting of the garments (Matt. xxvii. 35; Mark xv. 24; Luke xxiii. 34).
11. *Dial.* c. 105; vol. ii. p. 376: Incarnation and miraculous birth (John i. 1–4; Luke i.; Matt. i.).
12. *Dial.* c. 105; vol. ii. p. 378: Father, into Thy hands I commit My spirit (Luke xxiii. 46).
13. *Dial.* c. 105; vol. ii. p. 378: The righteousness of the scribes and Pharisees (Matt. v. 20).
14. *Dial.* c. 106; vol. ii. p. 378: The hymn sung after the holy supper (Matt. xxvi. 30; Mark xiv. 26).
15. *Dial.* c. 106; vol. ii. p. 380: The surnames given to Peter and to the sons of Zebedee (Mark iii. 16, 17;[3] John i. 42).

[1] We quote after the third edition of Otto, *S. Justini Opera*, 1876–77.

[2] This passage cannot properly be reckoned as *quoted* after the *Memoirs*; but it is a very important *mention* of these writings.

[3] According to Credner, derived from the *Gospel of Peter.*

16. *Dial.* c. 106; vol. ii. p. 380: The star of the Magi (Matt. ii.).

17. *Dial.* c. 106; vol. ii. p. 382: Arabia, country of the Magi.

18. *Dial.* c. 107; vol. ii. p. 382: The sign of Jonah, and the announcement of the resurrection on the third day (Matt. xii. 40).

These are the cases in which Justin makes appeal to the *Memoirs*; beyond this he also quotes our four gospels very often, without expressly naming them. But one can already certainly establish by this list *that there is not one of the traits of the life of Jesus quoted by Justin as contained in these apostolic Memoirs that is not found in our gospels*; this is a fact that of itself already suffices to prove the close relation that must have existed between the *Memoirs* and our gospels. There is more: Justin quotes some features of the gospel history, very secondary, it is true, that are not found in our gospels: thus *Arabia* as the country whence the Magi came (*Dial.* c. 77, 78, 88, 102, 106); the birth of Jesus in a *grotto* (*Dial.* c. 78); the *fire* lighted in Jordan at the baptism of Jesus (*Dial.* c. 88); the little ass of Bethany fastened to *a vine-stock* (*Apol.* i. c. 32; *Dial.* c. 53); besides some words that are no more found in our gospels, such as: "There shall be schisms and divisions" (*Dial.* c. 35); "You shall be judged in the things in which I shall find you" (*Dial.* c. 47); "Thou art My beloved Son; *this day have I begotten Thee*" (c. 88, 103). But what is very remarkable is that *not one of these facts, and not one of these words foreign to our gospels, is quoted by Justin as contained in the apostolic Memoirs.* This second fact, complementary to the first, seems to me to complete the demonstration of the perfect conformity of the *Memoirs* with our four gospels. In effect, if not one of the traits that Justin says are borrowed from the *Memoirs* is lacking in our gospels, and if not one of those that are lacking in the gospel narrative is mentioned by him as being found in the *Memoirs,* it would be a very strange chance if these books called by him *Memoirs of the Apostles* were not the same writings as our gospels.[1]

[1] It cannot be denied that Justin has borrowed some of the traits mentioned by him either from oral tradition or even from certain extra-canonical writings. But from these traits, often quoted, we must, I think,

Besides, Justin has himself taken care clearly to explain himself, at least once, on this point. In the first *Ap.* c. 66, i. p. 156, he writes: "This is what the apostles have transmitted to us in the *Memoirs* composed by them *which are called gospels* (ἐν τοῖς γενομένοις ὑπ' αὐτῶν ἀπομνημονεύμασιν ἃ καλεῖται εὐαγγέλια)." After having designated these writings by a name appropriate to his non-Christian readers, Justin would characterise them, at least once, as being just the same as those that commonly bear among the Christians the name of *gospels*. Only this name was then lavished on so many writings, that it might be asked whether, by those gospels, he just means *our* gospels actually regarded as canonical. The answer seems to me to emerge in a pretty certain way from the following explanation found in *Dial.* c. 103: "For in the *Memoirs* which I say were composed *by His apostles and by those that accompanied them* (ἃ φημι ὑπὸ τῶν ἀποστόλων αὐτοῦ καὶ τῶν ἐκείνοις παρακολουθησάντων συντετάχθαι)"; words that harmonise exactly with the composition of our canonical collection (on the one hand Matthew and

deduct a good number. Thus, 1st, those he thinks he can derive from a prophecy, as the little ass of Bethany fastened to a vine-stock, after Gen. xlix. 11; the birth of Jesus in a grotto, a fact also mentioned in some non-canonical writings, and for which Justin himself appeals to Isa. xxxiii. 16; the words, "This day have I begotten Thee," added to the divine allocution after the baptism, a reading that is also found in some manuscripts, and the true source of which seems to me to be Ps. ii. 7 which Justin himself quotes in this connection, saying (*Dial.* c. 88): "And a voice from heaven was uttered, *that which had been announced by David as to be addressed to the Christ by the Father.*" 2nd, Other details are derived by induction from our gospel texts themselves; thus Arabia as the country of the Magi; Justin defines thereby the vague expression of Matthew: "*from the East*"; he is led thus to express himself by the nature of the presents offered, and by the prophecies (Ps. lxxii. 10 and Isa. lx. 6). The mention of the ploughs and yokes that Jesus made is deduced from Mark vi. 3, "*the carpenter,*" and from Matt. xiii. 55, "*the son of the carpenter*"; the saying: "There shall be schisms and divisions," is a logical conclusion drawn from the announcement of ravening wolves, false Christs, and false apostles "seducing the faithful"; words that are quoted after Matt. vii. 15 and xxiv. 5 by Justin himself before and after the one we speak of, always with a probable reminiscence of 1 Cor. xi. 19; the maxim: "I will judge you after the things in which I shall find you," appears to me deduced from Luke xvii. 34–36 and Matt. xxiv. 40–42: "In that night the one shall be taken and the other left.'

John, and on the other Mark and Luke). And as we do not find, which we have seen above, any passage attributed by Justin to the *Memoirs* which is not read precisely in these four, it seems to us that their identity is not only probable, but certain.

As regards Christian extra-canonical works, Justin quotes by name only the *Acts of Pilate* (*Apol.* i. c. 35 and 48); it is possible that the *Protevangelium* is used by him (*Dial.* c. 78); but what a contrast between this small number of extra-canonical writings,—writings so rarely quoted, on the one hand, and the frequent quotations of our four gospels that we have established, on the other! Besides the eighteen express quotations indicated above as derived from the *apostolic Memoirs*, we find indicated in the register of Otto, for Matthew about a hundred, for Mark about fifteen, for Luke about sixty, for John about twenty quotations (pp. 587–590). Admitting that by a severe scrutiny one may reduce these numbers by a fourth or even by a half, it is no less true that the use made by Justin of our canonical gospels leaves

After all that there only remains, it seems to me, a single extra-biblical trait: the fire kindled in Jordan at the baptism of Jesus. That is a legend derived either from oral tradition or from some work that Justin did not judge worthy to be quoted; for he does not attribute it to the *Memoirs*. If it be objected that in the passage (*Dial.* c. 88), after having mentioned the two circumstances of the fire kindled in the river and of the descent of the Holy Spirit under the form of a dove, Justin quotes the apostolic *Memoirs*, it has to be observed that it is in relation to the second trait, *and to it alone*, that he adds these words: "This is what the apostles of our Christ have written." The mention of the two facts is separated by a significant change of construction, which does not allow us to refer the testimony of the apostles to the first. The unmentioned source of the latter appears to be (after the *De rebaptismate*, a writing wrongly placed among the works of Cyprian) an apocryphal book, entitled the *Preaching of Paul.* Again, two little extra-canonical details have been brought out, mentioned by Justin. After (*Dial.* c. 41, 59, 88) John the Baptist spoke *sitting* in the desert; but this was then the custom (Matt. v. 1; Luke iv. 20). Then Justin adds to the mocking of the Jews (*Dial.* c. 101) certain insulting grimaces with which they accompanied it. This trait is found, according to him, *in the Memoirs*; and, in fact, it really is found in the ἐξεμυκτήριζον of Luke (xxiii. 35). Besides, the quotation of the *Memoirs* on this point bears not on the mocking in act, but solely on those words of Jesus that they ironically parodied (εἰρωνευόμενοι): "He called Himself the Son of God."

infinitely behind it that made by the various writers of the first half of the second century, of the other analogous writings, in particular of the Gospels of the Hebrews or the Egyptians.[1]

There have been alleged, against the use of our gospels by Justin, the *differences* that there sometimes are between his quotations and the gospel texts. But we have already noticed a very free way of quoting in Clemens Romanus and Polycarp. This need not surprise us if it be admitted that these Fathers often quoted from memory and blended together analogous texts. Justin quotes with the same liberty the texts of the Old Testament while adapting them to his subject. He even quotes certain texts of the New in several and different enough ways. Westcott, in his book, *On the Canon* (6th ed. 1889), gives thirteen examples of this (pp. 129, 130). The most remarkable is the double quotation of Matt. xix. 17, found in the *Apol.* i. c. 16 and in the *Dial.* c. 101.[2] He even commits numerous mistakes in quoting one author of the Old Testament for another: thus, Zephaniah for Zechariah, Jeremiah for Daniel, Zechariah for Malachi. Nothing was more natural at that time, when the external form of the manuscripts rendered more difficult than at present the search for a passage that one wished to quote. The form of the roll, the continuous writing with no space between the words, and with no division resembling our verses, prevented one from readily finding the desired words. And one must take account

[1] The use of the three Synoptics by Justin, previously totally denied by some theologians, has been gradually recognised as regards the three; it is now a fact generally admitted. Some still refuse to recognise it as regards John. Volkmar, renouncing the denial of certain evident relations between this gospel and the writings of Justin, has sought to reverse the relation by making Justin the model and the author of John the copier. This stroke of ingenious audacity has not succeeded. Another scholar, also of the extreme left, Thoma, fully recognises the dependence of Justin in regard to John; he has even gone so far as affirm, in Hilgenfeld's *Zeitschrift*, 1875, that there is not a single chapter of John the impression of which one does not find again in the writings of Justin; only he thinks he reads between the lines that Justin quoted this writing without attaching to it the least idea of authority.

[2] In *Apol.*: "None is good but God only, who has created all." In the *Dial.*: "There is but one good, My Father, who is in heaven."

of the numerous variants that already existed in the texts of our gospels in the second century. We have even now in the Cambridge Manuscript (D) numerous examples of these ancient variants, more or less considerable; for, although dating from a much later time (fifth century), this manuscript, as Tregelles and Credner have acknowledged, reproduces the readings of much older manuscripts, and represents most exactly the text generally received in the second half of the second century (see Westcott, p. 177). We can thus by means of it form some idea of the differences of texts that already existed at that epoch. We have perhaps an instructive example of them in the following passage of Justin. In the first *Apol.* c. 35, he shows us the Jews seating Jesus on the tribunal of Pilate, while saying to Him in irony: "Judge us." This account is in itself so strange, so absurd even, that one cannot for a moment give it credence. How is it to be explained? In a simple enough way, if, on the one hand, one supposes in the text of John xix. 13 a slight variant, the plural form ἐκάθισαν ("they [the Jews] seated [Jesus]") in place of the singular ἐκάθισεν ("he [Pilate] sat down"),—there is but the change of one letter,—and if, on the other hand, one takes account of the lively desire that Justin had to show here the fulfilment of a prophecy, that of Isa. lviii. 2: "They seek to know my ways . . . and they require of me just judgments," words that Justin himself is careful to quote on this occasion. We see what a difference in meaning a very insignificant mistake in copying could produce. But if this explanation is well founded, it concurs in proving the use of John by Justin and by the Gospel of Peter.

Another still graver difficulty results from a certain number of cases where these differences between the quotations of Justin and the gospel texts recur almost identically in the gospel quotations of the *Clementine Homilies.* Had Justin and the author of the *Homilies* both drawn from a gospel different from our canonical writings, such as the Gospel of the Hebrews or of Peter, as Credner and Renan have supposed? Or, as Bousset has developed in a recent writing,[1] had Justin, while drawing from the editions of Matthew and Luke, been influenced by remembrances of the text of the Logia, the primitive work of the Apostle Matthew? Or had Justin drawn from an already existing Harmony of our gospels, as Sanday had supposed,[2] and as Rendel Harris concludes from certain relations between the Arabic *Diatessaron* and the Syriac version of Cureton? Or in fine, might it not be supposed that the author of the *Clementines*, writing at Rome sometime after Justin, knew his works there, and there drew from them? It is evident that we cannot here enter on this complicated problem. There can be no question of the Gospel of the Hebrews, the fragments of which known to us present no relation to the quotations of Justin;[3] and as little of the Gospel of Peter, which is quite posterior to Justin.[4] As regards the hypothesis of Bousset, Schürer, while paying homage to the exactness of his work, is unable to give him his assent, and thinks that this writer has let himself be too much influenced by the desire to recover a written source anterior to our Synoptics. According to him, "the problem is not yet solved."[5] However it may be with this question, its solution cannot compromise the result to which we have been led by the close relation we have established between the quotations of Justin and our four gospels. If it is true that there is not a single trait quoted by Justin *as derived from the Memoirs* which does not occur in our gospels, and not a single trait unknown to our gospels that he presents *as borrowed from the Memoirs*, it may doubtless be the case that he had derived this trait or that saying from oral tradition, or even from

[1] *Die Evangelien-Citate Justin's des Märtyrers, in ihrem Werthe für die Evangelien-Critik*, 1891.

[2] See Sanday, "A Survey of the Synoptic Question," *Expositor*, June 1891.

[3] See Westcott in *On the Canon*: "The fragments of the Gospel of the Hebrews that have been preserved to us do not present any particular resemblance to Justin."

[4] See Kunze: *Das neu aufgefundene Bruchstück des sogennanten Petrus Evangeliums.* The author places this writing between 160 and 170.

[5] See the review given by this scholar, *Literatur-Zeitung*, 1891, pp. 62–67.

some extra-canonical writing; but what is certain is that such a writing did not form part of the *Memoirs* of the apostles quoted by him. And, in effect, why should not it have been preserved as well as the others, if it had formed part of these *Memoirs*, the reading of which in all the churches of Christendom had been reported by Justin? And how should it have been the case that immediately after Justin, Tatian (by the very term Diatessaron), then Muratori's Fragment, and finally Irenæus, only speak now of our four?

We have yet to examine more closely a passage that we read in the first *Apol.* c. 67, and the whole value of which we can now estimate. Justin says:

> For all the things that we offer, we bless the Creator of all things by His Son, Jesus Christ, and by the Holy Spirit. And on the day called Sunday, all those who dwell in the city or in the country assemble in one place, and there are read the Memoirs of the apostles or the writings of the prophets, as far as the time permits; then, when the reader has ended, he who presides addresses a warning and exhortation to the assembly to imitate the good things that have been heard.

This picture of the ordinary worship of the Lord's day is completed by the account of the celebration of the Lord's Supper in the preceding chapter. From this it results that our gospels were placed, in the public worship of the churches that Justin had passed through from the East to the West, in the same rank as the writings of the Old Testament. It is even to be noticed that Justin places them before these last. As regards the expression: *The writings of the prophets,* to designate the whole Old Testament, it must be remembered that Justin himself (*Apol.* i. c. 32) calls Moses the *first of the prophets* (Μωϋσῆς, πρῶτος τῶν προφητῶν). Besides, wherever he had found Christianity established, that is to say, as he says, *Dial.* c. 117, "among the barbarians and among the Greeks, among the Scythians and among the nomads," he there also had found the gospels known and read in the public assemblies of the Church.

From all that precedes, it seems to me to result with certainty that it is neither to Justin nor to his time that the formation of the collection of our four gospels can be attributed. He never says a word leading us to suspect that this collection could have been his own work, or even that he had only used it privately. On the contrary, he speaks of it as a book known even by his Jewish interlocutor, and bearing in the Church the usual name of *Gospel*. Aristides the Athenian philosopher, who presents an *Apology* to the emperor, also employs this term *Gospel*, and constantly refers his reader *to the books* (γραφαῖς) of the Christians. This writer is so near Justin, that he could not speak of other writings than he did; and the résumé that he gives of them in beginning his book is so exactly conformed to the contents of our gospels, that one can think of no other books. Going back still farther, we have found them quoted, sometimes the one, sometimes the other, by the ecclesiastical and heretical writers of the different countries of the Church. This uninterrupted chain that attaches the fourfold gospel of Justin to all the writings quoted, from the year 100 to the year 150, continues, as we shall see, until Irenæus and Clement, towards the end of the second century.

A sanctuary with four fronts of harmonious beauty had arisen at the end of the apostolic age; a host of unpleasant structures in bad taste had been raised around this edifice, and had for the moment masked its beauty. The day came when, by a superior will, these surrounding structures were razed and swept away. The principal edifice then appeared to all eyes in its primitive grandeur and its harmonious beauty. That is what took place for the gospels in the time of Justin; there was not creation, but reappearance.

## V

Following upon the martyrdom by which Justin paid for his Christian fidelity and boldness (about 165–167), one of his disciples, named Tatian, of Assyrian extraction, probably converted by him, wrote, under the influence of the master whose admirer he had become, several works, in particular, an *Apology,* addressed to the heathen, and entitled *Πρὸς Ἕλληνας*, in which he three times quotes the Gospel of John, in particular these words of the prologue: "All things were made by Him," etc. (John i. 3); then another writing of exegetical nature, which Eusebius speaks of in these terms (*H. E.* iv. 29): "Tatian having composed, I know not how (οὐκ οἶδ' ὅπως), a certain combination and union of the gospels (συνάφειάν τινα καὶ συναγωγὴν τῶν εὐαγγελίων), called that (τοῦτο) by the name of τὸ διὰ τεσσάρων" (an expression signifying composed by means of four). We have seen that the master of Tatian had, in a remarkable passage, spoken of the *apostolic Memoirs* as "composed by the apostles and their fellow-workers" (*Dial.* c. 103); but he had not expressly indicated the number of these narrations: one must have supposed at least four of them. The title of the book of his disciple gives us to understand that these gospels were really four in number. In fact, it seems to me, after all we have ascertained of the intimate relation between the *Memoirs* of Justin and our four canonical gospels, that it is impossible to doubt that *the four* of Tatian were these latter. Yet this identity has been disputed. Thus Renan admits, indeed, that Tatian employed our three Synoptics, but not John. For he says: "Tatian did not know or did not admit this last" (*L'Église chrétienne,* p. 503). In speaking thus, Renan did not know, or else entirely forgot, the quotations of John in the *Apology* of Tatian. He thinks that besides the Synoptics, Tatian employed either the Gospel of the Hebrews or the Gospel of Peter. In fine, he assures us that the term Diatessaron is in Greek a musical expression, denoting *perfect accord,* and that, consequently, it in no way implies the fourfold number of the writings with which Tatian had composed his. But the accord of all the tones is called διὰ πασῶν (χορδῶν), and the two analogous expressions, διὰ τεσσαρῶν and διὰ πέντε, indicated the accord of two tones separated by an interval of two or three tones, the third or the fourth (see Passow's *Dict.* i. pp. 626, 653, 667), so that this musical use does not in any respect agree with the term designating the work of Tatian. A Greek expression that would have more analogy with the true sense of this title would be the example quoted by Salmon (p. 83), after which the term *Diapenté* denoted an unguent much used, and composed of *five ingredients.* The relation of this expression to the title of Tatian's *Harmony* is clear as day.[1] We only knew, till a a little while ago, two things about the *Diatessaron*: 1st, That Theodoret, bishop of Cyrrhus, near the Euphrates, had found at the beginning of the fifth century two hundred copies of this writing, and had replaced them by our detached gospels, because he had ascertained the suppression in it of the genealogies, and of all that implied the descent of Jesus from David. For the rest, he did not accuse it of any addition contrary to the gospel verity (comp. *Hær. Fab.* i. 20). 2nd, Besides that, there was known the affirmation of a Jacobite

[1] Jülicher (p. 101), while declaring "that all that we know of the *Diatessaron* shows that it rests on our four gospels alone," maintains the musical explanation of this title given by Renan, that of *accord* or *harmony*, without any relation to the number four; and in support of this general sense he adduces the passage of Dion Cassius, bk. xxxvii. 18 (p. 24, ed. Basil. 1858). But it seems to me this passage proves precisely the contrary of what it would have to show. The first words, "*Harmonia ea quæ Diatessaron vocatur*," would of themselves prove that this Greek term denoted a very special accord, and not at all an accord in general. The following explanation confirms it. "Let one begin," says Dion, "from tone one, and passing over the two following (*sequentes duos præteriens*), pause on tone four [to harmonise with one], then once more starting from tone four, and passing over the two following (*duobus proximis præteritis*), pause on tone seven [to harmonise with tone four]," that is, after Dion, the rhythm called Diatessaron, a rhythm that he applies to the seven days of the week as well as to the seven musical tones, with an object that it is needless here to explain. It is evident the rhythm thus described clearly rests on the number four. The quotation of Jülicher thus goes in a contrary direction to his object. The true explanation of the title adopted by Tatian, it seems to me, must be derived from another region. The famous physician Galen (second century), after having described an unguent composed of four ingredients, adds: "That is the Diatessaron (τὸ διὰ τῶν τεσσαρῶν [δ'])" (*Works*, vol. xiii. p. 851). This medical use of the word Diatessaron must have been much more popular and wider than its musical use, of a less usual and more scientific nature; and it agrees in a very striking way with the mode of composition of Tatian's *Harmony*, while, if one kept to the musical sense (according to Dion Cassius, agreement of tones one and four), the title of Tatian's work would denote a harmony of the first and fourth gospels alone, not of the four.

priest of the twelfth century, named Bar-Salibi, who spoke of a commentary on the *Diatessaron*, composed by Ephrem, the most illustrious Father of the Church of Syria (fourth century). Such a work, due to so great an author, sufficiently proved the public use that was made of this writing in those countries. The Syriac original of this commentary was lost: but there existed an Armenian translation of it, which was published in 1836 by the Armenian Mechitarist Institute, founded at Venice. This publication only attracted general attention, when a Latin translation of it appeared in 1876. Now this writing unanswerably proved that the work of Tatian really began, as Bar-Salibi had said, with the first verses of the prologue of John, the explanation of which Ephrem gave. Then followed the baptism of Jesus after Luke iii., then the narrative of the temptation after Matt. iv., from that the narrative passed to the calling of the first disciples (John i. 35 and fol.), then to the first return to Galilee and to the scene of Cana. The narration then continued without following a particular gospel, but using the four alike, and ended with a glance at the activity of the apostles in the world.[1] After that there was no more room to doubt the fact that the *Diatessaron* was indeed really a harmony of our four canonical gospels. This writing was in the Syriac language, according to Zahn, for the reason that it was long the gospel reading book in the churches of Syria, in particular in that of Edessa (now Orfa, that unhappy city recently given over to massacre and pillage by Turkish fanaticism). But, according to Harnack, it was rather written in Greek, as the very title and yet other signs seem to prove.[2] The gospel had, it seems, reached this remote country as early as the year 170.

To the discovery of the Armenian translation of Ephrem's

[1] This has been shown with success by Th. Zahn in *Forschungen*, i. pp. 113 to 219. See also the *Diatessaron* published in English in 1888 by Hemphill, after new documents more recently discovered. It results from the Arabic translation that this book finished with John xxi. 2, as it had begun with John i. 1 (Zahn, *Gesch. des K.* ii. p. 556).

[2] *Das Neue Testament*, etc. pp. 104, 105.

commentary there came to be added, a little later, that of two Arabic translations of the *Diatessaron* itself, one of which was published in Latin, in 1888, in honour of the jubilee of Leo XIII. These discoveries drew the attention of the learned to a Latin harmony of the gospels which had fallen, in 545, into the hands of Victor, bishop of Capua, and had been introduced into the C. *Fuldensis* of the Vulgate (sixth century). In reading the passage of Eusebius that refers to the *Diatessaron*, Victor had rightly supposed that this Latin *Harmony* might well be the work of Tatian. By means of the documents recently discovered, the conviction has been reached that it was really so, and thus one may now hope to possess approximately the work of Tatian. Doubtless the texts newly discovered are far from entirely agreeing. The substance, however, is so well established, that one can no longer have any doubt about the course followed by the author of the *Diatessaron*; it was just a combination (συνάφεια) of our four gospels. No doubt the word of Victor has been objected, which is as follows: "Unum ex quatuor compaginavit Tatianus evangelium, cui titulum *Diapenté* composuit." How are we to explain this title *Diapenté*, which nowhere else appears, and how could Victor, without contradiction, derive this title, signifying "composed *from five*," from the fact that Tatian had combined *four* writings? It must, perhaps, be supposed that Victor had remarked in this Latin translation some words or details that seemed to him foreign to our gospels, and which he had referred to another source, as has often been done regarding Justin. However this may be, it is quite certain, from all the testimonies, and from all the facts discovered, that even if it were so, the *four* of Tatian were none the less our four gospels, as his master had delivered them to him under the title of *apostolic Memoirs*. The *Diatessaron* of Tatian continued during more than a century the public reading book of the churches of Syria, till the time when, as we have seen from the example of Theodoret, there was substituted for this gospel, called *mixed*, our gospels, called *separate*.

About the time when Tatian published the *Diatessaron*, after 160, there was composed the strange book that has played since Baur's time an important part in criticism, and that bears the name of the *Clementine Homilies*. The author, who belonged to a semi-gnostic, Judaising party, lets fly sharp darts at Paul, whom he presents under the mask of Simon Magus. Although issuing from a medium quite foreign and even hostile to the church of Rome, the author of this writing, not less than Justin and Tatian, employs our four gospels, and quotes them as authorities. According to the table drawn up by Westcott,[1] Matthew is there quoted sixty times (seven times in a nearly literal way), Mark twice, Luke six times, John four times. He does not quote them alone, or nearly alone, as Justin and Tatian do; he alleges more frequently than they facts and words derived either from oral tradition or from writings of a more or less apocryphal character, like the Gospel of the Hebrews. In his quotations he does not expressly mention our gospels, and sometimes varies from the text of our Synoptics; but this way of doing is conformable to the plan of this religious romance, according to which Peter is supposed to report from memory the things of which he has himself been witness, and he behoves not to compromise that rôle by quoting writings composed later.

In 1740 the learned librarian of Milan, Muratori, published a Fragment in rude (some think African) Latin, written in the seventh or eighth century, which had been brought there from the Irish convent founded by Columbanus at Bobbio, in Lombardy. This Fragment formed part of a collection of various tracts, and contained a list of the writings that were read in the worship of the church in whose name the author was writing. This list was doubtless designed to serve as directory to another church not yet definitely organised, and to answer a question addressed by the latter to the former. The time when this correspondence must have taken place is determined by what the author of the Fragment says of the composition of the *Shepherd* of Hermas. He declares

[1] *On the Canon*, p. 522.

that that writing has been composed *quite recently* (nuperrimè) *in our days* (temporibus nostris), in the city of Rome by Hermas, brother of the bishop Pius, who was then at the head of that church. Now Pius occupied the see of Rome from 142 to 157 according to some, from 140 to 155 according to others. In estimating the interval denoted by the words *quite recently* and *in our days* at about thirty years, one reaches the date 170 to 180 for the composition of the original of this Fragment. Salmon (p. 52) and Zahn (*Gesch.* ii. pp. 134–136) allow the date 210, which does not seem to me compatible with the author's declaration we have just quoted. The omission of such writings as the Epistles to the Hebrews, 1 Peter, and James, corresponds to a time anterior to Irenæus rather than to the time of Clement and Origen. Scholars are not agreed on the original language of this writing. Hesse (*Das muratorische Fragment,* 1873) gives pretty strong reasons (pp. 25–39) in favour of the Latin original. But it is impossible not to discern across this rude Latin the traces of a Greek original, such as that which Hilgenfeld has succeeded in reconstituting (*Der Kanon*, ad p. 40). Comp. the accusative Luc*an*, and turns such as these: *nihil differt credentium fidei* (οὐδὲν διαφέρει τῇ πίστει), or *se publicare* (δημοσιεύεσθαι), or again, *alia plura quæ recipi non potest*, etc. What confirms this opinion is the observation of Zahn and Westcott, that other tracts contained in this collection use the same rude and semi-barbarous Latin style in reproducing in a Latin rendering fragments of Chrysostom. According to Zahn (*Gesch. d. K.* ii. 131), this Latin was pretty similar to what was spoken in Gaul in the fifth or sixth century. He so concludes from its analogy to that of the narrative of the journey to Palestine (*Peregrinatio*) of a Gaulish lady in 390.[1]

The Fragment begins with the last words of a phrase evidently relating to the Gospel of Mark, for it continues with these: *The third, the book of the gospel according to Luke,*

[1] One finds there the forms *per giro, per valle, per toto anno, in honore*, etc., and many other analogies with the forms of the Fragment.

which leaves no doubt of the mention of Matthew and Mark in the preceding lost part. Then follows the mention of the Gospel of John, as fourth, with a narration of the composition of that writing analogous to the account of Clement of Alexandria (see pp. 22 and 23). An apologetic tendency has been found in this passage, as if the author would labour to introduce into the Church this gospel, which was quite recent, and against which doubts had been raised. For my part, I cannot discover any trace of such an intention in this passage of the Fragment. If the author says: "What is there astonishing in this, that John declares himself in his epistles not only an eye-witness, but also writer of the admirable works of the Lord"? there is nothing in this reference to 1 John i. 1 and following, implying doubts raised regarding the gospel. This is also the opinion of Hesse, who says (pp. 123, 124): "The *quid mirum* of which the author speaks, and which he denies, does not concern the gospel but the first epistle, and applies to those who might wonder at the assurance with which the author declared himself in this beginning of the letter not only a witness, but reporter of the facts." The author of the Fragment confirms, by means of the epistle, the quality of witness that the author of the fourth gospel attributes to himself in the course of his narration. From the beginning of our Fragment it clearly appears that, in the collection containing these four writings, they followed each other in some sort numbered in the order indicated, and that this collection consequently already formed a closed and strongly fixed whole. They are the *Memoirs* of Justin and the gospels united in the *Diatessaron* that reappear here expressly *designated and counted.*

To this first group there succeeds a second, comprising the Acts and the epistles. While the history of Jesus was contained in four books, the labours of the twelve apostles are narrated in a single one, the Acts. Luke has here retraced the events of which he had himself been witness, and this is proved by the fact that he does not speak of the martyrdom of Peter, nor of the departure of Paul for Spain, in which he had not taken part. The author then enumerates thirteen epistles of Paul that are addressed by name to seven churches, in the same way as the *seven* of John in the Apocalypse. This symbolic number proves, in his view, that both the one and the other are designed for the universal Church. The Epistle to the Hebrews is omitted. Then he passes to the letters addressed to individuals, that to Philemon, that to Titus, and the two to Timothy, which, although dictated by personal affection, are yet held in honour by the Church, and consecrated by her to direct her administration. The author sets aside two letters falsely published under the name of Paul, the one to the Laodiceans, evidently fabricated by occasion of the epistle mentioned by Paul (Col. iv. 16); the other to the Alexandrians. The author says they were composed on behalf of the heresy of Marcion. The second consequently cannot be our Epistle to the Hebrews, as some, Hug for instance, have thought. The first is a flat compilation, but very innocent, of Pauline phrases. Jerome speaks of it in his *De Viris*, and that to reject it; it has, however, sometimes got access into the Canon for itself, and is still found in some biblical documents of the Middle Ages.

After the Pauline epistles, the author only names three catholic epistles, that of Jude and two (perhaps the three) of John; for sometimes the first and second of this apostle were regarded as but one. Then the Epistle of James and the two of Peter are completely omitted. The author here mentions "*the Wisdom* (*sapientia*), written in honour of Solomon by his friends." It has been thought that this expression applied to the Book of Proverbs, to which is sometimes given the name of Wisdom. But what would that book of the Old Testament have to do in this list of writings forming the Canon of the New? (See the notes following the text of the Fragment.)

There follows the third group, that of the Apocalypses. The author names two of them, John's and Peter's, while adding regarding this latter that some of the members of his church refuse to let it be read in the assembly. The Fragment of this writing that has recently been discovered in Egypt, in the tomb of the priest of Akhmîn, sufficiently justifies that opposition. To these two Apocalypses the author attaches what he has to say on the pretended revelations contained in the *Pastor* of Hermas. He declares that this writing must indeed be read (no doubt he means to say, be used privately or in the instruction of the catechumens), but that it ought not to be read publicly in the assembly, since it belongs neither to the prophets, whose number is complete, nor to the apostles, to whom has been granted the revelation of the last times. These words recall this saying of Justin: "They read the Memoirs of the apostles and the writings of the prophets"; a passage that proves that already, twenty years before the drawing up of this Fragment, those writings were read, and read alone, or nearly alone, in the weekly worship of the churches.

The Fragment ends as it began, with an interrupted phrase, the sense of which evidently is a summary declaration of rejection in regard to the writings of a certain number of heresiarchs. Among those names one clearly perceives at the beginning that of Valentine, and at the end, conjointly with the name of Basilides, the mention of Montanus, as chief of the sect of the Cataphrygians or Montanists.

I deem it useful here to give the complete text of the Fragment as, or nearly as, it is found in Westcott, *On the Canon*, pp. 534–538, as reproduction of the facsimile published by Tregelles, while correcting the barbarisms, whether of the translator or of the copier, which sometimes would render the text nearly unintelligible. This recension of Westcott is almost entirely conformed to Hilgenfeld's. A literally exact reproduction is found on pp. 523–527, and in Zahn, *Gesch. des K.* ii. pp. 5–8.

The most usual faults in this already corrupt Latin proceed from the confusion of the letters *u* and *o* (visurem, foit, numeni for nomine); the confusion of *c* and *g* (calatas, concruit); of *b* and *p* (scribta, obtime, apocalybsi, puplicare); of *e* and *æ* (directe, Jude, catholice); in fine, of the rude alteration of the terminations (proferam in place of proferat, ordine in place of ordinem, circumcisione for circumcisionem, duas for duæ).

A more complete list is given by Westcott (work quoted) and by Zahn (*Gesch. des Kanons*, vol. ii. p. 6).

*Text of Muratori's Fragment.*[1]

. . . Quibus (1) tamen interfuit, et ita posuit.

Tertium (2) evangelii librum secundum Lucan. Lucas, iste medicus, post ascensum Christi (3) cum eum Paulus, quasi ut juris (4) studiosum, secundum (5) adsumsisset, nomine suo (6) ex opinione (7) conscripsit. Dominum tamen nec ipse (8) vidit in carne, et idem prout assequi potuit (9), ita et a nativitate Johannis incepit dicere.

Quarti (10) evangeliorum Johannis ex discipulis (10[a]). Cohortantibus condiscipulis et episcopis suis (11) dixit: Conjejunate mihi hodiè triduo; et quid cuique fuerit revelatum, alterutrum (12) nobis enarremus. Eâdem nocte revelatum Andreæ ex apostolis (12[a]) ut, recognoscentibus (13) cunctis, Johannes suo nomine (14) cuncta describeret. Et ideo, licet varia singulis evangeliorum libris principia doceantur (15), nihil tamen differt credentium fidei, cúm uno ac principali Spiritu declarata sint in omnibus omnia de nativitate, de passione, de resurrectione, de conversatione cum discipulis suis ac de gemino ejus adventu, primum in humilitate, despectus quod fuit, secundum potestate regali præclarum (16), quod futurum est. Quid ergo mirum (17) si Johannes tam constanter singula etiam in epistulis suis proferat, dicens in semetipsum: "Quæ vidimus oculis nostris et auribus audivimus et manus nostræ palpaverunt, hæc scripsimus vobis." Sic enim non solum visorem, sed et auditorem sed et scriptorem omnium mirabilium domini per ordinem profitetur (18).

Acta autem omnium apostolorum sub uno libro scripta sunt (19). Lucas optime Theophile (20) comprendit quia (21) sub præsentia ejus singula gerebantur, sicuti et semotè passionem Petri evidenter declarat, sed et profectionem Pauli ab urbe ad Spaniam proficiscentis.

Epistulæ autem Pauli, quæ, a quo loco, vel quâ ex causâ directæ sint, volentibus intellegere ipsæ declarant (22). Primum

[1] The figures placed in the text refer to the explanatory notes that follow the text of the Fragment.

omnium Corintheis schisma hæresis interdicens (23); deinceps Calatis circumcisione (24), Romanis autem ordine scripturarum, sed et principium earum esse Christum intimans, prolixius scripsit; de quibus singulis necesse est (25) a nobis disputari, cum (26) ipse beatus apostolus Paulus, sequens prodecessoris sui Johannis ordinem, nonnisi nominatim septem ecclesiis scribat ordine tali: ad Corinthios (prima), ad Ephesios (secunda), ad Philippinses (tertia), ad Colossenses (quarta), ad Calatas (quinta), ad Thessalonecenses (sexta), ad Romanos (septima) (27), verum Corintheis et Thessalonecensibus licet pro correptione iteretur (28), una tamen per omnem orbem terræ ecclesia deffusa esse dinoscitur; et Johannes enim in Apocalypsi, licet septem ecclesiis scribat, tamen omnibus dicit. Verum ad Philemonem una, et ad Titum una, et ad Timotheum duas, pro affectu et dilectione, in honore tamen ecclesiæ catholice in ordinatione ecclesiastice discipline (29) sanctificate sunt. Fertur etiam ad Laodicenses, alia ad Alexandrinos, Pauli nomine finctæ ad hæresim Marcionis (30), et alia plura, quæ in catholicam ecclesiam recipi non potest. Fel enim cum melle misceri non concruit.

Epistula sanè Jude et superscriptio Johannis duas in catholica habentur (31); et Sapentia, ab amicis Salomonis in honorem ipsius scripta (32).

Apocalypses etiam Johannis et Petri tantum recipimus, quam quidam ex nostris legi in ecclesia nolunt (33). Pastorem vero nuperrime, temporibus nostris, in urbe Roma Hermas conscripsit, sedente cathedra urbis Romæ ecclesiæ Pio Episcopo, fratre ejus (34); et ideo legi cum quidem oportet, se publicare (35) vero in ecclesia populo neque inter prophetas, completum (36) numero, neque inter apostolos in finem temporum potest.

Arsinoi autem seu Valentini (37) vel Mitiadis (38), nihil in totum recipimus. Qui (39) etiam novum psalmorum librum Marcioni conscripserunt (40), una cum Basilide Assianom Cataphrygum constitutorem . . . (41).

### *Notes on Muratori's Fragment.*

1. *Quibus* might refer to the words *narrationes Petri* in the preceding missing phrase,—for it is certainly about Mark,—but this *quibus* may be also the end of the word *aliquibus*, that is to say, some of the scenes of the life of Jesus, in which Mark, although not an apostle, had been present. The *tamen* is better understood in the latter sense.

2. *Tertium*, either adjective of *librum*, as object of an *accipimus* that was to be found at the beginning of the piece, —this sense would suppose that the *Evangelium* denotes an unique whole of which the writing of Luke is the *tertius liber*;

or to be read *tertio* as an adverb, or, finally, object of the *conscripsit* that follows.

3. *Post ascensum.* These words do not depend on the verb *conscripsit*, which would give an idle sense, but on the verb *adsumsisset.*

4. *Ut juris. . . .* One can hardly refuse to accept Bunsen's correction, *itineris socium.* However, Zahn thinks it possible to maintain the word *studiosum*, occupied with zeal in the arrangements of the journey.

5. *Secundum*; perhaps as successor of Mark, who had fulfilled a like task in the preceding journey of Paul.

6. *Nomine suo.* On his own responsibility; comp. the *it has seemed good to me* (ἔδοξε κἀμοί), in the prologue of Luke.

7. *Ex opinione*: rather read *ex ordine* (by order); comp. the καθεξῆς of the prologue of Luke.

8. *Nec ipse*; no more he than Mark.

9. *Prout assequi potuit*: an illusion to the information that Luke in his prologue says he had gathered (παρηκολουθηκότι πᾶσιν ἀκριβῶς).

10. *Quarti evangeliorum.* It is doubtless most simple to read *quartum evangeliorum* (est) *Johannis* (the fourth gospel is John's). Westcott thinks we must read *quartum evangelii librum.*

10ᵃ. *Ex discipulis*; of Andrew it is said farther on, *ex apostolis.* This difference has appeared to be a sign of the fact that the author of the Fragment did not regard the author of the fourth gospel as one of the apostles. But he himself designates that John as the author of the first epistle and of the Apocalypse, which can only apply to the apostle. Besides, the name *John*, in brief, like that of Peter, in brief, can only designate the apostle. How many times is not the general term μαθητής employed in place of the special title ἀπόστολος, above all in the fourth gospel![1]

11. *Suis*: perhaps the translation of the word αὐτοῦ of the original. This pronoun depended only on the first substantive (*condiscipulis*). The Latin translator had falsely referred it to both, which has no sense as regards the second (*his* bishops)!

12. *Alterutrum*, for *alterutro*, taken adverbially and used, as often, for *invicem.*

12ᵃ. *Ex apostolis.* Andrew is intentionally qualified as one of the *apostles* and not merely of the *bishops* present, which implies a more solid guarantee of the divine message transmitted through his mouth.

[1] There is here no denial of the *apostleship* of John. Could not a historian designate Ney as Napoleon's ablest *general*, and a little farther on speak of *Marshal* Davoust, without thereby meaning to deny the marshalate of Ney? The special title suits the less known man; the more general does not ill become the more famous.

13. *Recognoscentibus*: all the other witnesses establishing the truth of the narrative and bearing witness to it; comp. the "And we know that he saith true" (John xxi. 24).

14. *Suo nomine*: without other authority than the knowledge of things that he possessed as immediate witness.

15. *Principia doceantur.* The question is about the different *beginnings* of the four gospels—in Mark, the ministry of John the Baptist; in Matthew, the birth of Jesus; in Luke, the annunciation of the birth of John the Baptist; in John, the eternal pre-existence. This difference might raise doubts, but the same directing spirit (no doubt in Greek ἡγεμονικὸν πνεῦμα) that animates and unites the four narratives, must dispel all suspicion.

16. *Præclarum*: doubtless we must read *præclarus* et *despectus* (Christus).

17. *Quid ergo mirum?* If the things took place as has just been said, it is not surprising that in one of his letters (1 John i. 1–4) John declares himself in order and persistently (*constanter*) *visor, auditor, palpator*, and, in fine, *narrator* of the wonderful life of the Saviour.

18. *Per ordinem profitetur*; these words seem to me to refer to the preceding minute enumeration of John's qualities; to it also the *singula* already referred. The author would thereby prove, not the authenticity of the fourth gospel, but the perfect competence of its author to compose it.

19. *Acta omnium apostolorum*; there is here a double opposition, between four books and a single agent on the one hand, and a single book and twelve agents on the other.

20. *Optime Theophile*: for *optimo Theophilo* as indirect object of *comprendit* (he has comprised for him in a single book . . .).

21. *Quia*: in the sense of *quæ*, even though it results from this, that in the opinion of the author Luke himself was present during the whole contents of the book of the Acts. This fact, which is not so impossible as it may seem, the author certainly concludes above all from the *we* in the second part of that book; then he finds the confirmation of it (*sicuti*) in the omission of the two following facts—the martyrdom of Peter and the departure of Paul for Spain—which Luke has not related, because he was not himself a witness of them. We must read *semotâ passione . . . sed et profectione*, two ablatives as governed by *declarat*; he declares by the very omission of these two facts.

22. *Declarat*: the author does not deem it necessary to explain in detail what refers to the epistles of Paul, for they themselves teach what concerns them to those who wish to understand them.

23. *Interdicens*: the two participles *interdicens* and *intimans*

lean on the verb *scripsit.* The author begins by summarily indicating the subject of the four great letters written to three churches.

24. Read *circumcisionem* and *ordinem.* The *order of the Scriptures* denotes the succession and progress of the revelations contained in Scripture, as they are set forth in the Epistle to the Romans (Adam, Abraham, Moses, Isaiah and the prophets, Jesus Christ).

25. *Necesse est*: it is absolutely necessary to read "*non* necesse est," to put the author in agreement with himself, for he has just said this that these letters explain themselves to him who would understand them. The omission of the negative is a frequent fault with copiers. The N. T. itself offers frequent examples of it; comp. Rom. iv. 19, v. 14; Gal. ii. 5; Col. ii. 18, etc. The *cum, since,* that follows permits no other explanation.

26. *Cum*: this conj. is the translation of an ἐπειδή, *since,* the action of which extends to *dinoscitur,* several lines farther on, which properly ought to be *dinoscatur.* It is not necessary to discuss specially the epistles of Paul, *since,* in only addressing them by name to seven churches, after the example of John in the Apocalypse, Paul meant to show, like the latter, that they were addressed less to those particular churches than to the one and universal Church, of which, in virtue of that number, they are the representatives. The word *prodecessoris* reads in various ways. The anteriority of John in relation to Paul might be that of the *apostleship,* but the context only allows us to think of a *literary anteriority.* The idea that the Apocalypse had been written *before* Paul's letters recurs in Epiphanius (*Hær.* 51. 33), who places its composition under Claudius (41–54).

27. *Septima*: in this second list the author intercalates the churches not yet named among those already mentioned who had received the principal letters — three between the Corinthians and the Galatians, one between the Galatians and the Romans. This order is no way chronological; it is without analogy. Zahn thinks it simply reproduces the succession of the epistles as it existed in the document the author made use of.

28. *Iteretur*: the double letters addressed to two of these churches make no change in their number of seven.

29. *Ecclesiastice.* The four letters addressed to individuals and not to the Church would seem to have no place in the Canon of the latter, for they belong to a merely private relation. Yet by reason of the consideration of which they have been the object in the Church, and of their utility for church government, they also form part of the Canon.

30. *Marcionis*: on these two apocryphal letters attributed to Paul, see above. Zahn (*Gesch.* ii. p. 586) quotes a poor

enough fragment that seems to have belonged to this letter to the Alexandrians: absolutely nothing Marcionite is to be noticed in it.

31. *Et superscriptio . . . habentur.* The word *superscriptio* has no meaning; the last two letters doubtless proceed from a confusion with the first two of the following word *Johannis.* We must read *superscripti*, a term that might refer to the fact that John has already been *named* above; but the meaning rather is that the name of John is inscribed at the head of these letters (ἐπιγεγραμμέναι Ἰωάννου). Are they two letters *besides* the first already named, and does this word contain also the third? Or again, are the first two regarded as a single one? That would amount to the same thing in the end. But the most natural sense is to see here only what we call the *first and the second* letters of John.

32. *Scripta*: the reference here can only be to the Judæo-Alexandrian book, often called *Wisdom of Solomon*, where that king is supposed to address the kings of the earth to require them to renounce idolatry and to govern justly; see Reuss, *La Bible, Philosophie des Hébreux*, pp. 503–560. This writing, composed, according to Reuss, between 150 and 50 before Jesus Christ, was highly esteemed by the Fathers. According to Jerome, some attributed it to Philo; and if it has never been canonised, it has not been the less recommended by some, by Athanasius, for example (with Sirach, Esther, Judith, the Didaché, and the Shepherd), as *books to be read* (ἀναγινωσκόμενα). It is in virtue of this that it is mentioned here. But who are those *friends of Solomon* who are said to have composed it in his honour? Here comes happily in a conjecture of Tregelles, who, in place of ὑπὸ φίλων, by *friends*, proposes to read ὑπὸ Φίλωνος, by *Philo.* This writing, attributed to the Jewish philosopher, contemporary with Jesus, would be a tribute rendered to Solomon, with whom in it Wisdom is identified. Thus all the suppositions of *ut* or *et ut* which had led to incredible hypotheses on the subject of the epistles of John, mentioned before, fall to the ground.

33. *Nolunt*: the omission of the two epistles of Peter has occasioned several attempts at correction, among which the least bad would be that of Thiersch (*Versuch*, etc. p. 386): "Petri unam recipimus; secundam quidam ex nostris legi in ecclesia nolunt." This is a very unlikely expedient, designed to reinstate in this list the two letters of Peter which remain decidedly unknown to it. And the rejection thus expressed regarding 2 Peter would be still more grave than the omission through ignorance.

34. *Fratre ejus*: the author relies on the quite recent composition of the *Shepherd* in order to shut against it the door of the collection of apostolic writings.

35. *Se publicare*: evidently a barbarous rendering of the middle δημοσιεύεσθαι.

36. *Completum*: read either *completo* or *completos numero.*

37. This paragraph is nearly indecipherable. The famous gnostic Valentine was an Egyptian, perhaps of Arsinoë, a city near Lake Mœris. Zahn therefore proposes to read τοῦ δὲ Ἀρσινοεΐτου τοῦ καὶ Οὐαλεντίνου ("of the Arsinoïte, namely, Valentine"); thus the two names would only denote one and the same person. The two names, Bardesanes and Marcion, have also been conjectured.

38. *Mitiadis*: a name hardly legible. Harnack has conjectured *Tatiani*; it would refer to the *Diatessaron*; this attempt has not succeeded. There was a writer Miltiades (Eus. v. 17), but he does not seem to have been heterodox, and the letter *l* awanting in the first syllable renders this reconciliation improbable. It would rather refer, according to Zahn, to some unknown collaborator of Valentine. Nolte has conjectured, in place of *vel Mitiadis*, as the Greek text: ἢ τῶν μετ' αὐτοῦ (or of those that are with him).

39. Credner has proposed to read *quin etiam*, as aggravated gradation, passing from heresy as teaching to heresy in the form of adoration: new psalms substituted for the biblical psalms! In fact, the psalms of Valentine are often spoken of.

40. *Conscripserunt*: if one does not change *Marcioni* into *Marciani* (the Valentinian branch of which Marcus was the head), the subject of this verb would be Valentine and Mitiades, who would have together composed that new book of psalms for Marcion, which has no meaning. Zahn proposes to read μακράν in place of Marcioni, giving this word the sense of *length* which it sometimes has, applied to the rolls of ancient writings. He reads: οἵτινες καὶ νέων ψαλμῶν βίβλον μακρὰν συνεγράψαντο (who have even composed a great book of new psalms).

41. The sense is perhaps, understanding at the end the verb *rejicimus* or *reprobamus*: We condemn all together (*una*, at once), Basilides and the Asiatic founder of the Cataphrygians (Montanus); that is to say, the African and the Asiatic, the speculative and the mystical, however different they are from each other.[1]

What did the author of this writing intend? It seems to me that he set himself the task, in reply to the question addressed to his church (probably that of Rome), to distinguish,

[1] Consult particularly on this whole Fragment the monograph of Hesse, *das Muratorische Fragment*, 1873; Westcott, *On the Canon*, pp. 211–220 and 521–538; and Zahn, *Gesch. des Kan.* vol. ii. pp. 1–143.

in the whole crowd of Christian or semi-Christian writings that were then circulating, the three following classes: 1st, the writings that ought to be *read in the worship* of the Church with an entire faith, as being above all discussion: these are the four gospels, the Acts, thirteen epistles of Paul, three epistles belonging to the group of the catholic epistles, and the Apocalypse of John; 2nd, those that ought to be *absolutely rejected*: several apocryphal epistles of Paul, of which two are denoted by name, and the Apocalypse of Peter (at least according to the opinion of some), then all the writings of the heresiarchs, of which several are named, precisely those that we have seen figuring between the years 100 and 150; 3rd, certain books which, although *orthodox* in contents and deserving to be read privately by the faithful, ought not to be *admitted to public reading* in the assemblies of the Church. The example given of this third class is the *Shepherd* of Hermas, a book much esteemed in the West. Why does the author exclude it from the public reading? Because he who composed it belongs neither to the number of the prophets nor to the circle of the apostles. We see this criterion agrees with that established by Justin, when he spoke solely of the *Memoirs of the apostles* and of the writings *of the prophets* as books used in the public reading.

It seems to me we find in this classification the symptoms of a significant movement of reaction. They had begun by reading publicly in worship, along with the Old Testament, what each church possessed of apostolic writings. Our readers recollect what we have said above of the designation of the Gospels of Matthew, of Mark, of John, and of the book of the Apocalypse to be read in the assemblies for worship. But there had soon been added to these apostolic writings, with a view to a more varied and actual edification, respectable Christian writings, such as the Epistle of Clement at Corinth and doubtless at Rome, the Didaché in Syria, the so-called Epistle of Barnabas at Alexandria, the so-called Apocalypse of Peter in the churches of Palestine, the Shepherd of Hermas in those of the West, etc. Then, as happens, the door thus set ajar had always been more widely opened. To those writings, non-apostolic in origin, there had come to be joined in many churches other edifying writings, such as letters received from other churches, accounts of martyrdoms, and soon interesting narrations, more or less fictitious and even heretical, which threatened to infect the Church. The danger of this invasion could not fail in the end to be keenly felt. A reaction was bound to appear. The abandonment of the primitive purely *instinctive* principle led, by its troublesome consequences, to a *deliberate* return to that same principle. We have found the first signs of this fact, as regards the gospels, in the severe delimitation marked by the writings of Justin, and, more clearly still, in the title of Tatian's work. But in these two writers the reaction only appears as yet in a purely practical form. In Muratori's Fragment it presents itself with the character of a deliberate and self-conscious principle, *that of apostolic origin*, direct or indirect: no writing must be admitted to public reading in the midst of the Church which does not belong to the prophetic collection, or which does not proceed from the apostolate, even were it for the rest, like the *Shepherd* of Hermas, of real utility. Some have raised the objection, as inconsistent with this principle (see especially Jülicher), of the admission of the Gospels of Mark and Luke and the Epistle of Jude. These three men, in fact, were not apostles in the proper sense of the word. But it must be recollected that the position made for the Twelve by their intimate and daily relation with Jesus during His earthly life had ceased with His visible presence, then soon, still more positively, by the call of Paul to the apostleship. Around the latter there had gradually formed a new apostolic circle, consecrated to labour in the heathen world; and the Church found in the community of life of these fellow-workers with the apostolic men the conviction that their writings could only be the faithful reproduction of the preaching of the apostles themselves. But it is clear that the extension of this secondary participation in the apostleship could not pass the restricted circle of those who had lived and wrought with the Twelve and with Paul. It is on this fact that the very profound difference rests that the author of the Fragment establishes between the writings of Mark, Luke, and Jude and that of Hermas, and one well understands, in this point of view, the reason why the time of the composition of the *Shepherd* is so exactly indicated; for it is precisely that date that excludes this book from admission into the sacred collection. For the rest, the need felt by several Fathers to make Mark the writing of Peter, and Luke that of Paul, well shows with what force the principle of apostolic origin continued to act in the Church. The only real inconsistency with which the author of the Fragment can be reproached is the mention of the book of *the Wisdom* (if the text be not corrupted); one cannot really well account for this fact, even if the book was attributed by the author to Philo, considered by him as a prophet. But in any case it is a great exaggeration to say, as Jülicher does (p. 310), that, "according to the Fragment of Muratori, the sole principle of the Church, in the formation of the Canon, has been the absence of all principle." Muratori's Fragment certainly signalises an important phase in the history of the Canon. This phase is that of limitation and exclusion, succeeding that of increase and adjunction. And it is even thus, it seems to me, that the important fact of *canonisation* was brought to pass, or the quite special consecration of a certain number of writings, and in particular of our gospels. The formation of the collection was a fact long accomplished when canonisation took place; and the latter consisted much less in the *admission* of these four writings than in the *exclusion* of others like them from all parity with them.

We have arrived at Irenæus, who closes this first period of the formation of the gospel collection. This Father is one of the last bearers of the personal memories bequeathed to the Church by the members of the apostolic circle, memories that he had brought with him from Asia Minor into Gaul. He calls the collection of the canonical gospels "the pillar and support of the Church." The authenticity and authority of these four writings, which for him form but one, *the Gospel with four faces*, are in his eyes facts as incontestable as in the order of nature are the four cardinal points, and in the domain of history the four forms of the divine covenant, those of Noah, Abraham, Moses, and Jesus Christ. Certainly it is not from the analogies drawn from these two domains that he concludes the necessity of four gospels, neither more nor less; but because that number was given him in an absolutely certain manner by the tradition of the whole Church, he believes he can establish the analogy of it with those not less divine and immovable facts of nature and history.

About the epoch of Irenæus we meet two statements, written, the one in Egypt, the other in Syria, that agree with the declarations of this Father; the one, already quoted, of Clement of Alexandria, who on occasion of a passage of the Gospel of the Egyptians mentioned by him expressly adds this remark: "But this writing is not of the number of the *four gospels that have been delivered to us*" (*Strom.* iii. p. 553); the other, of Serapion, bishop of Antioch about 190, who having found the so-called *Gospel of Peter* in a parish of his diocese, called Rhossus, approved it at first, then rejected it after a more thorough examination, while giving this explanation: "For us, brethren, we receive Peter and the other apostles, as the Christ; but, as circumspect people, we reject the writings falsely published under their names, well knowing that those writings *have not been transmitted to us*" (γινώσκοντες ὅτι τὰ τοιαῦτα οὐ παρελάβομεν, Eus. *H. E.* vi. 12).

It can be affirmed with certainty that this recognition of our four gospels, and of them alone, was a fact definitely gained from thirty to forty years before the end of the second century. The following ages changed nothing in this. At the beginning of the third century, Origen expresses himself thus (Eus. *H. E.* vi. 25): "According as I have learned it by the tradition touching the four gospels, that are also alone received without contradiction in the whole Church of God which is under heaven." A century later a quite similar declaration of Eusebius proves that, in the interval, nothing had been changed, either by the excision of one of the four, or by the addition of a fifth. He says (iii. 25): "In the first rank of the books universally received one must place the holy quadriga of the gospels (*τὴν ἁγίαν τῶν εὐαγγελίων τετρακτύν*)." Then when, towards the middle and in the last years of the fourth century, official decisions were interposed for the first time, the bishops, assembled in synods at Laodicea, at Hippo, and at Carthage, had nothing else to do than to ascertain and sanction what tradition and history had done before them.

## VI

### *RESULT*

I believe I have fulfilled the task I had set myself, of setting forth at what time, and in what manner, the collection of our four gospels was formed. Before concluding, I must still examine some opinions that have been recently advanced on this subject, and which differ from that which I have maintained.

And first, to listen to Renan, it would seem that this collection, so important for the life of the Church, had formed itself spontaneously, and as by a happy accident. "The gospels," says this scholar, "remained till about the year 160, and even later, private writings, designed for small circles. Everyone had his own, and for long no scruple was felt in completing, combining the texts already received . . . Men added, curtailed, discussed this or that passage. . . . In reality, across all this chaos, order was forming. . . . In the midst of the host of gospels, four texts tended more and more to become canonical, to the exclusion of the others. Mark, pseudo-Matthew, Luke, and pseudo-John advanced towards an official consecration." (*L'Église chrétienne*, pp. 498–500). But to speak thus is simply to signalise a fact (true or false), not to explain it. Even Renan happens to make a statement soon after, which renders the fact, so lightly advanced by him entirely inadmissible. After having stigmatised "the fatiguing verbiage of the apocrypha," and, as he adds, "the basely familiar tone of that nursery literature" (*ibid.* p. 507), he explains "this sad deterioration by a total change in the way of understanding the supernatural." But who will not ask himself how, in that case, it could have been that the epoch, when the taste for the supernatural became warped in this way, was precisely that in which our four gospels, so moderate and sober, "those masterpieces," as Renan himself calls them, have survived from the midst of all that miserable literature in which the grossest supernaturalism abounded, in such sort that at the very time when the taste was further changing, what is purest and most elevated definitely obtained the honour of canonisation and received the seal of divine authority!

Ad. Harnack, in his writing, *Das Neue Testament um das Jahr* 200 (1889), is nearly in agreement with Renan regarding the epoch of the formation of the collection. Only he tries to give a serious explanation of this phenomenon that he also regards as new at that epoch. He thinks that the exclusive prerogative accorded to our four gospels between 150 and 180 proceeded from the necessity in which the Church then found herself, to oppose a dam to the invasion of Montanist and gnostic doctrines. For this end there were chosen from among the host of Christian writings that had been admitted indiscriminately to public reading in the principal churches, those that could best serve to maintain the traditional doctrines, and that while taking account less of the origin of those writings than of the nature of their contents and of the services they could render the Church in that great struggle. This explanation no doubt enables one to understand the reason why (supposing that the gospel collection already existed) men were impelled to give it, at that epoch, an entirely new importance. But it cannot account for the formation of the collection itself from the point of view of the writings that were admitted to form part of it. As Herr Barth, professor at Berne, has shown, in a judicious work on this question,[1] it is difficult to believe that, if the collection of the gospels had been formed in view of the polemical need signalised by Harnack, there would have been admitted into it, by common consent, the Gospel of John, which had received so favourable a reception on the part of the gnostics, and which, from Basilides to Valentine, was used in their schools; so much so, that it was among them it was first commented on. The party of the Alogi even rejected this writing as imbued with gnosticism. A like objection would arise regarding Luke, that gospel which the dangerous use that Marcion made of it must have rendered suspicious to many churches. It may be said that at this epoch the *sacred quadriga*, if it already existed, was, as it were, quartered by the opposite parties. As Irenæus said (*Hær.* iii. 11. 7), the Ebionites appropriated Matthew, the Marcionites Luke, the Docetæ Mark, the Valentinians John; and, strange to say, at this very time we see arising, with unanimous and in some sort simultaneous agreement, from one end of Christendom to the other, the collection of our four gospels! What Harnack says of the New Testament in general (p. 110), applies quite specially to the gospel collection: "The New Testament" says this author, "wherever it arises, is something sudden." In the third quarter of the second century the agreement is found made as by a stroke from one end of the Church to the other. In Syria Theophilus and Serapion, in Egypt Clement, in Asia the bishops, who, although not in agreement in the dispute about Easter, "all equally proceed on the supposition that John and the Synoptics *cannot contradict each other*, and are unassailable witnesses of the gospel history" (Zahn, *Gesch. d. K.* i. p. 192); in

[1] *Der Streit zwischen Zahn und Harnack über den Urprsung des* ***N. T*** *Kanons* (*Neue Jahrbücher*, ii. pp. 56–80). I eagerly seize this occasion publicly to express to Professor Barth my gratitude for the invaluable services he has been so good as render me in the composition of this work, and that even though, on more than one point, his ideas differ from those I express in these pages.

Greece Hegesippus, who after his journey from the East to the West, and a sojourn at Corinth, declares that he has not met, in any of the churches visited by him, the least dissent as regards the things of the faith; in Italy Justin, who finds there, as well as in the other churches of Christendom, the "apostolic Memoirs, called gospels," read in the Sunday assemblies; in Gaul Irenæus, for whom the authority of this collection equals the certainty of the most patent facts of history and nature; in Africa, in fine, Tertullian, who, despite his dissents from the Church, fully shares the general conviction regarding the gospels. How are we to explain so prompt and unanimous an agreement? No central authority universally recognised then existed from which could proceed a word of command valid for the whole Church. This is established in the dispute about Easter, where Rome herself encountered an opposition she could not conquer. Harnack has appealed to a passage of Tertullian in the *De pudicitiâ*, c. 10, where that Father, addressing the bishop of Rome, speaks of *assemblies of churches* which have been occupied with the question of the Canon, and have ranked the *Shepherd* of Hermas in the number of *apocrypha* and *falsa*. But, first, the question there is not of a *general* council, of which history would not have failed to preserve the memory; Tertullian expressly says: "By every assembly *of your churches* (ab omni concilio ecclesiarum *vestrarum*)." He only means to speak then of certain *provincial* assemblies of churches nigh to Rome, or, at the very most, of the churches of Italy; and nothing in the words of Tertullian leads us to suppose that those assemblies had dealt with the question of the Canon in general; he only speaks of a decision taken with regard to the *Shepherd* of Hermas.

Holtzmann does not admit Harnack's explanation. For the decisions of an ecclesiastical assembly he substitutes mere conferences, exchanges of views between the bishops. But how much time would have been needed to produce by this complicated means an agreement so unanimous and simultaneous between so many churches, so different in their ecclesiastical customs, so remote from each other, and so jealous of their independence! Irenæus, one of the chiefs of the episcopal body at that epoch, could not have been ignorant of such confabulations, nor consequently have expressed himself regarding the gospel collection in the sense naturally resulting from his testimony quoted above (p. 6).

It seems to me evident that a result so firm, prompt, and universal as that we have ascertained, can only have been, especially in matter of religion, the work of time. The fact must have already existed in a latent way, to appear so abruptly outside as an institution generally admitted. As Jülicher says (p. 314): "There is no need to exaggerate the influence of Montanism and the gnosis on this development of the Canon. . . . Even if there had never been a single gnostic, the books of public reading of the year 100 would probably have become the sacred books of the year 200. . . ." And again: "It is not the idea of a Canon that brought about the formation of collections designed for church use; but it is from the existence of these collections that the canonisation of the writings they contained proceeded." That is the fact that Zahn seems to me to have established, with a vast display of erudition, in his *History of the Canon of the New Testament*. It is equally the fact I have sought to prove in these pages. It is not in the second half of the second century, but towards the end of the first, that we must place the formation of the collection of the four gospels; and what evoked it was not at all the appearance of the Montanist or gnostic sects, which only took place a quarter of a century later; but simply the perfection given by the composition of the fourth gospel to the narrative of the greatest event of history, incompletely contained in the first three. The latter had circulated in the Church during about twenty years, alongside of the oral tradition, "the *living and still remaining* voice" of which Papias spoke; this voice was now silenced with the death of the last witnesses of the life of Jesus, such as Aristion or the presbyter John. The necessity was then felt more and more of attaching oneself to written documents, emanating from the very medium of which the person of Jesus had been the luminous focus. These writings were spread, whether detached or united. The confidence of the churches resulted from the knowledge men had of their origin, and this confidence was confirmed by the impression due to their own internal characters, whereby they formed so complete a contrast to the contemporary apocryphal products. They were thus received and publicly read in the principal churches of Christendom, Ephesus, Antioch, Alexandria, Rome; and it was this use, already long established in the great metropolis, that, at the desired moment, when circumstances made the need of it more keenly felt, rendered possible the unanimous appearance and general canonisation of this collection. Jülicher says excellently (p. 317): "The primitive Canon [that is to say, doubtless, the group of the four gospels] was essentially the *codification* and *legalisation* of that which *custom* had consecrated."

Renan much admires the Church, "that with a light heart put herself thus in the most cruel embarrassment, by uniting writings whose contradictions it was impossible not to see" (*L'Église chrétienne*, p. 101). He adds: "One never sees better the honesty of the Church than in this circumstance." This praise would be better applicable to the epoch of 180, where this author places the formation of the gospel collection, than to that where we ourselves place it; for, at the earlier of these two dates, exegetical and critical discussions had not yet been raised, as they soon were by the Alogi, Marcion, Celsus, etc. It remains no less true that the calm assurance of the Church, braving without wincing all the striking differences between our gospel narratives, is a splendid proof of her perfect loyalty.

But if Harnack errs in bringing down the formation of the collection of our four canonical gospels to about the years 160 to 180, does not Zahn, on the other hand, exaggerate the truth of his thesis by putting back to the end of the first century, not only the collection of the gospels, but that of nearly all the New Testament? May it be permitted to me, who know not, to think that these two illustrious scholars have shared, on this question, both error and truth? If it is impossible to bring down, with Harnack, the formation of the gospel group to the time when it appeared in full daylight from one end of the Church to the other; on the other hand, it is not less impossible, as it seems to me, to put back, with Zahn, to the end of the first century, the canonical collection of the greatest part of the writings of the New Testament. In the formation of the Canon there was a gradual development which one can imagine in the following way: Towards the end of the first century, and as the ripest fruit of the apostolic age, that had reached, if I dare say so, its autumn, appeared the quadruple gospel, that remained the principal aliment of the Church during the first part of the second century. Around this nucleus are soon grouped the collections, more or less rich, of apostolic writings that are gradually formed in the churches. The first of these writings that were added to the gospels were doubtless the Epistles of Paul, of a collection of which we have already found a trace in Ignatius (p. 43), then in Aristides (p. 58), and the list of which is at last expressly to be read in Muratori's Fragment. To this collection, more or less complete in the different churches, was early joined the Apocalypse of John (see Justin), with some of the catholic epistles (1 John and 1 Peter, in Polycarp). This third group also contains the Epistle of Jude and the record of John in Muratori's Fragment. It was doubtless completed, towards the end of the second century or at the beginning of the following one, by the admission of the Epistle of James and of 2 Peter.

It seems to me that one can apply quite specially to the group of the four gospels what the late Professor Landerer has so well said of the Canon of the New Testament in general (Herzog's *Encyclop.* 1st ed. vii. p. 278):—

"It is self-evident that the canonisation of the writings of the New Testament did not take place in virtue of an express convention between the chiefs of the principal churches. It is in the nature of things that this development proceeded at once from different points, among which, as Reuss thinks, Asia Minor perhaps played a principal part. The fact that a result so identical was produced, proceeded essentially from an internal necessity, not that we would pretend to claim for the Church a sudden inspiration by which it arrived at clearness; but there really was in her an instinct, that instinct of the truth in which is enveloped providential direction, and which, across all apparent incidents and all human errors, to which free course is left, yet holds the reins of the progress of the Church."

And certainly the Church of all ages has had ground to congratulate herself and to give thanks that the thing followed this course. In the measure in which man had put what was his into the formation of the gospel collection, in that same measure party spirit, local tendencies, individual sympathies and antipathies, would have played a part in the composition of this the most important portion of the Canon. In place of finding Christ there in His fulness, as God gave Him to earth, we would there find Him as man with his prejudices and his narrownesses would not have failed to make Him, mutilated and diminished. The Church would not have possessed that complete Christ, that Christ *with four aspects*, whom the quadruple gospel, with its apparent contradictions and its real unity, presents to us; that Christ of Matthew, in whom is revealed all the riches of the work of God in the *past* of Israel; that Christ of Luke, a living germ of *the future* of the regenerated world; that Christ of Mark, acting, speaking, living before our eyes in His glorious and incomparable *present*; in fine, that Christ of John, hovering above the past, the present, and the future, like the eternal God whose visible image He is.

Harnack finishes his instructive and interesting work with the quotation of this word of Clemens Romanus: *῾Ο Χριστὸς ἀπὸ τοῦ Θεοῦ καὶ οἱ ἀπόστολοι ἀπὸ τοῦ Χριστοῦ*: let us add: *καὶ τὰ εὐαγγέλια ἀπὸ τῶν ἀποστόλων*, and we shall have the genealogy of the writings that are to occupy us.

## VII

The *titles of our gospels* differ from those that we ordinarily find at the head of ancient Greek classical and even biblical works. The ordinary titles are composed of but two terms, the one indicating the subject, the other (in the genitive) the author of the book (*Πλάτωνος Συμπόσιον* ; *Θουκυδίδου Συγγραφή* ; *Παύλου ἐπιστολαί*; *'Αποκάλυψις 'Ιωάννου*). In the titles of the gospels, the genitive of the name of the author is paraphrased and replaced by the preposition *κατὰ*, *according to*, governing the accusative. Whence comes this difference? It is certainly not accidental; its aim is to make it be felt that in this case the subject treated is not, as usually, a free conception of him who is designated as the author, but that only the editing belongs to him, and that the contents are given him from without. The true name of the author would properly be *Θεός*, as we expressly read in Rom. i. 1: "Paul, separated for the *gospel of God*"; and 1 Thess. ii. 8: "To give you not only the gospel *of God*, but our own lives." In effect, as St. Paul says (1 Cor. ii. 6–8), the gospel is not "a wisdom of this age, or of the princes of this age, but a *wisdom of God*, who conceived it before the ages for our glory." This eternal design of God, realised in the person and work of the Christ, that is the subject given from Above, which each evangelist has set forth in his manner (*κατὰ*, *according to*). This form serves at the same time to bring out the unity of the subject of these four writings, which are in reality but *one and the same* gospel, a sole divine message, and as Augustine says: "*Libri quatuor unius evangelii*. The evidently deliberate uniformity of these titles seems to me to prove that they have not been formulated by the authors of the gospels, but really by those, or one of those, that formed the collection of them.

In these titles, what is the meaning of the word *Gospel?* It does not designate these books themselves, as we might be led to believe from the sense that we are accustomed to give in ordinary language to the word gospel. In the whole New

Testament this word denotes *the publication* of the good news of divine salvation, due to the coming and work of the Christ. But one can easily understand the transition whereby this term has come to denote the *writings* themselves, in which this news is set forth. It is only, however, in the second century that this meaning of the word *gospel* appears; as in this phrase of Basilides (about 125): "What is said in *the gospels*," and in this word of Justin (about 150): "The Memoirs of the apostles, which are called *gospels*" (ἃ καλεῖται εὐαγγέλια). There is only, I believe, a single passage in the whole New Testament where this word might appear to denote a gospel *writing*, namely, the first words of Mark i. 1: "Beginning of the gospel of Jesus Christ." But would not this be a very idle sense: "Beginning of the book that is to follow"? I regard them rather as the apposition to the fact that will be mentioned in ver. 4, as the point of departure of the preaching of Jesus Christ. Ver. 1: Beginning of the preaching of Jesus; vers. 2 and 3: Beginning conformable to the prophecy of Isaiah; ver. 4: John appears . . . In other words, the beginning of the preaching of salvation was, as Isaiah had announced, the coming of the forerunner. — The term gospel is most frequently applied to the *contents* of the good news, rather than to the *act* of publishing it; so Meyer, in his Commentaries. But the word εὐαγγέλιον is not entirely synonymous with the fem. ἡ εὐαγγελία, which (2 Sam. xviii. 20, and Jos. *Antiq.* xviii. 6. 10) denotes the good news itself; they differ nearly as σωτήριον, means of deliverance, differs from σωτηρία, the deliverance itself. It is true that it is often difficult, when it concerns news, to distinguish between the *announcement* of the event and the event announced; as when it is said (Mark i. 15) that Jesus began to preach, saying: "Believe the gospel," one might equally well explain: "Believe in the salvation that I preach," or "Believe in my preaching of salvation." But it is not always so. There are, whatever may be said about it, a great number of passages where the word εὐαγγέλιον exclusively denotes *the act* of gospel preaching, and not its *contents*. For example: Rom. i. 1, where Paul declares himself "set apart for the gospel of God," which in the context certainly does not mean: to share in it himself, but: to announce it; Rom. xv. 19, where Paul says that "he has fulfilled the gospel of the Christ, from Jerusalem even to Illyricum" (that is to say, assuredly the preaching of the gospel); 1 Cor. ix. 18: "My authority in the gospel" (that is to say, in virtue of the office of preaching it, with which I have been charged); *ibid.*: "That I may make the gospel without charge," that is to say, my preaching (by the fact that I refuse any salary); 1 Thess. i. 5: "Our gospel came not unto you in word only, but in power," etc. (evidently our gospel preaching). This very frequent meaning of the word *gospel* in the New Testament seems to me to be also that which it has been meant to bear in our titles: "The beneficent message of God to mankind by the coming of Jesus Christ, related after the manner of Matthew, Mark," etc. An ancient Manichean writer, named Faustus, whom Augustine refuted, advanced the idea that the *κατὰ* used in these titles denoted, not the editors of these narratives, but the authorities after whose tradition they had been drawn up. This sense cannot be applied to the Gospels of Mark and Luke. For these two authors, possessing only a mediate knowledge of the life of Jesus, could not have formed an original conception of it to become an authority for others. Besides, it appears from the writings of the Fathers that the Church, to which these titles are due, attributed the gospels to the writers themselves whose names are governed by *κατὰ*. For the rest, in the later Greek it is not uncommon to find the *κατὰ* applied directly to the very author of the writing. Thus in these expressions: *ἡ καθ' Ἡρόδοτον ἱστορία* (Diodorus), *ἡ κατὰ Μωϋσέα πεντάτευχος* (Epiphanius), and above all: *Μαθθαῖος γραφῇ παραδοὺς τὸ κατ' αὐτὸν εὐαγγέλιον* (Matthew having given by writing the *gospel according to him*), Euseb. *H. E.* iii. 24. Several moderns, Credner, Volkmar, nevertheless maintain, even now, this explanation of Faustus. Reuss did the same (in the *Gesch. d. N. T. Schr.* § 177), especially urging the expression: *the Gospel according to the twelve apostles*, which can only denote the author in the moral point of view. But the very evidence of this sense in this case, prevents it from being quoted as an example for the use of *κατὰ* with an author's name in the singular. Reuss himself afterwards renounced this sense (*Hist. évangél.* p. 14).

It has also been sought to explain the *κατὰ* as a translation of the *Lamed auctoris* in the titles of the Psalms; but the LXX rendered that Hebrew form, not by *κατὰ*, but by the simple dative: *τῷ Δαυΐδ, τῷ Ἀσάφ, τοῖς υἱοῖς Κορέ*. In fine, let us notice that the use of the *κατὰ* in the formulæ *εὐαγγέλιον καθ' Ἑβραίους, κατ' Αἰγυπτίους*, which has equally been urged, can prove nothing; for here it is the *κατὰ* serving to indicate *the place*, as in the expression *τὴν καθ' ὑμᾶς πίστιν* (Eph. i. 15), or in the classical expressions *καθ' Ἑλλάδα, κατὰ λαόν, κατὰ πόλιν*, etc.

## VIII

According to *the order of the writings of the New Testament* most generally admitted, the gospels are at the beginning. This arrangement does not arise from the idea that they were composed before the other books of the Canon, —such was certainly not the opinion of the Fathers,—but simply from the fundamental importance that the person of Jesus Christ has in the religion of which the New Testament is the document. *Ἀπαρχὴ τῶν πασῶν γραφῶν τὰ εὐαγγέλια*, said Origen; and Paul, after having called the apostles the *foundation* of the Church, at once added: "Jesus Christ being the *chief corner-stone*," in some sort the bearing-surface of the two sides of the foundation-layer of the building (Eph. ii. 20). The gospels form the natural basis of the New Testament, as the Apocalypse naturally became the copestone of it. There are only some worthless exceptions to this first place given to the gospels. Some minuscules place them after the Acts and the epistles; others, behind the Acts and the catholic epistles only; others, even behind the Apocalypse. The only exception of some apparent importance is that of Chrysostom, who follows this order in the Synopsis: epistles of Paul, gospels, Acts, and catholic epistles. It seems to me evident that, working as an exegete, he has sought to preserve in this enumeration the historic order of the composition of these writings, and that one cannot thence draw any conclusion about the Canon of his church.

*The order of the gospels among themselves* presents more complicated differences. It presents itself in nine forms. The order that is by far the most generally admitted, and that from the earliest times to the present day, is the following:—

1st, *Matthew, Mark, Luke, John.*—This order is found in Muratori's Fragment (170), in Irenæus (180), Origen (at least, according to Eusebius, *H. E.* vi. 25), Gregory of Nazianzus, Athanasius, in the catalogues of the Councils of Laodicea (about 363) and of Carthage (397 and 419), in the oldest Greek uncials B ℵ A C (fourth and fifth centuries), in Augustine, many other Fathers, and, in fine, Jerome, who introduced it into the Vulgate, whence it has passed into our modern translations, and even into the Greek editions of the New Testament. Was this order determined, as Origen seems to say, and as Tischendorf thinks, by the date that was attributed to the composition of these four writings? But the historical order, as we have just seen, did not govern the general arrangement of the books of the Canon; it is equally absent from the arrangement of the epistles of Paul; in fine, it is different from that which the tradition of the ancient presbyters, reported by Clement of Alexandria, indicated, after which the composition of Matthew and Luke had preceded that of Mark. I think this very ancient and constant order was dictated by reasons of a more practical nature. If Matthew is almost everywhere at the beginning, this is because men saw in it the natural transition from the Old Testament to the New, and that it thus forms the normal opening of this latter. Matthew being once placed at the beginning, Mark and Luke naturally followed it, as having in general the same course, belonging as regards form to quite a similar genus, and being in some sort its two complements. John, which forms a genus apart, thus came to be thrown back to the end; it became at the same time the *apostolic* counterpart to the first gospel. It may be said that Matthew represented the step that behoved to lead the Jews from the ground of the ancient revelation to the higher stage of the new,—a stage that Mark and Luke enlarged in such a way as to bring in the heathen to it, John forming a still higher step, and as it were the open terrace, whence the outlook embraces the whole earthly and heavenly horizon. Or else, if this explanation appears strained, it may be said more simply, with a writer of the ninth century, Druthmar, quoted by Credner: "At the beginning, an apostle; at the end, the other apostle; between the two, those who have to derive their authority from them" (p. 393).

The variations that this order has undergone bear chiefly on the place given to John, then secondarily on the respective positions of Luke and Mark. John passes from the fourth place either to the third, to the second, or even to the first. As regards Luke and Mark, Luke is often placed first of the two, doubtless as the more considerable; but at times also second, perhaps to bring it nearer the Acts.

Among the orders differing from the preceding one, we place first the one that comes nearest to it, in that John here also occupies the fourth place; only Luke is here placed before Mark.

2nd, *Matthew, Luke, Mark, John.*—This order is only found in Ambrosiaster (the Roman deacon Hilary, in the fourth century), the commentator of the epistles of St. Paul.

In the following order, the third rank is assigned to John:—

3rd, *Matthew, Mark, John, Luke.*—Each apostle is thus accompanied by an apostolic assistant. This order occurs in this (exceptional) passage of Origen (*Hom. I in Lucam*):

"Matthæus quippe et Marcus et Johannes et Lucas scripserunt evangelia"; then in the manuscript of the Syriac translation (450–480) published by Cureton; in fine, at the other end of the Church, in the African catalogue published by Mommsen, and in the Latin version of the Commentary of Theophilus.

John occupies the second place in the two following arrangements, by which doubtless men had it at heart to place at the beginning the writings of the two apostles, while preserving the first place to Matthew:—

4th, *Matthew, John, Mark, Luke.*—So in the stichometry of the Cod. Claromontanus (sixth century), and in a Greek MS. of the ninth century (probably copied from a MS. of the fourth).[1]

5th, *Matthew, John, Luke, Mark.*—This is the order of the Cod. Cantabrigiensis, and of several MSS. of the Itala (*a, b, f, ff, n, o*); it occurs also in the Gothic translation, in some MSS. of the Peschito, and in Ambrose (see Zahn, ii. p. 371).

In fine, in the four following orders John occupies the first place:—

6th, *John, Matthew, Mark, Luke.*—After Zahn, this was the most ancient order in the church of Egypt; it occurs in two vocabularies, the one of Upper, the other of Lower Egypt; Zahn (ii. p. 371 and fol.) inclines to attribute this order to the collection of Origen.[2]

7th, *John, Matthew, Luke, Mark.*—An order that occurs in Chrysostom, and in a Latin MS. of the fifteenth century.

8th, *John, Luke, Mark, Matthew.*—This was probably the true order of Codex X (tenth century), and of the very ancient Latin Cod. (*k*) of Bobbio, which contains only fragments of Mark and Matthew.[3]

[1] Druthmar, who had just indicated as the known order *Matthew, Mark, Luke, John*, relates that having found this Greek MS., which was said to be Hilary's, he asked a Greek scholar whence came this order, and that the latter replied to him: "It is just as the good ploughmen do; they yoke in front the oxen they regard as the strongest."

[2] Volkmar equally attributes this order to Tertullian, because he says (*Adv. Marc.* iv. 2): "Fidem ex apostolis Johannes et Matthæus insinuant, ex apostolicis Lucas et Marcus instaurant." But this saying proves nothing as regards any canonical order whatever.

[3] Volkmar believed that these fragments formed the *beginning* of the

9th, There is yet found *John, Luke, Matthew, Mark,* in the MSS. 90 and 399.

It is a fact that Mark and Luke are not at the beginning in any document, and that Matthew and John are pretty regularly placed, the one at the beginning, the other at the end, according to the explanation given by Druthmar (p. 106).

The order indicated in the first place is so constant and general, that one is led to ask if it is not that which was adopted from the first by those that formed the collection of the four gospels. This is Credner's opinion, who says (p. 92): "Simultaneously with the admission of the four gospels, and of these four alone, there was also fixed from the first the order of these books in the canonical collection." There will be found in the appendix at the end of this chapter ancient narratives affirming this view as a fact.[1]

As regards the very numerous orders, different from this the most general and ancient one, they are easily explained by the fact that, after the formation of the collection in which the four gospels were for the first time united, these writings continued to be diffused, all four separately, in the churches, and might thus be found differently placed in the collections designed for public reading.

manuscript, and found therein an interesting precedent in favour of the hypothesis of the priority of Mark. But it results from the more exact study made by Zahn that the Gospels of John and Luke were placed *before* these fragments, instead of following them, as Volkmar believed.

[1] Consult on this subject especially Credner, *Gesch. des N. T. K.*, published by Volkmar, 1860; Zahn, *Gesch. des N. T. K.* ii. pp. 367–372; Gregory, *Prolegomena* to the *eighth edition* of Tischendorf, pp. 137, 138.

# APPENDIX

Recollections, legends, fictions? I know not in which of these categories one must rank the following statements, which seem to me to have in many respects an apocryphal character, even though some of the writers that transmit them to us, such as Theodore of Mopsuestia or Photius, are not ordinary persons. In any case, they present a certain interest, as a testimony of the sentiment of the ancient churches on the matter of fact that we have sought to elucidate in the preceding pages.

In the *Acts of Timothy*, a writing composed in the course of the fourth century (Lipsius, *Die apocryphen Apostelgeschichten*, vol. ii. pp. 372–400, especially p. 378), we read as follows:—

For those who had accompanied the disciples of our Lord Jesus Christ, not knowing how to unite in one whole the detached leaves composed in divers places by them (the apostles) in different tongues (οὐκ ἐγνωκότες συνθεῖναι τοὺς παρ' αὐτῶν σποράδην συνταγέντας χάρτας, διαφόροις γλώσσαις συγγεγραμμένους) on the marvellous deeds performed in their presence by our Lord Jesus Christ [these companions of the apostles, I say], having met at Ephesus, brought them with one consent to John, the famous theologian, who, having well considered all, and, urged by them, having inserted in the three gospels the things said by them, copied them according to the order, Matthew and Mark and Luke, putting their names at the head of the gospels. But finding that they had related what concerns the dispensation of the incarnation with genealogy, John, writing as a theologian, joined thereto the things that had proceeded from the divine heart (ἐκ τοῦ θείου στήθους), which were not to be found in them, then he also filled up the wonderful divine works that were only to be found incompletely related in them, as regards the beginnings (ἐν τοῖς κεφαλαίοις); therefore he gave his name to this writing or gospel.[1]

Photius gives an account of this narrative of the Acts of Timothy in the following manner (*Bibliotheca*, Cod. 254):—

Then, having received the detached pieces (τοὺς τόμους), which described in different tongues (διαφόραις γλώσσαις) the saving Passion of the Master and His works and teachings from the hands of those that brought them to him, he [John] arranged and distributed them (διέταξέ τε καὶ διήρθρωσε), and applied to each of the writings the name of the three evangelists (τὸ ὄνομα τῶν τριῶν εὐαγγελιστῶν ἐνηρμόσατο).

In the Commentaries on the Gospel of John, collected by Fritzsche (*Commentarii in Novum Testamentum*, Zurich, 1847, p. 19 and fol.), there occurs a similar narrative, from the pen of Theodore of Mopsuestia:—

Thus the blessed John comes to dwell at Ephesus. . . . At this time took place the publication of the other gospels, of Matthew and Mark, then also of Luke, who wrote each one his own gospel; and they were diffused in a moment (ἐν ἀκαρεῖ) through all the earth, and all the faithful, as was just, exerted themselves in promoting this diffusion. But the faithful dwelling in Asia, esteeming the testimony of the blessed John on the gospel worthier of credit than that of the others, for the reason that he had been with Him from the beginning, and even before Matthew, and because he had enjoyed greater favour as a result of love, brought him those books, wishing to hear from his mouth what opinion he had of them. He praised those who had written them as regards their veracity, then said that few things had been omitted by them as regards the miracles most necessary to be reported; but as regards the

[1] It seems to me that one cannot fail to recognise in this narrative an imitation of that of Eusebius (iii. 24. 7), namely, that the first three gospels, having already come to all, and also to John, it is said that he affirmed the truth of them, while pointing out that they lacked the account of the things that had taken place at the beginning of the preaching of Christ, before the imprisonment of John the Baptist; then that, on the request that was made to him, John related those things in his gospel (ἐν τῷ κατ' αὐτὸν εὐαγγελίῳ); and that in return he omitted the genealogy of the Saviour according to the flesh, for the reason that it had already been written by Matthew and Luke, and began with the theology that had been entrusted to him, as to the most excellent (οἷα κρείττονι), by the Holy Spirit.

teachings, very nearly all (μικροῦ ἅπαντα).[1] Then he declared that doubtless the things related touching the sojourn of Christ in the flesh must not be omitted, but just as little the words relating to the divinity. Whereupon a prayer was addressed to him by the brethren to edit with care the things most necessary for instruction, and that he found omitted in the others; which he also did.

It is evident from these accounts that there reigned in the churches of the first centuries a settled conviction on this point, that the organisation of the collection of the gospels was due to John himself, and that the composition of his own gospel had been closely connected with this important act, whether as occasioning cause, or as effect. These narratives even attribute to John a part in the arrangement and completion of the first three gospels, which had only been delivered to him in the form of reported pieces (τόμοι, χάρται). They seem even to go still farther; for they speak more than once of the *different tongues* in which these detached leaves were written (doubtless for Matthew, Hebrew; for Mark, Latin (?); and for Luke, Greek). In uniting these leaves into a whole designed for publication, the editor had naturally to draw up the work in a single language, the Greek, in which it was diffused. The apostle had thus not only copied (ἀπεγράψατο), but also translated the first gospels, at least Matthew and Mark. This detail seems to me absolutely incompatible with the unity and originality of style of each of the three Synoptics. But this very exaggeration proves how deep in the churches was the conviction of the main fact, the fact of the co-operation of John in the formation of the gospel Canon.

It is with surprise and pleasure that, while finishing these pages, I read in No. 3 of the *Theologische Literatur-Zeitung*, 1897, p. 70, this statement of Professor Bousset: "It seems to me not improbable that the collection of the gospel Canon was produced in the Johannic circles of Asia Minor, and that perhaps at the time when the publication of

[1] This translation, that necessitates one or two slight corrections of the certainly corrupt text, seems to me alone to give a sufficiently clear sense.

the Johannic gospel took place; to this we are led by the only account we possess on this matter (*Acta Timothei*)." I would only have to substitute for the vague expression, "in the Johannic circles," the words, "by the care of the Apostle John," to find in this phrase the summary of my own writing.

## CHAPTER II

### THE GOSPEL ACCORDING TO ST. MATTHEW

WE shall indicate here the titles of—

1. Some works of Introduction to the New Testament: Hilgenfeld, 1875; Bleek-Mangold, 1886, 4th ed.; H. Holtzmann, 1886, 2nd ed.; B. Weiss, 1889, 2nd ed.; G. Salmon, 1889, 4th ed.; Reuss, *Gesch. d. N. T. Schriften*, 1887, 6th ed., and *La Bible*, 1874, vol. i. pp. 3–112; Schaff, *History of the Christian Church*, 1882, i. 612–627; Nösgen, *Gesch. d. christl. Offenbarung*, 1891–1893; Zahn, *Gesch. d. N. T. Kanons*, 1888–1892; Weizsaecker, *Das apostolische Zeitalter*, 1886; Jülicher, *Einleitung*, 1894; A. Harnack, *Das N. T. um das Jahr* 200, 1889, and *Die altchristl. Literatur*, 1897, vol. i. pp. 651–700.

2. Some special works on the Synoptics: H. Holtzmann, *Die synopt. Evang.* 1863; Weizsaecker, *Untersuchungen über die evang. Geschichte*, 1864; Sabatier, *Essai sur les sources de la vie de Jésus*, 1866; B. Weiss, *Das Markusevang. und seine synopt. Parallelen*, 1872, and *Das Matthäusevang. und seine Lukas-Parallelen*, 1876; Volkmar, *Marcus und die Synopsis*, 1878; Westcott, *An Introduction to the Study of the Gospels*, 1881, 6th ed.; G. Meyer, *La Question synoptique*, 1878; Wetzel, *Die synopt. Evang.* 1882; Renan, *Les Evangiles*, 1877; Paul Ewald, *Das Hauptproblem d. Evangelienfrage, etc.* 1890; Gloag, *Introduction to the Synoptic Gospels*, 1895; Roehrich, *La composition des quatre évangiles*, 1897; Holtzmann, *Handcommentar zum N. T.* vol. i. 1892, 2nd ed.

3. Some critical works on Matthew: Sieffert, *Ueber den Ursprung des ersten canon. Evang.* 1832; A. Réville, *Etudes*

*critiques sur l'évang. selon saint Matthieu*, 1862; J. Morison, 1870; Bonnet, *Le N. T.* 1880, 2nd ed. by A. Schroeder, 1895; Lutteroth, *Essai d'interprét. de l'évangile selon saint Matthieu*, 1876; Keil, *Das Ev. Matthaei*, 1877.

The name *Synoptics*, given to the first three gospels, was introduced into science by Griesbach. Derived from the Greek word σύνοψις, *combined view*, this term characterises them, in opposition to the Gospel of John, as three narratives sufficiently similar in their general course, and often even in their details, to admit of being arranged in parallels and thus included in a single view and easily compared.

The three narratives have often been published in this parallel form. One of the oldest works of this kind, and which is still, as it seems to me, the best arranged of them, is the *Synopsis of de Wette and Lücke* (Berlin, 1818). For the Galilean ministry in particular, these authors have taken care to repeat the texts three times, placing successively, as basis, that of each of the three Synoptics with parallel accompaniment of that of the two others. The *Synopses* that followed are those of Tischendorf, 1848, 4th ed.; of Roediger; of Anger, 1868; of Schultze, 1884; of Sevin, 1886; they do not afford the same advantage as the first. Unhappily the text of this old synopsis is a little behind date, because of the great progress since made by textual criticism. The work that at present may be regarded as the most remarkable, and which may even be called magnificent, is the *Synopticon* of Rushbrooke (1880). For practical use, the work of Huck, *Synopse der drei erst. Evang.* 1892, and that of Veit, *Die synopt. Parallelen*, 1897, may be recommended.—As regards the patristic quotations, I specially recommend the work of Charteris, *Canonicity*, 1880. This book, which is founded on that of Kirchhofer, is superior to it in several respects.

We have treated in Chap. I. pp. 104–108, of the *order* of the gospels in the Canon. The order evidently the most ancient, which is also the most generally received, has appeared to us at the same time the most rational. It is it that we shall follow in the study of the three Synoptics.

# I

## The Apostle Matthew

Our first gospel is placed at the beginning of the gospel collection and of the whole New Testament, as forming the transition from the writings of the old covenant to those of the new. To it is applicable very particularly the saying of St. Augustine: "The New Testament hidden in the Old; the Old unveiled in the New."

The author to whom the unanimous tradition of the primitive Church attributes it, the Apostle Matthew, is one of those of the Twelve who remained in the background during the earthly life of the Saviour. He is only named twice in the gospel that bears his name, in the account of the calling of him (ix. 9) and in the list of the apostles (x. 3). His name only appears three times in the other writings of the New Testament, and that merely in the lists of the apostles (Mark iii. 18; Luke vi. 15; Acts i. 13). Despite this very obscure part, Matthew has turned out to be one of the two apostles that have exerted the greatest influence on the development of the work of Christ in the world down to the present time.

His name is written in two ways in the Greek documents. The most ancient MSS. (א B D) write it with two *θ* (*Μαθθαῖος*); this form has been preserved in many modern editions (Lachmann, Tischendorf, Tregelles, Westcott and Hort, etc.). But the form *Ματθαῖος* is found in the more recent uncial MSS. (C E K L, etc.); it was adopted by Griesbach, and is read in general in the editions of the Received Text. This orthographic difference is not entirely without importance. If one reads this name with two *θθ*, it proceeds evidently from the Hebrew, for we find in the Old Testament the names Maththan (gift) and Maththanja (gift of Jehovah). This last, abridged into Maththija, is rendered into Greek sometimes in the form *Μαθθίας* (Acts i. 23, 26). But it may have been reproduced also with the termination *αῖος*. There are many examples of this form. Hilgenfeld (*Einl.* p. 453) cites in particular *Jehoudi, Kenaani,* rendered in the New Testament in the forms *Ἰουδαῖος* and *Χαναναῖος*. Keil cites also *Zabdi,* rendered 3 Esd. ix. 21 by *Ζαβδαῖος*. The instance of this kind most conformable to the present case is that of the Hebrew name Chalphaï (Alpheus), which is found rendered into Greek in the two forms **Κλωπᾶς** and *Ἀλφαῖος*. If this is indeed the etymology of the name of Matthew, one should conclude from it the Jewish origin of this apostle. It would not be entirely the same if we accepted the form *Ματθαῖος* as Blass (*Grammatik d. N. T. Griechisch,* 1896, § iii. 11) and Schmiedel (*Grammatik des N. T. Sprachidioms,* 8th ed. by Winer) are disposed to do. According to the first, if I rightly understand him, the true Greek form would be *τθ*, and the reading *θθ* would proceed from an assimilation of the *τ* by the following *θ*, as in *Βάκχος* becoming *Βάχχος*, *Ἀτθίς* becoming *Ἀθθίς*, *Σαπφώ* becoming *Σαφφώ*. I should rather think with Curtius (*Grundzüge der griechischen Etymologie,* p. 418), that the primitive orthography was really that of the two *θθ*, but that, as the Greek language always seeks to mollify, the two consecutive aspirates seemed too harsh, which led to the change of the first into a mute (tenuis). In this case the form *Μαθθαῖος* would be more conformable to the etymology and the form *Ματθαῖος* to the pronunciation, which agrees well with the probably Hebrew origin of the name and of the person of the apostle, as well as with the character of his whole writing.[1]—Two other etymologies equally derived from the Hebrew have been proposed; the one by Ewald, who would see in this name the reproduction of the name Amitthai (Jonah i. 1), the other by Grimm, who makes it come from Matthim, plural of the unused singular Math (*vir*). The name would mean in the first case the *faithful,* in the second, the *virile* one; but these suppositions have not been accepted.

[1] I express here my thanks to MM. J. Lecoultre and G. Attinger, professors at Neuchâtel, for the information they have kindly procured me on this subject.

Another more important question is raised by the parallel narratives of Luke and Mark, which, while relating nearly in the same terms the calling of a toll-collector at Capernaum, both call him *Levi* (comp. Matt. ix. 9 with Mark ii. 14 and Luke v. 27). Clement of Alexandria (*Strom.* iv. 9, 73) reports that the Valentinian Heracleon regarded this Levi as a different person from the Apostle Matthew, the former being only some toll-collector turned Christian. This distinction has been admitted by many modern critics, Grotius, Neander, Sieffert, Hilgenfeld, Reuss, etc. Clement himself appears to share this opinion; for among the apostles who did not suffer martyrdom, he names *Matthew*, Philip, Thomas, *Levi* (provided this last name does not denote Lebbaeus). Origen also; for he instances as having been toll-collectors Matthew *and Levi* (*Contra Cels.* i. 62). According to Sieffert, tradition had applied to the Apostle Matthew the circumstances that had marked the call of the toll-collector Levi. But if the explanation that supposes two different persons is not impossible, it is very improbable. For: 1st, The three accounts are perfectly similar in substance and in form, save the name of the toll-collector. 2nd, In the three narratives this call is placed after the same miracle, the healing of the paralytic. 3rd, In all the three alike it is followed by one and the same narrative, that of the feast offered by the newly called one, to Jesus, the apostles, and his friends, the toll-collectors of the place, with the same conversation after the repast (fasting, the Bridegroom taken away, the old and new garments, the new wine and the old bottles). We have to do, then, in the three narratives with one and the same fact, and must admit that the name Matthew was a surname given to this toll-collector by Jesus Himself, at the time he was called. In surnaming him *gift of God,* Jesus had signalised the value He attached to this sudden adhesion, so promptly obtained; comp. numerous examples of double names (Simon = Peter; Lebbaeus = Thaddaeus; Thomas = Didymus; Joseph = Barnabas; Judas = Barsabas). Only it seems to me it is not necessary to refer the word λεγόμενον (*named*, Matt. ix. 9) to the moment when the calling of the toll-collector took place; the author may thus designate the apostle by the name by which he was known in the Church at the time when he was writing (comp. the use of this participle, Matt. i. 16, x. 2, xxvii. 17, 22; Eph. ii. 11): "the man known by the name of . . ."

It has often been held that this call of Matthew was a vocation to the *apostleship*. I do not think so. The apostleship as such only existed later. Jesus only invited him, at this time, to accompany Him habitually as one of His intimates, as His permanent disciple; it was a permission that He gave him to take a place in the privilged circle in which He afterwards chose His apostles. A scruple of delicacy doubtless induced Mark and Luke not to recall expressly the past of the apostle, which had in it something degrading; they preferred to cover it by resuming his original name, for the most part forgotten.[1] Matthew, on the contrary, did not fear, in his evangelising work, to set forth to the glory of the grace of his Master his profession of toll-collector (ix. 9), and frankly designated himself by his name, saying: *ἄνθρωπον Μαθθαῖον* λεγόμενον, and *Μαθθαῖος* ὁ τελώνης (x. 3).

The character of Matthew must have been firm and decided. This appears from the narrative of Luke: "And *leaving all*, he arose and followed Him." We thus perhaps understand why Jesus had associated him with the scrupulous and sceptical Thomas, who formed with him the fourth pair of apostles.[2]

[1] Let it be remembered how the author of the Epistle of Barnabas, so called, derives from the calling of Matthew the proof that Jesus came to call sinners, even greater sinners that all other sinners (ὑπὲρ πᾶσαν ἁμαρτίαν ἀνομωτέρους).

[2] Resch, in the *Aussercanonische Paralleltexte zu den Evangelien* (Matt. Mark, 2tes Heft, 1894), has put forth the opinion of the identity of the Apostle Matthew with Nathanael (John i. 44 and fol.); and in fact the narrative of John is certainly that of the calling of a future apostle (ver. 50 and 51); comp. John xxi. 1). But the name Nathanael is not found in any of the lists of the apostles, and must consequently recur in that of one of the Twelve; and as the names Nathanael and Matthew have

Immediately the call of Jesus was accepted, Matthew performed his first missionary action. He offers Jesus a repast in his house, to which he invites his old colleagues, the tax-collectors of the place, doubtless in order to bring them into relation with his new Master. That is the only possible sense of the narrative of Luke (v. 29). It is certainly also that of the narrative of Mark (ii. 15), where the express repetition of the name of Jesus after the words *in his house*, forces us to refer the pronoun **αὐτοῦ** (*his*) to Matthew and not to Jesus. In Matthew (ix. 10), Meyer-Weiss refers the words *in his house* to the house *of Jesus* Himself. But why establish here a difference with the other Synoptics? Had Jesus then a dwelling of His own, where He could offer a feast? This feast day, when Matthew made his entry into the divine kingdom, was, as Schaff observes, that of his farewell to the world and to his earthly occupations.

After the election of the Twelve, which the first gospel has not related,—we know not why,—Matthew belonged to

absolutely the same sense (Matthew: *gift of Jah* [abbreviation of Jahvé], and Nathanael: *God* [El] *has given*; comp. the names Theodore and Dositheus), we understand what has led Resch to see in them one and the same person. However, this opinion does not seem to me tenable. The scene of the calling of Nathanael (John i.) has nothing in common with that of the calling of Matthew (Matt. ix. 9), neither in place nor time nor manner. The first belongs to the first return journey from Judea into Galilee; the other takes place at Capernaum, and consequently a certain time after that return to Galilee, when Jesus had already transferred His home from Nazareth to Capernaum (Matt. iv. 13) and was in full activity. Then Nathanael makes objections; Matthew, on the contrary, obeys the first call. Let us add that the two inaccuracies, the confusion of the first two returns to Galilee and the omission of the long sojourn in Judea that separated them (Matt. iv. 12; comp. John iii. 22–24), are more difficult to explain if Matthew was present at the first return than if he was only called later. I rather think therefore with most expositors that Nathanael ought to be identified with Bartholomew (son of Tholmaï), a patronymic name that assumes for him who bore it another personal name. This last name is that which John uses (chaps. i. and xxi.) as that by which he had at first known Nathanael and then continued familiarly to designate him, while the name of Bartholomew was that by which he was designated as apostle, as it appears in the lists of the apostles and in the narrative of Eusebius on Pantaenus, where he appears under this name as the apostle of *southern Arabia* (properly India). Comp. Eus. *H. E.* v. 10. 3.

the second of the three groups of four of which the apostolic college was composed, and of which he formed with Thomas the first pair. According to Clement of Alexandria (*Paedag.* ii. 16), he had led a kind of ascetic life, abstaining from fermented liquors and from all animal food. It is the same kind of life that Hegesippus attributes to James, the brother of Jesus, and that St. Paul mentions of certain Jewish Christians of the church of Rome, whom he calls the weak (chap. xiv.). Without taking their side, the apostle protects their liberty; which he would assuredly have done regarding these two men. As the first gospel expressly recalls the principle of Jesus, after which it is not what enters into the man that defiles the man (Matt. xv. 16 and fol.), one cannot see in this practice a proof of the legal spirit. Some have thought also to find in it a trace of Essenism. But Essenism admitted a number of other practices and abstentions having in that system a religious and obligatory character, and that would not have been compatible with the apostolic life. It may be thought that these two men did in this as do our present vegetarians. There is sometimes attributed to Matthew the mention of an alleged saying of Jesus: "If the neighbour of an elect sin, the elect has sinned; for had he conducted himself as the Word prescribes, his neighbour would have been filled with such respect for his life that he would have been led not to sin." But it proceeds from an extra-canonical book, the *Traditions of the Apostle Matthias* (Clement, *Strom.* vii. 13, 82, ed. Klotz). We find again in this saying the studied and strained character of almost all those that the extra-canonical writings attribute to Jesus.

In the work entitled the *Preaching of Peter* (see chap. i. pp. 61 and 62) it was said that Matthew had remained in Palestine for twelve years after the Ascension, which would bring us to the year 42. What is certain is that in 59 Paul no longer found any apostle in Jerusalem (Acts xxi. 17 and fol.). Harnack in his *Chronologie* even tries to prove that the dispersion of the apostles in general took place from the year 42, but after data not very solid, as it seems to me.[1] According to Eusebius (*H. E.* iii. 24. 6) it had been on the occasion of his departure that Matthew had composed his Aramean gospel to indemnify his compatriots of Palestine for his removal.

Whither did Matthew then repair? To Ethiopia, according to the historian Socrates (19. 2); after others, to the Parthians or to Macedonia or to India. Later legends represent him preaching with Andrew among the Anthropophagi, probably the half-barbarous peoples inhabiting the regions near the Black Sea (Lipsius, *Die apocryphen Apostelgeschichten, etc.* 1883, i. pp. 28, 545 and 598).

The Roman martyrology fixes the martyrdom of Matthew on 21st September; the Greek Church celebrates it on 16th November (Credner, *Einl.* § 35). But Clement (*Strom.* iv. 9, 73), seeking to prove that one may be saved without having been a martyr, cites the name of *Matthew*, Philip, Thomas, Levi (Lebbaeus ?).

## II

### Contents and Plan of the Gospel

The course of the narrative is quite natural: the history is divided into seven parts—1st, the accounts of the infancy (chaps. i. and ii.); 2nd, the Messianic advent (chaps. iii.–iv. 11); 3rd, the Galilean ministry (chap. iv. 12–xviii. 35); 4th, the journey from Galilee to Jerusalem (chap. xix. 1–xx. 34); 5th, the ministry at Jerusalem (chap. xxi. 1–xxv. 46); 6th, the Passion (chaps. xxvi. and xxvii.); 7th, the Resurrection (chap. xxviii.).

The first verse of the gospel indicates the subject of it, and clearly characterises its spirit. Jesus is there presented, first as the descendant of David and heir of his royalty, then as He who should realise the salvation promised to Abraham and to his posterity for all the families of the earth. The

[1] After *Kerygma Petri*, *Acta Petri*, *Pistis-Sophia*, and other extra-canonical sources.

ripe fruit of the theocratic particularism is to become the seed of the universalism which was its goal from the beginning.

## § 1

### NARRATIVES OF THE INFANCY

This first part comprises three pieces: 1st, the genealogy of Jesus (i. 2–17); 2nd, the fact of His birth (vers. 18–25); 3rd, some circumstances of the first period of His life by which He was signalised as the promised Messiah (ii. 1–23).

A. *The genealogy* (i. 1–17).

By reason of the close connection which has just been mentioned (ver. 1) between the appearance of Jesus and that of His two great ancestors, it is not surprising that the narrative begins with a genealogy intended to establish the reality of that providential connection.

It is certain that the author of this genealogical document derived the first two parts of it from the genealogies of the Old Testament. The third, referring to the generations between the return from the Exile and Joseph, the adoptive father of Jesus, has perhaps been borrowed from the public tables (*δημόσιαι δέλτοι*), of which the historian Josephus speaks at the beginning of his autobiography, and from which he says he had derived his own; or had the author had in his possession some family document? In any case he did not draw those twelve names from his imagination, a thing that would be a jest unworthy of a serious writer.

Regarding this document let us notice:

1. That the form of the proper names is most frequently derived from the LXX, not from the Hebrew: thus Phares (Matthew and LXX) for Perets (Hebr.); Naasson for Nachson (Hebr.); Zara for Zerach, etc.

2. The author deviates from the form of the Hebrew genealogies by the singular fact that four times names of women are introduced in the genealogical list (Tamar, ver. 3; Rahab and

Ruth, ver. 5; and Bathsheba, this last mentioned as the wife Uriah (ver. 6), so as expressly to recall her adultery). The exceptional mention of these four women may be explained in several ways. Three of them—Tamar, Rahab, and Bathsheba—having had a life stained by impurity, it might be supposed that the mention of them is intended to give an idea of the character of merciful compassion of the Messiah's work; but the fourth? On the other hand, Rahab the woman of Canaan and Ruth the Moabitess, being strangers to the Hebrew people, it might be admitted that they are mentioned as a prelude to the entrance of the Gentiles into the kingdom of God: they would be named as types of the future universalism. But this explanation does not apply to the two other women. Perhaps it is better to suppose that the exceptional mention of these four women in the genealogy of the Messiah is related to the special part of woman in the fact of His birth.

3. The author has divided the genealogy into three periods of the same duration, each measured by fourteen generations. Scanning in some sort the history of the kingdom of Israel down to the birth of the Messiah, he reckons the first phase from Abraham to David as the preparation for the kingdom; the second, from David to the Captivity, is the time of its typical realisation, but also of its fall; the third, finally, is the time of its temporary disappearance, but that which clears the way for its real and definitive reappearance.

This is the ingenious rhythm under which the author contemplates the whole course of the theocratic history; it results evidently from it that the hour to raise again the throne of David has now sounded. It is quite true that, to attain such symmetry he is obliged to exclude four names from the list of the kings of Judah and to count twice the king who was led captive to Babylon, and under whom the return from the Exile took place. But two or three generations matter little in a history comprising more than two thousand years; and this view, on a large scale of the course of things, remains no less striking and approximately exact.

4. However, this whole account appears to rest on a contradiction. On the one hand, indeed, the Davidic filiation is only important so far as he was the real father of Jesus. And, on the other hand, the whole of the following piece, by attributing to Jesus an exceptional birth, without the concurrence of a human father, seems to contradict this carefully demonstrated filiation. The opponents of the miraculous birth have made use of this contradiction to deny the fact. Cerinthus already did so, and a similar tendency can also be shown in the Syriac translation of the gospels recently discovered at the convent of Sinai by Mrs. Lewis. In ver. 16 this translation actually reads in place of the words: "Joseph, the husband of Mary, of whom was born Jesus," the following words: "Joseph, to whom the Virgin Mary bore Jesus"; then at ver. 21, in place of "She shall bring forth a son," she "shall bring forth a son *to thee*"; lastly, at ver. 25: "And she brought forth *to him* a son whom he called Jesus." Evidently the translator, not daring openly to change the text, modified it so as to suppress the supernatural birth. But all the rest of the narration, the anxieties of Joseph, the intervention of the angel, and the quotation from Isaiah, condemns these evidently intentional changes. As regards the apparent contradiction pointed out above, it is resolved by the fact that, on the one hand, Jesus, in order that He might be acknowledged by the people and their heads as the Messiah had necessarily to be regarded as descended from David, which was in fact the dominant opinion; and that, on the other hand, as the gospel narrative proves, the mystery of His miraculous birth could not be published till a later time, when faith in Him should be already established. Till then he who was held as His father had to be recognised as proceeding from the royal family. Otherwise faith in Him would have been rendered almost impossible to the Jewish people. Even the fact of the adoption of Jesus by Joseph could only confer on the former the quality of son of

David on condition that the latter possessed that quality himself.

B. *The miraculous birth* (i. 18–25).

1. It must be observed that, properly speaking, the fact itself is not related; it is tacitly supposed by the first words of ii. 2. What is important to the narrator is less the historical side of the fact than its religious value. Here is the difference between the narrative of Matthew and that of Luke. This also appears from the expression: "the birth of *the Christ*" (i. 18), in place of: "the birth of Jesus."

2. The narrative of the annunciation of this birth is presented solely from the point of view of what occurred to Joseph, and not to Mary; another difference from Luke. There are here two traditions proceeding from different sides.

3. It has been alleged that the idea of the supernatural birth of Jesus was due to the prophecy of Isaiah recalled (ver. 23). But the details relating to the conduct of Joseph are not connected with anything in that prophecy; thus it is rather the fact itself that drew attention to the prophecy.

4. From the beginning of the second century there is found an effort to maintain the virginity of Mary; so in the *Protevangelium of James*, while Matt. i. 25 shows how entirely the first gospel is still free from this tendency.

5. There is nothing wonderful, as we have seen, in the difference of the genealogies in Matthew and Luke. On the one hand, Jesus could only be recognised as Messiah on the condition of being *regarded* as the son of a descendant of David; that is shown by the genealogy of Joseph (Matthew). And, at the same time, that this appearance might not be deceptive, the Davidic filiation of Jesus could only be real if it was a truth at the same time on the side of Mary, by whom alone the blood of David really flowed in His veins. In these conditions a double genealogy was necessary, the one provisional, valid in the eyes of the immediate contemporaries of Jesus, the other real and definitive for the faith of the Church, when the mystery of that exceptional birth could be unveiled.

C. *Some Messianic signs in the course of the infancy* (ii. 1–23).

The four facts enumerated in the sequel are in no way a connected account of the infancy. The author is not thinking of relating the history of that period, but only to bring out the Messianic character of some of the facts that marked it. That is the essential difference between the account of Matthew and that of Luke (chaps. i. and ii.).

1. The adoration of the Magi (ii. 1–12).

The name of Bethlehem had not yet been mentioned; it is here alone that this place of the birth of Jesus is named, on the occasion of the arrival of the Magi, and by reason of the prophecy of Micah (v. 1), and of the part that it played on this occasion. Hilgenfeld points out, no doubt rightly, the importance of this whole account as a prelude, on the one hand, of the disposition to faith in the Gentile world, and, on the other, of the unbelief and hatred that would be developed in the Jewish people. This first fact is thus, as it were, the prelude of the whole history of the Messiah.

2. The flight into Egypt (ii. 13–15).

It is mentioned in like manner in reference to the prophecy of Hosea (xi. 1). It has been inferred from this that this was a fictitious circumstance imagined by reason of this text of the prophet. That is hardly probable; for it was necessary either to substitute the form *my son* for that of *his sons* (of Jacob) in the LXX, or to deflect in a forced way on the child Jesus the sense of the Hebrew *my son* (Jacob). It is not then the text of Hosea that can have suggested a flight into Egypt, but the well-known fact of that flight that suggested the word of the prophet.

3. The massacre of the children (ii. 16–18).

The same observation applies as to the preceding citation. The prophecy of Jeremiah (xxxi. 15) cannot have given rise to the idea of the massacre of the children of Bethlehem. That crime, which had made a sensation, recalled to the author a word of the prophet that presented a remote analogy to it.

4. The settlement at Nazareth (ii. 19–23).

The efforts of exegetes to explain this passage do not seem to me to have succeeded. The *nazir* of Gen. xlix. 26 that Hilgenfeld quotes, does not suit, since "nazir" (distinguished) contains an idea of elevation, and the word Nazarene, on the contrary, contains one of abasement. The word *netser* (shoot), Isa. xi. 11, only leads to complicated and hardly natural explanations. I think the name Nazarene, just like that of Galilean given to Jesus by His contemporaries (Matt. xxvi. 71; Acts xxiv. 5), was a term of contempt, a species of nickname corresponding to the numerous passages announcing the humiliations of the Messiah that had a prophetic value in the eyes of Christians.

## § 2

### THE MESSIANIC ADVENT

(iii. 1–iv. 11)

This piece contains three facts: the ministry of John the Baptist, the baptism of Jesus, and His temptation.

A. *The ministry of John* (iii. 1–12) behoved, by awakening in the people the feeling of their moral fall, and therewith the need of pardon and restoration, to prepare them to receive favourably the salvation that God was sending them. For this it was necessary that the desire of spiritual deliverance should, in the heart of Israel, take the place of the hopes of political greatness which were connected with the expectation of the Messiah (comp. Luke i. 77).

1. The singular expression: *In those days* (ver. 1), comprises not less than thirty years. The author is less concerned with the chronological aspect of the facts than with their religious value.

2. The name *John the Baptist*, used here without any explanation, assumes readers already aware of the existence and office of this personage.

3. The quotation of Isa. xl. 3 (ver. 3) shows anew the

Messianic and divine character of Him who is to succeed John.

4. The discourse that the author puts into the mouth of John appears to be rather the general summary of his preaching than the reproduction of one of his particular addresses. John gives an idea of the separation that the coming of the Messiah will effect in the mass of the Jewish people; but this judgment is presented, as in the Old Testament, in the form of an outward and sudden act. Yet the moral character of this preparatory separation is strongly asserted (iii. 9–12). John gives an idea of the imminence and gravity of this Messianic crisis, by describing it according to the prophecy (Mal. iii. 2, 3), which served at the same time as a basis for his own mission (iii. 1, iv. 5).

B. *The baptism* (iii. 13–17).

Jesus receives, by the communication of the Spirit, the gifts, that is to say, the light and the powers that are needful for Him to effect in mankind the foundation of the Kingdom of God. This is His solemn installation into the Messianic ministry. Two features distinguish Matthew's account from those of the two other Synoptics:

1. The conversation between Jesus and John preceding the act of baptism, of which Mark and Luke do not speak. It must be remembered that John and Jesus did not yet know each other personally (John i. 31 and 33), the former having lived in the wilderness until his appearance in Israel. But we know from Matt. ii. 6 and Mark i. 5 that those who requested baptism made first of all a confession of sin before John. What must that of Jesus have been? He had no personal sin to tell. He must have set forth the sin of the world that was weighing on His heart, and that He was beginning even then to make His own. One can thus understand how John could afterwards designate Jesus to two of his disciples as: "The Lamb of God that beareth the sin of the world," and can thereby also explain to oneself his immediate exclamation: "I have need to be baptized by Thee!"

2. The divine allocution is addressed, in Matthew, not to Jesus but to *John the Baptist*: "*This is* . . . (οὗτός ἐστιν) *in whom* . . . (ἐν ᾧ . . .)"; and not, as in Luke and also in Mark: "*Thou art* . . . (σὺ εἶ . . .); *in thee* . . . (ἐν σοί . . .)." John, called of God to bear witness officially to the divine mission of Jesus, had to receive the divine revelation of it as directly and personally as Jesus Himself. This revelation took place simultaneously, at the moment of the baptism, in the consciousness of both. The narrative of Matthew appears to come from a tradition emanating from the Forerunner himself.

C. *The Temptation* (iv. 1–11).

It seems that when once clothed with divine powers and conscious of His filial union with God, Jesus had now only immediately to begin His work in the world. But His manhood is not a mere appearance. Simply as a man, He has to be initiated not only into the holy beauty of the work He will accomplish (*the opened heaven*), but also into the forms of the evil that He will meet, and the diverse arts by which His great adversary will seek to turn Him from the true Messianic way. This second side of His preparation was realised by the Temptation, a struggle in which He gained a preliminary victory over all the particular seductions which were to occur later at each step on His path. The narrative of Matthew differs from that of Luke in this, that the Temptation, relative to the universal Messianic sovereignty, which in the latter is the second, is the third in Matthew, and forms the culminating point of the trial. This order is so conformable to the general Messianic character of the first gospel that one may thereby feel disposed to prefer the order of Luke.

## § 3

## THE GALILEAN MINISTRY

## (iv. 12–xviii. 35)

This part comprises in our gospel three groups of narratives: the beginnings, the central part, and the final excursions.

A. *First period: The beginnings* (iv. 12–vii. 29).

1. The first care of the author in beginning the account of the Galilean ministry is to place it under the patronage of a Messianic prophecy which should serve as its programme (Isa. ix. 2).

2. The return of Jesus from the banks of the Jordan to Galilee is occasioned (iv. 12) by the news that Jesus receives of the imprisonment of John the Baptist. On consulting the fourth gospel (John iii. 22–24 and iv. 1–3), we find that in this datum are blended into one the first return to Galilee, immediately after the baptism (John i. 44), and the second (John iv. 3), which was separated from the first by a pretty long sojourn of Jesus in Judea, a sojourn of which neither Matthew nor Mark speaks.

3. Matthew specially recalls Jesus' change of domicile, who came from Nazareth to settle at Capernaum. That city, from its more central situation and its position on the important route leading from the interior of Asia to the sea and to Egypt, was more suited to become the starting-point of the work of Christ; it corresponded exactly to the description of the Messianic scene drawn by Isaiah.

4. Ver. 17 sums up the first preaching of Jesus, which is closely connected with that of John the Baptist. Here is placed the first Messianic act of the Lord, the calling of four disciples, called to accompany Him henceforth in His evangelising journeys.

5. This itinerant preaching, and especially the miraculous healing that accompanies it, attracts from the surrounding regions, from Syria, from Perea, and even from Judea and Jerusalem, a great concourse of people, and thus there is formed the considerable audience to which Jesus addresses His first great public discourse reported by the evangelist: *The Sermon on the Mount.*

*The first discourse: The true righteousness* (chaps. v.–vii.)

Here is the programme of the moral life which must

become that of the new state of things, of the heavenly kingdom: it is the exposition of the true righteousness that must take the place of the quite external righteousness at present taught and practised in Israel. This discourse, as we possess it in our first gospel and in part also in the Gospel of Luke (vi. 20–49), raises many questions:

1*st question: To whom was this discourse addressed?* Was it to the disciples or to the whole multitude?—It might be inferred from the fact that, according to Luke, Jesus had just then chosen His twelve apostles, that it was for them that Jesus uttered it, in order to initiate them into their mission among the people and in the whole world (comp. Luke vi. 20). But Matthew has not even related the election of the apostles, and says at the beginning (ver. 1): "Jesus, seeing *the multitudes.*" No doubt His disciples surrounded Him more closely, as the regular representatives of all present or future believers; but the discourse has too much in view the moral life in general to refer to the commission of the apostles in particular; in chap. x. Jesus will handle this subject in an entirely different discourse. The Sermon on the Mount is not the installation of the Twelve, but that of the new people that is about to rise at the word of Jesus to take the place of the old. The mount where Jesus speaks is as the Sinai of the new covenant. Jesus there proclaims three things: first, the *condition of entrance* into this new order of things; then, the new *principle of life* that will rule there; and lastly, the *responsibility* of those who shall present themselves to form part of it.

2*nd question: At what time was this discourse delivered?* —Our gospel seems to place it in the first beginning of the Galilean ministry, for it only previously mentions three facts: the general preaching of Jesus, which is only as yet a confirmation of that of John, the calling of the first four disciples, and an active preaching and healing attracting the crowds to which He will address this discourse. Instead of these three facts, Mark mentions thirteen before the passage

iii. 13, where the place is clearly marked of the Sermon on the Mount, which he omits. He puts here, beside the three mentioned by Matthew: 1st, the healing of the demoniac in the synagogue of Capernaum; 2nd, the healing of Peter's mother-in-law; 3rd, the evening of this first Sabbath day; 4th, the first evangelising journey in the environs of Capernaum; 5th, the healing of the leper; 6th, the return to Capernaum; 7th, the healing of the paralytic; 8th, the calling of Levi the publican, with the feast and conversations that follow it; 9th, two Sabbath healings; and lastly, 10th, the election of the Twelve. Luke, before the Sermon on the Mount (chap. vi.), presents the same facts as Mark, and nearly in the same order. All this evidently supposes a much more lengthened activity than would appear from the narrative of Matthew alone. Besides, certain words in the discourse itself presuppose circumstances not justified by the previous accounts; thus the suspicions raised about the respect of Jesus for the fulfilment of the law (v. 17), suspicions which can only have been called forth by the Sabbath healings related afterwards by Matthew himself, or the warnings given to believers against a merely external profession (v. 13, vii. 21–23). Such words naturally presuppose a more advanced period.

3rd *question: Was this discourse delivered, in all its parts, as we read it in the first gospel?*—An attentive analysis of the discourse itself does not allow us to think so. One perceives at every moment either interruptions or words that are evident additions in the context. Even in the beatitudes that begin the discourse, one is struck with the discrepancy between the first four, stating, as the condition of entrance into the new state of things that Jesus is inaugurating, the feeling of all that man lacks for salvation, and the last four, which presuppose, on the other hand, salvation already possessed; not that the latter did not also proceed from the mouth of Christ, but this must have been at some other time, for here they are incongruous with the first ones. They are also lacking in Luke, where their place is occupied by the maledictions pronounced on those who do not feel the needs expressed in the first four. The exhortation to reconciliation (v. 25) interrupts the sequence of the antitheses between the old and the new righteousness. The same is the case with the exhortation to severity towards oneself (v. 29, 30), and the prohibition of divorce (v. 31, 32). In the condemnation of the pretended pharisaic virtues (vi. 1 and fol.), the warning against vain heathen repetitions and the teaching of the Lord's Prayer (vi. 7–10) are beside the subject. The piece regarding the contempt of riches (vi. 19 and fol.) and trust in Providence (ver. 24 and fol.) might well, in strictness, be a continuation of the polemic against pharisaic righteousness (comp. Luke xvi. 14). But nothing in the text indicates such an intention, and this whole piece does not appear to be connected with what precedes. Nor does it connect better with the following passage (vii. 1 and fol.), on the proud judgments which those allow themselves who think themselves better than their brethren. It rather seems that here recommences, after a long insertion of diverse precepts, the criticism of the pharisaic righteousness that had, as its specially repellant character, the judgment of others. The invitation to prayer that follows (ver. 7) can be attached to this warning only in a forced manner. The lack of natural connection continues in all that follows, on to the 14th verse. The warning to beware of false prophets (vii. 15–20) may, no doubt, be connected with the danger of Pharisaism; but that against lip-profession on the part of believers (vers. 21–23) supposes, as we have said, a more advanced time. On the other hand, the parable that ends the discourse, that of the wise or foolish builder, is certainly a suitable conclusion of this solemn appeal addressed to the people in these memorable circumstances, which has the character of a real taking of a position, and even, in some sort of a declaration of war addressed to the leaders of Israel. This close is found in Luke as well.

It results from this analysis that the report we find

in Matthew contains many elements foreign to the primitive discourse. What confirms this view is that we again find all these elements that have seemed to us doubtful, either in Luke, or in Mark, or in Matthew itself, in different situations in which they are quite in their place. Thus the passage (v. 25, 26) on reconciliation between brothers is (Luke xii. 58 and 59) applied quite differently, as an invitation to prompt reconciliation with God; that on severity towards oneself (v. 29, 30) recurs Mark ix. 43–50, where it is adduced very naturally; still more, it appears yet again in Matthew itself (xviii. 8 and 9) on quite a different occasion. The Lord's Prayer, so far from naturally placed in Matthew (vi. 9–13), has, on the contrary, a very good motive in the account of Luke (xi. 1–4). For the salt without savour, comp. Luke xiv. 34 and Mark ix. 50. The precepts on trust in Providence are much more naturally placed in Luke (xii. 13–31), following the picture of the rich fool, that picture where the mention of the overflowing barns and cellars contrasts so well with that of the ravens and the lilies of the field, which, without sowing or reaping, without spinning or weaving, yet live and thrive. This contrast, which gives to these precepts so great a charm in Luke, is entirely lost in the Sermon on the Mount, where Matthew puts them. The same is the case with the encouragement to pray: "Ask, seek, knock" (vii. 7–11), which Luke also quotes (xi. 5–10), but connecting these images with the parable of the friend who himself also goes to ask, seek, and knock at the door of his friend, and ends by obtaining. The fitness of these images is yet again lost in Matthew. We shall not continue these quotations; let us merely remark that eighteen times words placed by Matthew in the Sermon on the Mount are found mentioned elsewhere, in particular in Luke, where they stand with the advantage of a special situation that brings out their gracious fitness. We may conclude from these observations with a sort of certainty that the report of this discourse in Matthew is a work of a composite order, in which have been combined many heterogeneous elements; which does not deny that there was really a great discourse of Jesus delivered at the beginning of His ministry before a considerable crowd, and that we can easily disengage from the midst of these diverse elements the real subject of that discourse. We there perceive the installation of the true people of God on the earth by the proclamation of the only righteousness conformable to the holy nature of God, which should characterise the true members of His people, in opposition to the formal righteousness cried up by the traditional teaching and the example of the doctors. This righteousness, far from being contrary to the law, is the very fulfilment of it, since the meaning of the law has been falsified by those who call themselves its interpreters.[1]

4*th question: What is the relation of this discourse to that which Luke has preserved to us* (Luke vi.)?—It has been thought that Luke reproduced another discourse than Matthew. Lange, in his *Life of Christ* (ii. 566–570), has called the one

[1] Here is, it seems to me, according to Matthew, the *course of the real inaugural discourse*, in which Jesus developed this fundamental opposition. The first *condition* of the true righteousness that God acknowledges is the feeling of the lack of it, and the ardent desire to obtain it (v. 3–6). If those who follow this way have to *suffer* from men (vers. 10–12), they should none the less persevere in giving the example of doing good (vers. 14–16). They should not be troubled by the reproach of *destroying the law* by this new manner of righteousness, which is, on the contrary, the fulfilment of the law rightly understood (vers. 17–20). Men must in fact abstain not only from murder, but from hatred; not only from adultery, but from covetousness; not only from perjury, but from falsehood; not only from revenge, but from the absence of support; and, instead of rendering hatred for hatred, respond to enmity by love. Thus they resemble the supreme model, God. In these five antitheses "Jesus does not oppose *His* law to *the* law," but His interpretation of the law, identical with the sense of the law itself, to the quite external interpretation of the rabbis (see Weizsaecker, *Untersuchungen über die evang. Gesch.* p. 348). Jesus then passes to the criticism of the *pharisaic good works*, so much admired, alms, prayers, fastings (vi. 1–18). Then (vii. 1–6) He stigmatises the proud mania of *judging* others to which those pretended righteous ones are addicted, and puts the people on their guard against present false prophets (the scribes and the rabbis), advising to estimate them after their works and not after their words (vers. 15–20). The conclusion (vers. 24-27) is a pressing *exhortation*, not only to hear His instructions, but to retain them and put them in practice.

the *Kulm-Predigt*, which had been a speech of an esoteric nature, addressed to the disciples alone; the other, the *Staffel-Predigt*, addressed to all the people. But the two discourses begin and end in the same manner, with the beatitudes and the parable of the wise or foolish builder. And at bottom the subject is essentially the same. The principal difference is that Luke substitutes for the notion of *righteousness*, which is properly Israelitish, the more generally human idea of *love*. He thus makes, for his Greek readers, of the contents of the last of the five antitheses of Matthew (v. 43 and fol.), the principal subject of the whole discourse, omitting the antitheses regarding the alteration of the true sense of the law. We here confine ourselves to these few words that the analysis of the discourse in Luke will complete.

Matthew finishes the report of the discourse, and resumes the course of the narrative by a formula that we shall again find several times in the sequel, at the end of several other similar discourses: "And it came to pass that, when Jesus had finished these discourses . . ." The plural, *these discourses*, is remarkable. Perhaps it betrays the feeling of the plurality of the teachings which are found collected in the great whole that we have just studied.

B. *Second period: The central part of the Galilean ministry* (chaps. viii.–xiii.).

In this part are reported the principal facts that made up the Galilean ministry. The narrative does not follow a chronological order; it is, on the contrary, systematically divided into two groups: the first comprising a series of *acts of Messianic sovereignty*; the second, a series of *words of Messianic wisdom*. Such a grouping is evidently the work of reflection, and not the reproduction of history; for the acts and the discourses did not form two successive periods in the work of Jesus; they were its constantly united and co-operating factors.

Two features confirm the fact of the grouping of which we speak: 1st, Each of the two collections ends in a great discourse forming the culminating point of it, namely, chap. x. (the instructions given to the Twelve) and chap. xiii. (the collection of parables on the kingdom of heaven). 2nd, Each of the two collections has as theme a prophecy that imprints on it the Messianic character; the first, Isa. liii. 4: "He took on Him our infirmities, and bore our sicknesses" (Matt. viii. 17); the second, Isa. xlii. 1–4: "Behold My Servant, whom I have chosen . . . I will put My Spirit upon Him . . . He shall not strive nor cry . . . He will not break the bruised reed, nor quench the smoking wick . . ." (Matt. xii. 17 and fol.). This symmetry is certainly intentional.

(*a*) The first group (chaps. viii.–x.).

This group contains twelve facts: 1st, the healing of the leper; 2nd, that of the centurion's servant; 3rd, that of Peter's mother-in-law; 4th, the injunctions addressed to three hesitating disciples; 5th, the stilling of the storm; 6th, the healing of the two demoniacs to the east of the sea; 7th, the healing of the paralytic; 8th, the calling of the toll-collector and the conversations that followed; 9th, the healing of the sick woman and the raising of the daughter of Jairus; 10th, the cure of two blind men; 11th, of a deaf and dumb demoniac; 12th, the compassion with which Jesus was filled at the sight of the abandonment of God's people, which naturally brings about the mission of the Twelve. This series of facts has as its conclusion the great discourse of chap. x., which is addressed to them on this occasion.

We remark, with regard to this series: 1st, that the facts 1, 2, and 3 are placed in Luke and Mark even before the Sermon on the Mount; 2nd, that the calling of Matthew and the injunctions given to the three disciples, without being miracles, are yet also acts of Messianic authority; 3rd, that in Mark and Luke the arrival and the prayer of Jairus immediately follow the return from Gadara, and are not separated from it by the account of the healing of the paralytic and the calling of Matthew; 4th, that in Matthew Jairus speaks of the death of his daughter as having already happened; 5th, that the sending of the Twelve, without being a miracle, is also an act decidedly Messianic, since it is in some sort the installation of a new patriarchate, and consequently the substitution of a new Israel for the old.

*The second discourse: The instruction of the apostles* (chap. x.)

The discourse of chap. x., which closes this part, presents the same features as the discourse on the mount. On the one hand, a discourse, such as this, was certainly delivered on the occasion of this mission, and, on the other hand, this report contains numerous additions borrowed from other teachings of Jesus. These two points are confirmed by a comparison with the analogous but much shorter discourses given on this same occasion by Mark (vi. 7 and fol.) and by Luke (ix. 1 and fol.). From eight to ten times we find in the discourse of chap. x. words placed differently in Mark and Luke, and which are certainly more suitable in these latter.[1] We do not speak here of certain sentences that Jesus may have spoken several times.

Despite these intercalations, it is not difficult to indicate the current of the original discourse. Weizsaecker has well summed it up in these three points: 1st, the instructions properly so called (1–15); 2nd, the announcement of the sufferings that the disciples will meet with on the way (16–25); 3rd, the encouragements (26–42). The last verses 41 and 42 are strikingly original, and have their parallel in Mark ix. 41. They doubtless formed the true conclusion of this discourse. What greater encouragement, indeed, could there be for the apostles than the hope of being the bearers of a blessing that will be communicated to all those who shall receive them with goodwill! Thus, then, the opening and the close of this discourse, as well as of the Sermon on the Mount, have certainly been exactly given.

[1] For example, the announcement of judicial persecutions (vers. 17–20); comp. Mark xiii. 9–13; Luke xxi. 12–15 and xii. 11, 12. Domestic hostilities (vers. 21, 22); comp. Mark xiii. 12; Luke xii. 51–53 and xxi. 16 and 17. Bearing the Cross (vers. 38, 39); comp. Mark viii. 34 and 35; Luke ix. 23 and 24; xiv. 27. Encouragements (vers. 40–42); comp. Mark ix. 41; John xiii. 20.

The author ends the reproduction of this discourse with a remark entirely similar to that with which he had closed the Sermon on the Mount: "And it came to pass that, when Jesus had finished giving His commands to the twelve disciples . . ." We must conclude from what precedes that these discourses were edited with a view to instruction and edification rather than with the intention of historical exactness.

(*b*) The second group (chaps. xi.–xiii. 53).

In this group are combined the Messianic teachings of Jesus. These are: 1st, His testimony on the person and work of John the Baptist, on occasion of the question that the latter addresses to Him by two of his disciples (xi. 1 and fol.); 2nd, the farewell addressed to the unbelieving cities of Galilee, and the very tender appeal to those who feel the need of consolation and pardon; 3rd, two teachings on occasion of two Sabbatic scenes; 4th, here is placed the prophetic theme forming the centre of this group; 5th, the great apologetic discourse of Jesus, in reply to the accusation of the Pharisees that He wrought His miracles, and in particular His cures of demoniacs, by the help of Beelzebul; 6th, the condemnation of Jewish unbelief by comparison with the Ninevites and the Queen of the South; 7th, on occasion of the arrival of the mother and brothers of Jesus, the revelation of the new spiritual family, superior to that which rests only on the tie of blood.

But all these occasional teachings were only preparing men's minds for the great revelation of the near establishment of the divine kingdom on the earth. This principal subject is set forth in its different aspects in the great discourse in which this series terminates.

*The third discourse: The revelation of the kingdom of heaven* (chap. xiii.)

This discourse contains seven parables, in which Jesus reveals for the first time to those who have received in a becoming spirit His first instructions, the true nature and the diverse aspects of the divine work that He comes to found. And first, its humble and peaceable *origin*, in the parable of the *sower*. The coming divine creation will not be effected by a great external and sensible act, like political conquests and revolutions, but solely by the adhesion of a small number of honest and upright hearts to the divine truth, preached by Jesus and the apostles. Then, the mode of its *development*. This will not be, as might be expected, a pure and irreproachable society; there will be associated with it heterogeneous elements, the presence of which we will have to learn to tolerate (parable of the *tares*). Two other parables, those of the *treasure* and the *pearl*, bring out the *supreme value* of this new state of things that Jesus institutes, and which deserves that we should endeavour to share in it, at the price of the greatest earthly sacrifices. Two others describe the *irresistible power* of this divine principle that Jesus introduces into the world, under the image of two perceptible facts: the profound action of the *leaven*, which, without noise or appearance, displays a marvellous efficacy of internal transformation, and the growth of the *mustard seed*, which slowly grows and spreads externally. Finally, the parable of the *net* announces *the final separation* which is to close this development by setting aside the false members, and raising the truly faithful to the perfect and glorious state that God has had in view in creating man.

This series of pictures terminates with a gracious image that Jesus applies to Himself, of a father of a family, who, to instruct and interest his children, draws from a mysterious closet all kinds of old and new objects, hitherto kept hidden and as in reserve.

It is clear that all these parables were not pronounced at one breath. Jesus was too good a teacher thus to accumulate images difficult to understand, and each of which ought to be pondered by itself. These pictures then are not placed here as the works of a master are found together in his studio; they are collected and co-ordinated, as in a sort of gallery. What suffices to prove it is that their parallels in Mark and Luke are placed in quite different positions. Mark has here but three of them (iv. 1–32), all of them borrowed from the vegetable kingdom, the parable of the sower, to which he adds that of the ear omitted by Matthew, and that of the mustard seed; Matthew's five others are omitted. Luke omits the parables of the tares, the treasure, the pearl, and the net. He has that of the sower in the same position as Matthew, and the mustard seed and the leaven (xiii. 18 and fol.) in quite a different position, on the occasion of the joy of the crowd rejoicing to see the adversaries of Jesus confounded by His triumphant reply to a ruler of the synagogue.

But although this collection of the seven parables on the kingdom of heaven is the work of the evangelist, it remains no less true that there was in the ministry of Jesus a decisive moment when this mode of instruction did not absolutely begin, but starting from which it played its whole part. That part was to reveal in an ineffaceable manner to the .nds of the new believers the true nature of the work in .e service of which they were to consecrate their life. The ıature of this work was in fact the antipodes of the idea that till then they had formed of it, as we have seen in rapidly expounding the meaning of the parables. There was not one of them that did not overturn from top to bottom what had been taught them on the coming kingdom. Jesus also said to them when beginning His explanation (Matt. xiii. 11): "*To you* it is given to know the mysteries of the kingdom of heaven." Till then He had sought by His essentially moral teachings, of which the Sermon on the Mount remains the type, to awaken in Israel the true idea of moral good, in order thus to lead the people to the national repentance that had been the aim pursued by the Forerunner and His own at the beginning. He shows that like His Forerunner He has failed, but yet not with all. There is a certain number who, as well as His disciples, have entered on the new way that He has opened to them. The time is now come to lead them further forward and initiate them in the knowledge of the superior state of things in prospect of which He has attached them to Himself. As regards the others, who persist in their impenitence and their merely earthly labour, nothing is now left but to leave them to their hardness. For if they learned more about the coming work of Jesus, that would profit them nothing and would but furnish them with pretexts for mockery. For this reason the choice must now begin, and teaching by parables is the means of it. This Matthew explains in the passage at which so many exegetes have wrongly been scandalised (Matt. xiii. 11–16). There is in the parable when it is well understood, in the light of the explanation that Jesus gives of it for believers, the means of engraving on their heart in an indelible manner the truths of the kingdom which abstract instruction would not enable them to grasp. There is at the same time in this figurative mode of teaching, which remains unintelligible to the rough crowd that continued carnal, what will turn it away from him with whom it cannot find what it is seeking. It is the prelude of the final judgment. Jesus here quotes the prophecy of Isa. vi. 9 and fol., which that prophet had uttered in like manner at the opening of an epoch of serious separation for ancient Israel.

C. *The last period of the Galilean ministry* (xiii. 54–xviii. 35).

Until now the ministry of Jesus had been in general exercised in the environs of Capernaum, which Matthew for this reason calls *His own city* (ix. 1). Henceforth He undertakes a series of excursions more or less considerable, and visits the entire country as far as the utmost borders of Galilee. First of all—(1) a visit to Nazareth in the south-west, a visit with which is connected (2) the expression of the sentiments of Herod on the occasion of the increasing fame of Jesus, which reminds that king of the person and the murder of John the Baptist; (3) the words of Herod give occasion to the evangelist to relate the murder of the Forerunner; (4) an excursion towards the north-east coast of the sea of Gennesaret, near the mouth of the Jordan, where the first multiplication of the loaves takes place; (5) the stilling of the tempest and the return to Capernaum; (6) the discussion on purifications; (7) an excursion towards the north-western extremity of Galilee, as far as the borders of Phenicia, and the healing of the ughter of the woman of Canaan; (8) the return to the sou h by the region situated to the east of the sea of Tiberia. and the second multiplication of loaves; (9) the arrival in the plain of Gennesaret, and various conversations with the Jews and the disciples; (10) a new excursion towards the northern extremity of the country, as far as the sources of the Jordan, and the conversation at Cæsarea Philippi: Jesus the Messiah, but the suffering Messiah; (11) the Transfiguration; (12) the healing of the lunatic child; (13) the second announcement of the Passion; (14) the return to Capernaum, and the payment of the didrachma; (15) the lesson of humility given to the disciples.

This series of facts recurs nearly the same in Mark on to No. 8, and in Mark and Luke from that on to the end. It terminates, like the preceding parts, in a great discourse, intended to regulate the relations between the members of the new spiritual community formed around Jesus.

*The fourth discourse: The Church and the relations between its members* (chap. xviii.)

This discourse, like the preceding ones, contains a certain number of heterogeneous elements, and, like them, is connected with the following narrative by the formula: "And it came to pass that, when Jesus had finished these sayings . . ." It begins with a lesson of humility given to the disciples on the occasion of a dispute that had occurred among them, and which Matthew had not mentioned, but of which Mark (ix. 33 and 34) and Luke (ix. 46) speak positively. The question was, which of them would be the greatest in the kingdom of the Master. The warning that follows on offences given to the weak is perhaps connected with another fact that Mark and Luke place at this same time (Mark ix. 38, 39; Luke ix. 49): the spirit of jealousy that the disciples had shown towards the man who was casting out demons in the name of Jesus without following them. The parable of the lost sheep, which follows in a very abridged form, is not easily connected with this context. Its true place and form appear in Luke xv. 1. If we think of the conflict between the disciples that had taken place on the way, one may well suppose that the person of Peter had there played the principal part, and can understand the question of that apostle on the pardon of offences, and the parable that ends the discourse (xviii. 21–35). But the essential part of this discourse is found in vers. 15–20. Jesus, beholding the group of those who have spontaneously gathered around Him, designates it for the first time by the name Church ("assembly convoked" by Him), and gives directions on the way to appease the conflicts that may arise within it.

This time and this discourse show in a very remarkable way the relation of dovetailing, if one may so say, that exists between our three synoptic narratives. Several sayings of Jesus in Matthew can only be explained by placing them beside facts only related in Mark and Luke.

This last period of the Galilean ministry gains quite particular importance from the conversation at Cæsarea Philippi (Matt. xvi. 13 and fol.). Jesus, after having shown by a question and by Peter's reply the degree of faith which the disciples have already reached, that is to say, their belief in Him *as Messiah*, opens quite a new chapter of His teaching, and begins to reveal to them the way in which He must fulfil that part by discovering to them for the first time the unexpected and formidable prospect of the *suffering Messiah*, and, as a corollary, that of the Church of the Cross. This is the third phase of the teaching of Jesus. The first had been the attempt to bring the people to the sense of its moral fall by replacing in their consciousness the knowledge of the true relations between man and God (chaps. v.–vii.). Then with the teaching in parables (chap. xiii.) had begun the revelation of the true kingdom of heaven, flowing from that idea of holiness. At Cæsarea Philippi begins the teaching of the painful way in which the Messianic salvation must be realised. In the first phase Jesus had called *the whole people*; in the second, He had instructed *the believers*; in the third, He prepares *the apostles* for that which must follow.

§ 4

## THE DEPARTURE FROM GALILEE AND THE JOURNEY THROUGH PEREA

(xix. 1–xx. 34)

Jesus had proclaimed the gospel of the kingdom at Capernaum and in the neighbouring regions; then He had extended His work by a series of excursions farther and farther to the east and west, and at last as far as the northern extremity of Galilee. The time had now come to visit the other parts of the Holy Land, and, in fine, to repair to Jerusalem, which He knew well would be the limit of His earthly activity (Luke xiii. 33). But He did not need to hasten. It was autumn (comp. John vii. 1, 2; Matt. xvii. 24, where the tribute is required of Him in arrear since the preceding Passover). Several months were still left to Him before the next feast of the Passover, which His death was to signalise. He set out then from Galilee: this important period of His life is strongly marked in Matthew, as well as in the two other Synoptics (comp. xix. 1; Mark x. 1; and especially Luke ix. 51). If this departure had been that of an ordinary journey to the feast, Jesus would have proceeded straight south, so as to cross Samaria, for that was the usual route of the Galileans when they repaired to the feasts (Jos. *Antiq.* xx. 6. 1; John iv. 4). But as on this occasion He had time before Him, He made use of it to preach the Word in the southern part of Galilee adjacent to Samaria, and then in Perea on the other side of the Jordan. There were there the descendants of the tribes of Gad, Reuben, and the half tribe of Manasseh, who had not yet known His presence. In the passage of Isaiah viii. 23, quoted as the prophetic programme of the

Messianic work, these words occurred: *beyond the Jordan* (*πέραν τοῦ Ἰορδάνου*). The author reproduces them expressly (xix. 1), doubtless to show that the fulfilment of the prophecy continues even after the departure from Galilee. The account of this journey from Galilea to Jerusalem occupies about ten chapters in Luke (ix. 51–xix. 28). In Matthew only seven points are mentioned: 1st, a conversation on divorce with the Pharisees; 2nd, the blessing of the little children; 3rd, the conversation with the rich young man, and the discourses that follow; 4th, the parable of the labourers successively called and paid alike; 5th, a new announcement of the Passion; 6th, the request of the mother of James and John; 7th, the cure of the two blind men at Jericho. The first point occurs in Mark; the two following are common to the three; the fourth is peculiar to Matthew; the fifth is found in all three; the sixth is common to Matthew and Mark; the seventh to all the three, except that Mark and Luke only mention the cure of one blind man. It is with the blessing of the children that Luke, after having followed his special course since the departure from Galilee (ix. 51), returns to the current of the common narrative.

## § 5

### THE MINISTRY AT JERUSALEM

(xxi. 1–xxv. 46)

The three days of the last week (from Monday to Wednesday) comprised under this head (see my *Comment. on the Fourth Gospel*, iii., on chap. xii. 1) embrace a series of detached facts (chaps. xxi.–xxiii.). This series ends, like several of the preceding sections, in a great discourse (chaps. xxiv. and xxv.). The facts mentioned are: 1st, the entry into Jerusalem with the expulsion of the traders (in all the three narratives); 2nd, the cursing of the barren fig-tree (Matt. and Mark); 3rd, the official interrogation by the Sanhedrin (all the three); 4th, the parable of the two sons (Matt.

only); 5th, that of the vine-dressers (the three); 6th, that of the great supper (Matt.; comp. Luke xix.); 7th, the tribute to be paid to Cæsar (all the three); 8th, the resurrection of the body (the three); 9th, the first commandment (the three); 10th, the question of Jesus on the son of David (the three); 11th, the address to the scribes and the Pharisees (the three).

Chap. xxiii. contains a severe apostrophe to the theocratic authorities of the time, and declares the condemnation that is awaiting them. As in other cases, the beginning of the discourse is also found in Mark (xii. 38–40) and in Luke (xx. 45–47); it is therefore probable that it really belongs to the situation indicated. Jesus first addresses the people (Mark) or His disciples before all the people (Luke). After that there follows in Matthew a vehement apostrophe addressed to the chiefs themselves (xxiii. 13 and fol.), in which seven subjects of condemnation are enumerated. Luke reports an analogous passage (xi. 37 and fol.), but in Galilee, at a meal to which Jesus was invited by a Pharisee, which agrees with vers. 24–26 of Matthew, that present figures suitable to the situation of a repast. The vivacity of the tone and of the censures that follow agrees also with this situation better perhaps than with that of Matthew. It would appear at the first glance that the striking allocution to "Jerusalem that killeth the prophets" (at the end of the discourse), better suits a scene in the temple than a repast in Galilee. I continue none the less to believe, as I have shown in my *Commentary on the Gospel of Luke*, that the situation indicated by Luke is preferable.

This chap. xxiii. is often closely connected with the discourses of chaps. xxiv. and xxv., as if it formed but one with them, so that Reuss, Reville, and others include it with them in the Logia. In my view this is an error; chap. xxiii. is positively separated from chap. xxiv. by the account of the departure from the temple and of the declaration of its destruction, as well as by an entirely new introduction.

The first part of the sojourn of Jesus at Jerusalem has

been rightly called the time of His reign in the temple; in effect He there exercises an absolute dominion by His personal ascendency and His sovereign word. And now, on the evening of the last of these days, which was, if I mistake not, the Wednesday, two days before His death, He withdraws with His four most intimate disciples (Mark) to the Mount of Olives. Then, sitting with them opposite that temple whose ruin He has just announced, He unfolds to them the vistas of the future that will follow His near departure, first for themselves, then for the Jewish people, and lastly for the Church and the whole world.

*The fifth discourse: The time that must elapse between the departure of Jesus and His future return* (chaps. xxiv. and xxv.)

Some months before, when Jesus had announced to the disciples His coming sufferings, He had confirmed the shaken faith of the three chief of them by associating them with His private prayer and with the sight by anticipation of His glorification (xvii. 1–8). Now, in view of the ignominious death He is about to undergo before their eyes, He strengthens them in like manner by revealing to them in a prophetic picture His glorious return as a King and a Judge, but also the painful circumstances that the Church will have to pass through before that time. From the midst of this future is specially detached the tragic event, the time of which they had asked of Him: the judgment of Jerusalem, the first act of the judgment of the world.

The discourse of chap. xxiv. contains five pieces, and not merely four, as is often thought:

1. In the first fourteen verses are described in a general way the external circumstances that will be, after His departure, the conditions of the life of the Church. There will be a kind of accumulation of the ordinary plagues of the earthly life (wars, famines, earthquakes), calamities in which the Church will naturally share. Besides that, she will have her own trials, attempts to seduce her proceeding from false

Christs and persecutions on the part of Jews and heathen. But the Church will none the less fulfil her task to bear witness to the gospel before all peoples.

The forty years that elapsed between the death of Jesus and the ruin of Jerusalem, in the year 70, were in fact one of the most troubled epochs of the history of mankind. There arose false Christs (ver. 5) and false prophets (ver. 11), like Simon Magus, who pretended to be the great power of God (Acts viii.); Dositheus, who called himself the son of God and pretended to be the Christ promised by Moses (Origen, *Cont. Cels.* i. 57, vi.); Menander, a disciple of Simon, who said he was the envoy of invisible powers; then rioters like the Egyptian who is mentioned Acts xxi. 38, and later Bar-Cocheba; these are some examples of those false prophets and Messianic impostors that Jesus announced. The scourges of the time equally justified His prophecy: wars raged both near (between Herod and Aretas) and far off, in the provinces (in Gaul) and at the extremities of the empire (Parthia). Famine also at times produced distress; frequent earthquakes kept the people in continual anxiety. "The globe itself," says Renan, "went through a convulsion parallel to that of the moral world. Never were earthquakes more common than in the first century; in 63 Pompeii was almost destroyed, Asia Minor was in a perpetual concussion, fourteen cities were destroyed in the region of Tmolus. From 59 onwards, there is not a year which is not marked by some disasters; in the year 60 Laodicea and Colossæ are swallowed up; men did not remember a time when the crust of the old continent had been so greatly disturbed" (*L'Antechrist*, ch. xiv.). Nor were persecutions awanting, neither on the part of the Jews (Acts iv. to viii., xii.; martyrdom of James and of the chiefs of the Church in 62, related by Josephus) nor on the part of the heathen (Nero, in 64). Finally, the preaching of Paul realised, as far as that was possible in so short a time, the commission, given by Jesus, to offer salvation in His name to all the peoples.

2. This discourse of Jesus had been evoked by the

question of the disciples (ver. 3) relative of the announcement of the approaching ruin of the temple. Now this question is thus formulated in our gospel: "Tell us when these things shall be, and what shall be the sign of Thy coming and of the end of the world." It referred, then, first to the ruin of the temple and of the Jewish State; but the disciples appear to have thought that this event would coincide with the glorious return of Jesus and the end of things; hence the last words of their question. It is solely upon the first of these two subjects that Jesus replies in what follows (vers. 15–22). From the midst of the extremely troubled course of things that has just been described, there arises as from an obscure depth, an event still more sombre, the destruction of that which they have hitherto regarded as the most sacred and inviolable of things. Matthew speaks of a sacred place invaded by an abominable devastation; but the sequel where Jesus recommends His people to flee from Judea excludes the thought that it regards the temple devastated by a hostile army, for it would have been too late to flee when the whole country was invaded, Jerusalem taken, and the temple occupied. Again, Mark uses a more vague expression: "The abomination of desolation standing *where he ought not.*" Luke says yet otherwise: "When you shall see the hostile army surrounding Jerusalem." Jesus would denote thereby, not the taking of the city and the temple, but the gradual invasion of the Holy Land by the hostile army; at this moment there would still be time to escape, and Daniel's term, quoted by Jesus, may apply to the profanation of that sacred soil by the Roman standards, symbols of idolatry adored by the soldiers. That is so true that, according to Josephus (*Antiq.* xviii. 5. 3), when Vitellius wished to lead his army from Antioch to Petra, instead of causing it directly to cross the Holy Land, he caused it to make a great detour, in order not to be stopped in its march.—The author here interrupts, quite exceptionally, the discourse of Jesus in order to accentuate energetically the Lord's warning (ver. 15).

3. Here occurs a transition piece (vers. 23–28), of which

sufficient account is not taken, and which is yet of the greatest importance. Holtzmann even divides it into two fragments (vers. 23–25 and 26–28); but how can we separate ver. 26 from vers. 23–25! The preceding piece expressed the idea that the days of the tribulation described above would be shortened for the preservation of the elect (ver. 22).[1] The piece that follows describes the state of things that is to succeed this end abruptly brought by Providence to the days of tribulation (vers. 23–28). To the ruin of the Jewish people will succeed a period of religious struggles and spiritual seductions (false Christs and false prophets), and, for the faithful, of anxious expectation of the Christ, whose appearance will be delayed: ("Lo, He is here or there").[2] The

[1] The tribulation of which Jesus speaks (ver. 21) cannot directly end in the Parousia; for He adds that after it there will not be the like, which supposes in its sequel the continuation of history. As regards the saying: "These days shall be shortened, otherwise all the world would perish," I think it refers to the bloody horrors of the siege and the war, properly so called, which, if it had not been promptly ended, would have achieved the destruction of the Jewish people. Paul says in this sense: "We would have become as Sodom and Gomorrah," those cities of which no inhabitant was left as a remnant (Rom. ix. 29). But this fate could not be that of the chosen people, since *the remnant* that is assured it (τὸ κατάλειμμα, ver. 27) cannot fail.

[2] The false prophets announced by Jesus for the period that He places between the ruin of Jerusalem and the Parousia are the false teachers inspired *by the spirit of this world*, as Paul says (1 Cor. ii. 12), who in all ages of the Church have falsified the gospel of Christ and His apostles. As regards the *false Christs*, it is said that a pretty large number of them have arisen in the Synagogue, who have not gained notoriety. The history of the Church does not present well-known personages of this kind, which does not prevent such pretensions from having arisen without leaving a trace. I myself have thrice encountered persons who claimed to be the Christ. One, a Hungarian advocate, admired the spiritual work of Jesus, but thought it had remained incomplete because He had not added social reform to it. Moses, he said, wrote the Old (das alte) Testament; Jesus the New (das neue); my part is to make the *quite new* (das neueste). From Constantinople, his future residence, he would cause justice and peace to reign over all the world. The second, an Alsatian, endowed with great beauty and talents, repaired to the first universal Exhibition at London, in 1851, where his manifestation should take place. The third, a venerable brother, known to many of us, thought he had come to save those who had not believed in Jesus, and to communicate new spiritual powers to those who had received Him. One may suppose that the point of departure of this state of mental

very short picture of this interval between the ruin of Jerusalem and the Parousia has parallels in Mark (xiii. 21–23) and in Luke (xvii. 22 and 23). But it should above all be completed by many other sayings reported in Matthew itself, and in the two other Synoptics, which cannot apply to any other time than the period in question. Thus the announcement of the state of wordliness and carnal security into which the world will fall, like that of mankind before the Deluge (vers. 37–39), or that of Sodom before its destruction (Luke xvii. 28–30), a state from the general influence of which the Church herself will not escape (comp. in Matt. xxv. the sleep of the ten virgins, the wise as well as the foolish, and this saying in Luke xviii. 8: "When the Son of Man cometh, shall He find faith on the earth?"). It is also the time when the servants that have received talents (Matthew) or pounds (Luke) are commissioned to employ them by working for the interests of their master, and thus themselves determine the degree of their reward or punishment at the time of giving account, when that master will come as king and judge after a long time, *μετὰ πολὺν χρόνον* (Matt. xxv. 19). The length of his absence is denoted in Luke (xix. 12) by the duration of the journey (*εἰς χώραν μακράν*). It is the time when (Matt. xxiv. 48) the unfaithful servant says to himself, "My lord delayeth his coming," and begins to eat and drink with the drunken. It is the time when the faithful servants, in the anxiety into which they are plunged by this long waiting, sigh for the blessing of seeing *one of the days* (a perceptible manifestation) of the Son of Man, to fortify their wavering faith, *but shall not see it* (Luke xvii. 22). It is the time of the persevering cry of the widow long vainly asking to be put in possession of her heritage, and who, despite all, perseveres till she has been heard.

alienation was the very real experience, but badly interpreted by an ill-balanced mind, of the truth formulated by Paul in these words: "It is no longer I that live, but Christ liveth in me" (Gal. ii. 20).—How many like facts may have occurred in the Church without having been noticed by history! And it may be presumed that the longer time advances the more will they be multiplied.

Only the Lord asks if the Church will to the end have this faith in the divine promises (Luke xviii. 1–8). It is the time of that long waiting of which Jesus speaks in Mark (xiii. 35) and Luke (xii. 38), which begins in the evening, continues till midnight, is prolonged till the cock-crowing and even perhaps till the morning, when all hope of seeing the Master arrive will seem lost. Is it not, lastly, the time needed in order that the seed may become a tree whose branches shelter the peoples, and that the leaven may pervade the whole of human life?

Such is the sum of the facts, each of longer or less duration, which, according to the words of Jesus scattered in our Synoptics, must be placed between His departure and His return, and consequently take place alongside of this third part of the discourse that we are considering. It is then a very grave error to pass lightly over these few verses, that in reality embrace the whole period of the life of the Church, in the actual absence of the Lord, the interval called by Luke by this striking name: *the times of the Gentiles* (**καιροὶ ἐθνῶν**). "Jerusalem," he says (xxi. 24), "shall be trodden down by the Gentiles, until the times of the Gentiles be fulfilled." This expression cannot denote the time of the *domination* of the Gentiles, for the phrase would be tautological: the Gentiles will dominate the Holy Land, as long as it will be given them to dominate it! It assumes, on the other hand, its full meaning if it be explained by the two parallel sayings (Matt. xxi. 41 and 43): "He will let his vineyard to other husbandmen, who will render him the fruits *in their seasons* (ἐν τοῖς καιροῖς αὐτῶν). . . . The kingdom will be taken from you, and given to a nation rendering the fruits thereof." The word καιρός denotes a *favourable* occasion, and the plural of the word an occasion prolonged in a series of periods. It is for the heathen nations the time of the free successive acceptance of salvation, a time corresponding, as regards the expression, to what Luke calls, as regards Israel (xix. 44), the time of *their visitation*, that is, the time of the presence of Jesus in the midst of His people to open to them the door of the kingdom. Doubtless it might be objected that this whole series of facts that we have just enumerated was placed in the thought of Jesus before the judgment of Jerusalem and of the Jewish people. But how should the marriage feast that ends the parable of the ten virgins have anything in common with the ruin of the theocracy? What would the settlement of accounts between Jesus and His servants have to do with the catastrophe of Israel? And what would the long cry of the widow and the slow penetration of human life with the leaven of the gospel signify, if the only question was of the interval between the death of Jesus and the ruin of the Jewish people? Certainly Jesus placed all the facts above enumerated before His final return, so that in His thought a long period, that of the Church, had to intervene between the end of the theocracy and the fourth phase, contained in the following piece.

4. The fourth piece (Matt. xxiv. 29–31) presents the picture of the Parousia. The first words of this passage contain the chief difficulty of the whole discourse: "Immediately after the tribulation of those days (εὐθέως μετὰ τὴν θλίψιν τῶν ἡμερῶν ἐκείνων)," says Matthew (ver. 29), "the sun will be darkened . . ." This expression: *the tribulation of those days*, occurred before in vers. 21 and 22, where it referred to the days that will immediately follow the ruin of Jerusalem. It seems then that in ver. 29 it should denote these same days. But how then are we to understand the words: "immediately after"?

Jesus cannot have *immediately* attached His Parousia to the great tribulation of Israel, except by suppressing the whole interval in which alone all the facts above recalled can be placed, and thus putting Himself in full contradiction with Himself. Such a supposition is impossible. Consequently there only remains this alternative:

Either admit inaccuracy in the Greek account of the discourse delivered by Jesus in another language, which supposition would be confirmed by the omission in Mark

(xiii. 24) of the word *immediately*, εὐθέως, which forms the chief difficulty of the text of Matthew. Was this word added by the one to the oral or written source, or removed by the other? But even granting that this word was removed in Mark, the relation between the destruction of Jerusalem and the Parousia still remains, even with him, very close.

Or else, without seeking to decide what were the exact terms that Jesus used, we must suppose, if we do not wish to make Him contradict Himself, that in this passage of the discourse our two texts do not exactly correspond with its primitive form. And if we consider, there would be nothing inexplicable in this. In the question addressed to Jesus by the disciples (ver. 3), we see that they thought the destruction of Jerusalem should be the signal of the glorious return of Jesus and of the end of the present dispensation. This view of theirs resulted from the prophecy of the Old Testament, in which the *day of the Lord* comprised at once the final judgment of Israel and the decisive chastisement of the heathen nations before the establishment of the divine kingdom (Zach. xiii. and xiv.; Mal. iii. and iv.). It appeared to them, then, that the ruin of Israel must be immediately followed by the consummation of things. In this spirit they questioned, and in this spirit they listened. When too small a vessel must receive contents that surpass it, these contents in order to enter it must of course be more or less strongly compressed and contracted. Possibly it has been thus with the thought of Jesus, which infinitely transcended the expectation of His disciples, and, in general, of all the other Israelites. Let us add that, when Jesus said to the apostles, "Watch, for that day will come upon you as a snare," they might easily apply to themselves, as individuals, what Jesus committed to them as representing all the generations of believers, the number of whom He Himself declares He knew not.

After that there remains, however, another possibility which ought not to be passed in silence, namely, that the expression, *the tribulation of those days*, contains in the thought of the evangelists not only the catastrophe itself, but that event with the whole state of things that has resulted from it: the disappearance of Israel from the number of the peoples, the occupation of their country by the heathen nations, and the transference to these of the kingdom of God. What Jewish heart would not recognise in this state, which still endures, the continuance of the great tribulation that began with the ruin of Jerusalem. In this large sense of the word *tribulation*, the word of Jesus in Matthew and Mark completely agrees with the term used by Luke: "The times of the Gentiles." The word *immediately* would not signify in this case *soon after*, as when it is preceded by the mention of a particular fact, but would be taken in the sense it should have after the description of a state of things: *suddenly, unexpectedly.* It thus exactly corresponds with the term ἐξαίφνης, *sudden*, of Mark (xiii. 36), and with the αἰφνίδιος, *unforeseen, rapid*, of Paul (1 Thess. v. 3). This word strongly contrasts with the terms εἰρήνη and ἀσφάλεια, *peace* and *safety*, by which the apostle characterises the moral state of society at that time. One may compare the expression εὐθέως μετὰ σπουδῆς of Mark vi. 25, following the interruption of the feast, caused by the deliberation of Herodias and her daughter.

5. The fifth piece, vers. 32–36, contains the practical application of the whole discourse; and is summed up in this word: Watch. The three Synoptics develop this application each in its own way. But all three agree in the tenor of the words of ver. 34, where Jesus declares that all these things shall be accomplished in this generation. As Holtzmann shows (*Hand-Commentar*, ad h. l.), after Herodotus, three generations were reckoned to a century, the time of a generation being equal to 30–40 years. If we explain hereby the date of ver. 34, Jesus had announced that the event to which it refers would take place, at the latest, some forty years after His departure. What is this event? Holtzmann, Weiss, and most others reply: the Parousia. To the objection that Jesus could not have hoped that the gospel would be preached to all nations in so short a space of time, Weiss does not hesitate to reply that Jesus did not realise the size of the globe. I do

not know what idea Jesus had of the size of the globe. Isaiah already speaks of the *Sinim*, whom he opposes to the peoples of the extreme West (xlix. 12). Does it refer to the Chinese, as has sometimes been thought? That would prove that the extent of the Asiatic continent was not unknown. But what is certain is that all the other passages we have quoted above suppose a much longer future for the Church on earth than the forty years that elapsed between the years 30 and 70. Klostermann has proposed an explanation that would remove the difficulty, which is, to apply the words, *this generation*, not to the generation contemporary with Jesus, but to that which will be living at the beginning of the last crisis. The men who will be present at the precursory signs of the Parousia will also see the end of them, so rapid will be the course of things. The parable of the fig-tree (ver. 28) agrees very well with this meaning, better certainly than the ordinary explanation; it even seems positively required by the expression, "When *you shall see*" (Luke xxi. 31). But two parallel passages forbid us to accept this meaning, however alluring. Jesus says (Matt. xxiii. 36), "that the punishment for all the innocent blood shed from that of Abel will come upon *this generation*," and (Luke xi. 50), "that the blood of all the prophets, shed from the creation of the world, will be required of *this generation*," which can only apply to the generation that crucified Him, and that thus filled up the measure of the enmity of the people against their God. Jesus was thinking then, doubtless, of the generation in the midst of which He lived, in declaring that the event of which He would speak would take place before it had passed away. But what is that event? The opinion of Weiss, Holtzmann, and so many others that it refers to the Parousia, is no doubt the sense to which the context most naturally leads. But the context cannot decide the question; for we know how often it occurs that the evangelists displace the words of Jesus. In the traditional apostolic account, they held less to the situation in which the words had been pronounced than to the tenor of the words themselves; and a change of situation might certainly modify the application of them. Thus the exhortation to reconciliation (Matt. v. 25 and fol.), which in that context can only refer to reconciliation between brethren, as it is placed in the context of Luke (xii. 58), evidently applies to reconciliation with God. So again the picture of the unclean spirit who returns to his dwelling and finds it well swept and garnished, after having left it for a time, applies (Matt. xii. 43) to the whole people of Israel, while, after the context of Luke (xi. 24 and 25), it refers to relapses following superficial cures of the possessed performed by Jewish exorcists. In these two cases the application resulting from the context of Luke is certainly preferable. Perhaps it is otherwise in the following cases: The words of Jesus on the blasphemy against the Holy Spirit seem better placed in the context of Matthew (xii. 31) than in that of Luke (xii. 10). So again with the exhortation not to go down into one's house to remove his goods, etc., which in the context of Luke (xvii. 30, 31) is connected with the time of the Parousia, in Matthew is referred with more probability to the time of the flight when Jerusalem is destroyed (xxiv. 17, 18).

Something similar, then, may have occurred regarding our ver. 34; its place may have been inverted, and its application thus modified, and that the more easily that the two discourses that Jesus spoke, the one on the end of the theocracy (Luke xxi.), the other on the end of the present dispensation (Luke xvii.), are found blended into one in Matt. xxiv. and Mark xiii. Immediately after the words of ver. 34 (in Mark ver. 30), these words occur in Matt. ver. 36 (Mark ver. 32): "But of that day and hour knoweth no one, neither the angels of heaven, nor the Son, but the Father only." Let us notice: 1st, that this verse which refers to the Parousia—as all agree—begins with the adversative particle δέ, *but*, which clearly opposes that day to the preceding day (ver. 34); 2nd, that in the two texts (Matt. ver. 36 and Mark ver. 32) the pronoun ἐκείνη, *that day*, is used in speaking of the day and hour of the Parousia, in opposition to the pronoun αὕτη, *this generation* (Matt. ver. 34;

Mark ver. 30); and, above all, 3rd, that the knowledge that Jesus denies He has regarding the Parousia (ver. 36; Mark ver. 32), is absolutely opposed to the knowledge of which He gives proof in reference to the event mentioned in ver. 34. This event cannot then be the Parousia, and can only have been, in the thought of Jesus, the other essential fact treated in this chapter, namely, the destruction of Jerusalem. This saying is then parallel to that which we have already noticed (chap. x. 23), where the idea of the return of Jesus is applied also to this event. The two texts of Matthew and Mark here present the same peculiarities.

Colani, desiring not to attribute to Jesus, in his view a mere man, the fantastic hope of a glorious return from heaven and of the holding of the last judgment of mankind, has proposed to regard this chapter as a little apocalypse composed by a writer of the time, a little before the destruction of Jerusalem.[1] This fly-sheet, of Jewish origin according to Colani, Judæo-Christian according to others, had fallen into the hands of the author of our gospel, who had inserted it in his work, as a discourse of Jesus. This hypothesis has obtained the assent of some of the most eminent of modern critics (Weizsaecker, Keim, Hilgenfeld, Weiffenbach, Mangold, Holtzmann, Renan in *The Antichrist*). It has even been thought to find in this prophecy the oracle of which Eusebius speaks (*H. E.* iii. 5. 3), which was published at the beginning of the Jewish war, and had determined the exodus of the Judæo-Christian Church. This is a way to spare Jesus the accusation of half-madness, which it is not easy for Him to escape from the dogmatic point of view of these critics. But it is evident that, as regards the evangelist personally, he viewed this discourse as spoken by Jesus, for the same reason as those of chaps. v.–vii., x., xiii., and xviii.; for at the end of it he resumes the narrative with the same formula with which he had concluded all the other discourses (xxvi. 1): "And it came to pass, when Jesus had finished all these words, He said unto His disciples." Could it be possible that

[1] *Jesus-Christ et les croyances messianiques de son temps*, 1864, 2nd ed.

he had derived this discourse from a source absolutely different from that whence he had drawn the four previous ones? That is the more improbable that this last discourse is absolutely like the others, whether as regards style, which nowise differs from that of the rest of the gospel, or as regards the mode of composition, which rests, like that of the four previous ones, on the same process of agglomeration of diverse elements. No more could one understand, if this discourse were the reproduction of a written document, the considerable differences presented by Mark's edition, whether one of the two editions has been derived from the other, or both proceed from the same supposed document. Then it would be still more difficult to understand how by means of this one oracle the idea occurred to Luke to compose two discourses completely different both in situation and contents (xvii. and xxi.). In fine, how can we believe that the first evangelist, who has reproduced in his whole writing in an incomparable manner the teaching of Jesus as the apostles transmitted it, would have granted without scruple so decisive a place to the contents of a fly-sheet that had accidentally fallen into his hands! An unprejudiced criticism cannot admit this. I am glad to find the proof of it in the recent work of Titius, *Das Verhältniss der Herrnworte im Marcus-Evangelium zu den Logia des Matthaeus*, published in the *Theolog. Studien* (pp. 284–331), where the author maintains that the discourse of Mark (chap. xiii.) has been derived from the Logia of Matthew, but not from a foreign source. In fine, What is gained by a supposition so arbitrary as that of this "little apocalypse" of unknown origin? What Jesus there attributes to Himself is only at bottom what He has declared about Himself in many other places. This fact of His return in glory to judge mankind we find affirmed in a host of other sayings that we shall presently quote. And as regards the oracle of which Eusebius speaks, it is natural enough to think that on seeing the preparation for the war with Rome, the chiefs of the Church recognised in solemn deliberation that the time to apply the warning of the Lord had arrived. Perhaps a decision in this sense was then taken and a prophecy uttered on this occasion. Did the body of the elders communicate this decision to the churches while pointing out to them as the place of refuge, the region of Pella beyond Jordan? I think with Weiss that some fact of this kind may have occasioned the report of Eusebius, without needing to resort to the very strange hypothesis of Colani.

The success of this bold hypothesis is doubtless due to the same cause as its origin, the desire not to make Jesus responsible for assertions which would have betrayed in Him, it is thought, an extreme enthusiasm. But this effort is of absolutely no use, since the same assertions recur in the rest of the gospel, and in so large number that no arbitrary operation can remove them from it; thus vii. 22 and 23: "Many will say to *Me* on that day, Lord, Lord! . . . *but I will declare unto them* . . . "; x. 33: "Whosoever shall confess Me . . . *I* will also confess him . . . and whosoever shall deny Me . . . *I* will also deny him before My Father . . . "; xvi. 27: "The Son of Man shall come in the glory of His Father with His angels, and then *shall He render* to every man according to his deeds . . . "; xiii. 30: "In the time of the harvest *I will say* to the reapers . . . "; and ver. 41: "The Son of Man shall send forth *His angels* and they shall gather those that do iniquity, and shall cast them out of His kingdom into the furnace of fire . . . "; xix. 28: "In the regeneration . . . when the Son of Man shall sit on *the throne of His glory* . . . "; xxv. 31: "When the Son of Man shall come in *His glory,* and all *His angels* with Him, then He shall sit on the throne of His glory, and before Him shall be gathered all nations, and He shall separate . . ." In fine, xxvi. 64: "Henceforth ye shall see the Son of Man sitting at the right hand of power, and coming on the clouds of heaven" (Mark xiv. 62). Jesus returning after a long absence to judge and hold the final assize—such are the contents of the discourse (Matt. xxiv.–xxv.), and these contents wholly recur, point by point, in the words which we have just quoted, so that the expedient proposed by

Colani, despite the success it has obtained, is not only arbitrary and improbable, but also completely useless.

Let us notice that, while in xxvi. 1 the author resumes the course of the narrative after this discourse exactly as after all the preceding ones, with the usual formula in such cases, he here adds exceptionally the word πάντας, *all*, as if to tell that he has reached the end of the collection from which he has derived them.

Before coming to this final formula, the author intercalates yet four pieces connected with what precedes as regards the subject, but not as regards the time where they are placed. The one is found again in Luke xii. 41–48, where it is connected with a warning given to the future leaders of the Church on the judgment that they will have to undergo. With this passage, transposed here by Matthew, are connected two parables describing the judgment of the Church, the parables of the virgins and of the talents (chap. xxv.), the first bearing on the necessity of an uninterrupted *spiritual* life; the second, on the obligation of *practical* activity for the cause of Christ. The latter has a brief parallel (Mark xiii. 34) in the same position. In fine, this grand whole ends (xxv. 31 and fol.) with the picture of the universal judgment: all the nations assembled before the glorified Christ to be judged by Him (ver. 32). It no doubt refers to the already evangelised nations, as that was predicted xxiv. 14. Active and practical love is stated in this solemn picture as the condition of salvation, faith being supposed as its principle (ver. 40).

## § 6

### THE PASSION (chaps. xxvi.–xxvii.)

In this part of the account, the chain of the events being much closer, the parallelism between the three narratives is also more constant than in all the rest of the gospel narrative. It approaches to what we have found in the last period of the Galilean ministry. Matthew and Mark in particular proceed in almost complete agreement, save little additions or omissions distinguishing the two accounts. The narrative of Luke is absolutely independent of that of the other two. What characterises Matthew's are the prophetic quotations that accompany the most of the facts reported. It particularly concerned this evangelist to justify by prophecy all the details of that death of the cross which was the great stumbling-block to the Jews, and thus to change into a motive of faith the principal reason on which their unbelief rested.

## § 7

### THE RESURRECTION (chap. xxviii.)

Here, again, the accounts of Matthew and Mark proceed in close union, while Luke's more and more departs from them. Matthew only relates two principal facts: the visit of the women to the tomb, which occasioned the knowledge of the great event, and the appearance of Jesus in Galilee, in which He Himself announced to the apostles His elevation to the universal sovereignty promised to the Messiah (Ps. ii. and cx.). He assured them also of His permanent help for the fulfilment of the task that He was confiding to them, namely, to lead all the nations to receive his Word. This solemn affirmation in the mouth of Jesus is the last word of our gospel; it is the seal set to His Messianic dignity proclaimed from the first word of this writing. The programme of the book is shown to be accomplished. Such is the unity, strongly conceived and executed, of this work: beginning, middle, end, the whole is pervaded by a single grand thought. The Old Testament said in closing (Mal. iii. 1): "*He is coming.*" The New, in opening with the first gospel, says: "*He has come.*" In these circumstances we can understand without great difficulty that the author, entirely dominated by this solemn thought, did not feel the need of pausing long to report all the detailed facts by which the apostles were personally brought to the subjective conviction of the reality of the resurrection. The detail of the diverse appearances that had so firmly raised and founded their faith did not necessarily come within the limits of a narrative so objective as that of Matthew. What he had to recall after the fact of the resurrection was the final declaration by which Jesus had announced to the apostles His supreme elevation while committing to them their future task.

The formula of *baptism* which the author places at this time in the mouth of Jesus is declared by many critics to be posterior to the apostolic age. According to them, the primitive form had been simply baptism *in the name of Jesus*, as the epistles and the narrative of the Acts would prove. But the use of the name of God (the Father) in this solemn rite was indispensable, for it served to separate the heathen neophyte from his old religion, just as the name of Jesus separated the Jewish neophyte from Judaism. And as regards the mention of the Holy Spirit, it cannot cause doubt, for it is positively recalled 1 Cor. vi. 11, where the formula indicated in Matthew is freely reproduced: "Ye were *washed* . . . in the *name of the Lord Jesus* and by *the Spirit* of *our God*." Another passage that forbids us to doubt the mention of the Holy Spirit in apostolic baptism is the fact related in Acts xix. 1 and fol., where Paul wonders that certain disciples of John, while having been baptized, had not heard tell of a Holy Spirit. The wonder of the apostle is only to be explained if the name of the Holy Spirit expressly figured in the primitive ceremony of baptism. If we compare 1 Cor. xii. 4–6 and especially 2 Cor. xiii. 13: "The grace of *Jesus Christ*, the love of *God*, and the communion of the *Holy Spirit*," we shall be convinced that the formula of baptism, as Matthew indicates it, was quite conformable to the consciousness of the apostolic Church.

## § 8

### THE PLAN

The plan is perfectly clear: it simply corresponds with the progress of the history without pretending to explain it or to give an account of it: the infancy, appearance, Galilean ministry, journey to Judea, ministry in Jerusalem, Passion, Resurrection. Besides, at certain points of this narrative are placed some great discourses, each corresponding to one of the principal teachings pronounced at that time, but all increased by the addition of elements homogeneous to the central subject and belonging to other situations. I do not think that a more systematic plan is to be sought, as Weiss does, who divides into five parts: after the accounts of the infancy and the preparatory circumstances (i.–iv. 22), (i.) Jesus teaches and heals (iv. 23–ix. 34); (ii.) unbelief is developed (ix. 35–xiv. 12); (iii.) from xiv. 13 there follows a series of facts of the Galilean ministry without a dominating idea on to xx. 16; (iv.) from xx. 17, the departure for Jerusalem and the activity in that city; (v.) Passion and Resurrection (xxvi.–xxviii.). This plan, cleverly explained by this author by means of the two sources which he believes to be combined in our gospel, is wrong in ignoring the final point of the Galilean ministry, so clearly marked in Matthew's narrative (xix. 1), as well as in the parallel passages of the two other Synoptics, after the last return to Capernaum (Mark x. 1; Luke ix. 51).—Keim especially insists on the parallelism of iv. 17 and xvi. 21; the first of these passages indicating the beginning of the preaching in general, and the second the first revelation of the suffering Christ, with which the second part of the book opens, entitled by him "the march to death."—Holtzmann recognises the well-marked division xix. 1, where the departure for Jerusalem is indicated. Before that, if I understand aright, he divides the facts of the Galilean ministry into three groups, which are connected with the great discourses as fulcrums: the first (iv. 23–ix. 34), with the Sermon on the Mount; the second (ix. 35–xiii. 58), with the discourse of chap. x.; the third (xiv.–xviii.) ends in that of chap. xviii. There follow the last two parts of the history: (1) xix.–xxv., and (2) xxvi.–xxviii. It is a division similar to that which I have proposed. See *Hand-Commentar*, pp. 5 and 6.

The following division has recently been proposed by M. E. Roehrich in his treatise, *The Composition of the Gospels*, 1897. After the preamble, six parts: I. The kingdom of heaven (v. 12–xii. 52); subdivided into: (*a*) the head; (*b*) the workmen; (*c*) the signs; (*d*) the progress. II. The opposition to the kingdom (xiii. 53–xvi. 4). III. The Church (xvi. 5–xx. 28); subdivision: (*a*) its foundation; (*b*) the duty of its members; (*c*) its social mission; (*d*) its prerogatives. IV. The prophecy of the kingdom (xx. 29–xxv. 46). V. The Passion (xxv. 1–xxvii. 66). VI. The Resurrection (xxviii.). This mode of grouping seems to me very artificial. It is easy to see that the pieces only come in a forced way under the titles indicated. Then, we again find here the fault committed by Weiss, that of effacing the principal division marked by the author himself (xix. 1). What is true in this plan, as in that of Weiss, is that it marks well from the first and happy beginnings of the work of Christ the development of the opposition to that work. But that was a matter of course. For my part I do not think that a *logical* scheme ruled in the mind of the author the general course of his narrative. This is what appears to me to be the plan of the first gospel:

The seven great parts have been indicated above (pp. 121–164). I only here resume the course of the third, that of the Galilean ministry, the most complicated part, and sum it up as follows:

A. The beginnings, ending with the Sermon on the Mount (iv. 12–vii. 29), and grouping around the prophetic theme (iv. 14–16).

B. The central part, comprising:

(*a*) A group of acts of Messianic sovereignty (viii. 1–x. 42), ending with the discourse of chap. x., and having as prophetic theme the words of Isaiah quoted in viii. 17;

(*b*) A group of words of Messianic wisdom (xi. 1–xiii. 58), ending with the discourse of chap. xiii., and having as prophetic theme the passage of Isaiah quoted in xii. 17–21;

(*c*) The journeys to the northern extremities of the Holy Land (xiv. 1–xviii. 35), ending with the discourses of chap.

xviii., and still resting on the prophetic text of chap. iv. relative to the ministry of the Messiah in Galilee.

The course of the other parts is understood of itself.

It is then with reason that Weizsaecker thus expresses himself: "It cannot be denied that the Gospel of Matthew is a composition well conceived and well executed from one end to the other" (*Unters.* p. 131). Keim, in like manner, says: "The plan of the book is careful, simple, of striking clearness, transparent, and very well executed" (*Gesch. Jesu,* i. p. 52).

## III

### Characteristic Features of the First Gospel

A. *From the historiographic point of view.*

Two principal features seem to me to distinguish this writing in this first connection.

1. The preponderance of the didactic over the narrative element: more than the half of the book contains discourses and conversations. And this preference does not appear only in the whole of the recital, but also in the way in which the particular features are related. One is struck at every moment by the absence of all details fitted to describe the facts and to reproduce their local colour. It is enough to compare the account of the cure of the paralytic of Capernaum (Matt. ix. 1 and fol.) with the account of the same fact in Mark (ii. 1 and fol.) and in Luke (v. 17 and fol.), or that of the cure of the centurion's servant (Matt. viii. 5 and fol.) with the corresponding account of Luke (vii. 1 and fol.), to show how little the first evangelist occupies himself with the description of the facts that he reports, and how from the first he hastens to the final words of Jesus as the really essential thing that reveals the religious meaning of the fact reported. Hence the absence as well of any pretence to chronological accuracy. The formulas: *after that, behold, at that time,* are mere transitions without historic value, and no greater mistake can be

committed than that of Ebrard, who tried to reconstitute what he calls the acoluthia (the historic sequence) of the facts by means of such formulas. If the author had even claimed to observe a chronological order, he would not have divided the central part of the Galilean ministry, after an order of subjects, into two groups, the one of acts of power, the other of words of wisdom, two elements that alternated at every moment in the activity of Christ.

2. This apparent negligence, in a historical point of view, shows that the evangelist was dominated by a superior preoccupation to that of the mere recital of the facts. What he wished was to bring out the meaning of the facts rather than describe the details of them. This is the second peculiar feature of this narrative. The author seeks above all to show in the facts of the history of Jesus the realisation of the Messianic picture distributed in scattered features in the revelations of the old covenant. In comparison with this chief end, the minute depicting of the facts had only a secondary interest in his view. There is constantly one thesis at the basis of the first gospel, which approximates it to the fourth and distinguishes it from the two other Synoptics. This thesis is the Messianic dignity of Jesus.

B. *From the doctrinal point of view.*

Baur and his school have thought they could show two contradictory points of view in this writing. On the one hand, they find in it the traces of a narrow Judaic particularism: the Mosaic law maintained in the midst of the Church to its minutest prescriptions (v. 17 and 18); the rigorous observance of the Sabbath (xxiv. 20); the prohibition to preach to the heathen and the Samaritans, who are compared to dogs and swine before which the gospel pearls must not be cast (vii. 6, x. 5); the preaching of salvation confined to the house of Israel (xv. 24); the condemnation of Paul and his adherents as men who work iniquity, while having on their lips the name of the Lord (vii. 21–23); Paul himself represented as *the enemy* who sows tares in the field (xiii. 28), and threatened with being relegated to the lowest place in the kingdom for not having respected the commandments of the law, even the very least (v. 19).—And then, on the other hand, in the same gospel a host of facts and words impressed with the widest evangelical spirit: the law had only to continue till John the Baptist (xi. 12 and 13); mercy preferable to sacrifice (ix. 13, xii. 7); the Son of Man Lord of the Sabbath (xii. 8); moral defilement proceeding not from what enters the man, but from that which issues from the heart (xv. 18, 19, a saying that contains in principle the abolition of the whole Levitical legislation); the announcement of the near destruction of the temple, and consequently of the abrogation of the whole system of sacrifices (xxiv. 2); the stones of the Jordan might be transformed by divine grace into children of Abraham (iii. 9); the kingdom ready to be transferred to another more faithful nation (xxi. 43); strangers from the East and West taking the place of the unbelieving Jews at the table of the patriarchs (viii. 11, 12); the pardon of sins granted to faith alone (ix. 2); the gospel destined for all peoples (xxiv. 14); all the nations admitted into the Church on the sole condition of baptism and the acceptance of the commandments of Jesus, without any further question of circumcision and any legal prescription (xxviii. 19); in fine, whoever labours and is heavy laden invited to come and seek rest with Jesus, without having to accept any other yoke than His (xi. 28–30).

How are two points of view in appearance so contradictory to be reconciled? The school of Baur has solved this question by holding that our gospel was composed of two strata; the primitive one belonging to a strictly Judæo-Christian writing; the second resulting from working it over in the Pauline sense, and intended to procure entrance for this writing into the Gentile churches.

Is this solution satisfactory? It would suppose on the part of the author a hardly admissible procedure. If he wished to substitute, without unmasking himself, the Pauline teaching for legal Judæo-Christianity, which formed the basis of the primitive writing, would he have left as they are the declarations belonging to the legal tendency, while merely adding to them others that contradicted them? Would not it have been more natural and effectual, if not entirely to suppress the former, at least to modify them sufficiently to facilitate their reconciliation with the latter? But to place pure and simply alongside each other the declarations belonging to the two opposite tendencies, was not to raise the Church to a higher point of view, but to throw her conscience into perplexity.

Moreover, it is entirely false that the words alleged by the school of Baur, which we quoted above, are the expression of a legal Judæo-Christianity. The words xxiv. 20 do not imply the maintenance of the legal observance of the Sabbath for believers. The difficulty for these to migrate on a Sabbath day might arise, not from a legal scruple, but from the indignant opposition of Jews who were present, and would see them set out on such a day. The difficulty, thus understood, agrees better with the other obstacle mentioned thereafter and proceeding from the external circumstance of a journey in the depth of winter. Besides, Jesus had always Himself till this time respected the Sabbath, and when He was speaking on the Mount of Olives He could not go before the time and suppose His disciples already convinced of the abolition of the Sabbath.[1]

The prohibition to preach the gospel to the heathen and the Samaritans (x. 5) was only temporary, in conformity with the merely preparatory character of that first mission of the Twelve. Besides it is softened in Matthew even by the word μᾶλλον (*rather*) in the following verse, and completely removed (xxviii. 19) in the definitive directions to the apostles. The limit that Jesus for the time imposed on the apostles was no other than what He had imposed on Himself during the whole

[1] Reuss and Réville are wrong in alleging that Jesus emancipated Himself from the observance of the Sabbath. The yoke that He rejected was never that of the fourth commandment; He only trod under foot the absurd excrescences with which Pharisaism had overloaded it. As for Him, He remained all His life, as Paul says, *subject to the law*, and a *minister of the circumcision* (Rom. xv. 8; Gal. iv. 4).

course of His sojourn on earth (xv. 24), and until the resurrection had freed Him from the Jewish mode of existence under the form of which He had assumed human nature (Rom. i. 4 and 5; Gal. iii. 4 and 5). The application of the word *enemy* to Paul in the parable of the tares (xiii. 25 and 28) is, according to Keim, "a mere fable." Jülicher rightly reminds us that at ver. 39 Jesus Himself explains this figure by saying: "The enemy is the devil." It is absurd to find in the prohibition (vi. 7) to throw what is holy to the dogs a forbidding to preach the gospel to the heathen. What would such a precept have to do in one of the first discourses of Jesus?—Finally, the threat Matt. vii. 22, 23 does not apply to Paul's party; for it recurs exactly the same in the Pauline gospel (Luke vi. 46, xiii. 25–27).

The passage most difficult to explain is certainly the words Matt. v. 17–19. We must here take account of an important fact: nothing was more delicate than the position in which Jesus found Himself in presence of the law of Moses, the divine origin of which He Himself recognised, and which all the people proclaimed with Him. On the one hand, He had the task to bring about or at least prepare for the abrogation of it, and, on the other, He could only effectually work for this result by testifying in word and action the most profound respect for that divine institution. What prudence and at the same time what clearness of sight were needful for Him in order not to compromise Himself in handling this question! He was guided, here as in all, by the penetrating eye of His moral conscience, which made Him early discern the distinction between the form of the Jewish commandment, the temporary and national envelope of the divine will, and the universal, permanent, shall I say human, foundation of the true law, of the essence of the real and permanent good. In this second point of view there was not a commandment of the law, even the smallest, the most purely ritual, the most insignificant in appearance, which did not appear to His conscience as an element of the perfect holiness to be realised by man. Thus when He read that every oblation of a meal offering should be seasoned with salt, He discerned at the first glance the permanent moral truth hidden under this transient form, the principle of energetic sacrifice and austere severity that ought to dominate the whole life of man (Mark ix. 49, 50); or, when He studied such another of these *least commandments* as the one not to mix honey with the meal offering, or not to seethe a kid in its mother's milk, He at once discovered with the eye of the heart the element of permanent human morality, the reflection of the divine holiness, that formed the foundation of it. And it was in virtue of this distinction between the Jewish form and the human foundation, that He could at once teach the permanence and the abolition of the law, because, as Weiss says, "He learned to understand and practise it quite otherwise than the scribes and Pharisees." To love God and one's neighbour as himself was in His eyes both to fulfil the law in its essence and to possess the means to dispense with it in its external form, exactly as Paul says (Rom. xiii. 8–10 and Gal. v. 14). Jesus then can abolish the legal commandment, but only by raising it to its higher truth. Paul did so again, when he found in the prohibition to muzzle the ox in the joyful time of harvest (1 Cor. ix. 10) the obligation on the Church to support those who had founded it by painful labour, or when he applied to the Christians of Asia Minor (Eph. vi. 2 and 3) the promise of a long life in the land that God had given them, as if they themselves were dwelling in the land of Canaan. The first gospel has often been represented—and Holtzmann and Jülicher still do so—as the expression of a Christianity already enfeebled and fallen from the primitive vigour of the Pauline spirituality, and as a transition to the legal Christianity of the following centuries. But there is in this writing a teaching that should suffice to show to what point the spirit of the most primitive spirituality, the spirit of Jesus Himself, has here been preserved intact and blameless. There are the parables of the old garment which it must not be sought to mend with a piece of new cloth, and of the new wine which it must not be desired to preserve in old wine-skins. It is true that this gospel strongly insists on the necessity of moral works. But does not Paul do so also in each of his epistles (Rom. ii. 6; 2 Cor. v. 10)? The question raised by the relation between the law and the gospel is not whether good works are or are not necessary, but what is *the true means* to produce them. The difficult and delicate task of Jesus was to effect without a revolution the transition from the legal régime to the pure evangelical spirituality, or, as Paul says (Rom. vii. 6), from the oldness of the letter to the newness of the spirit.

His ministry must then have constantly and simultaneously presented two aspects, the one respectful to the old economy, the other preparatory to the new. Jesus Himself characterised this difficult position when, in the sequel of the parable of the new wine and the old wine-skins, He added (Luke v. 39) this remark, with regard to pious Jews sincerely attached to the law, whom He met in great numbers around Him: "No man having drunk old wine immediately desireth new: for he saith, The old is good." Thus is explained the consideration with which He treated the question of the law, not ceasing to take account of the scruples of the well-disposed Israelites. We perfectly agree then with Jülicher when he declares "that there is nothing more false (*verkehrt*) than to regard the Judæo-Christian writer, respectful to the Old Testament, who wrote our gospel, as a narrow Judaiser, a strict antipaulinian." He kept himself, on the contrary, on the straight line that the Lord had drawn, respecting the law, but at the same time sowing with full hands the seeds that should, when the time came, burst that temporary form and raise the new life in its pure and eternal spirituality.

Weizsaecker seems to me to have admirably expressed the true way to regard this difficult question, when he wrote these words: "The principle of love, the true fulfilment of the law, applies to the smallest things of life as well as to the greatest. In the Sermon on the Mount Jesus seeks neither to confirm the legal institutions nor to attack them; He explains them so as to raise the thoughts of His hearers above them; and He can act so in regard to them, because they really contain a truth that transcends them; rather He had to act thus, because He had to take account of the profound respect that the attached Jewish conscience still retained to the Mosaic constitution (*Unters.* pp. 350 and 351).

A great historic fact confirms what we have just set forth, and proves that the teaching of Jesus must really have simultaneously presented this double aspect of a particularism that is dying and of a nascent spirituality that succeeds in giving it the deathstroke. This is the spectacle of the three parties that come out in the apostolic Church after the departure of Jesus. We see three branches growing almost simultaneously on the trunk of His teaching: the narrow Judæo-Christianity that pretends to maintain the observance of the law in the Church; the spirituality of Paul which, breaking with Mosaic forms, boldly displays all the riches of definitive spirituality; and, as a link between the two, the modified Christianity of the apostolic Judæo-Christian Church, which, without impeding the powerful Pauline movement, with good right takes advantage of the interim of grace, still granted for a time to the Judaism faithful to the law, until God, by the destruction of Jerusalem, put an end to that theocratic rule instituted by Him and piously respected by Jesus Himself.

Keim has energetically denied "the domestic conflict" that the school of Baur has pretended to find in our gospel; he even calls it "an outrage on the living organism of this book." For his part, he admits only some unimportant interpolations too arbitrary in my view to require me to pause on them.

M. Réville also rejects the idea of an internal doctrinal conflict; he only finds a contradiction between x. 23, where Jesus announces that the Son of Man will come before the persecuted disciples have made the tour of the cities of Israel, and chap. xxiv., where He speaks of the preaching of the gospel in all the world. But this contradiction disappears if, by the coming of the Son of Man of which Jesus speaks in chap x., He means the judgment of *Israel*, the destruction of Jerusalem, a judgment that will put an end to the apostolic mission in Palestine, inaugurated by the discourse contained in this chapter. The following words: "Ye shall not have gone *through the cities of Israel . . .*," do not allow us to suppose that Jesus is thinking of the universal preaching which must precede the Parousia.

We finish the study of this particular point with these striking words of Jülicher: "What irony would not this be in history, if a gospel of Judaising or Essene tendency had so rapidly vanquished the hearts of the Gentile Christians that it has remained till this day the chief gospel of Christendom, on the type of which the image of Jesus Christ is engraved in all our hearts!"

C. *From the literary point of view.*

1. The first question that arises here is whether our first gospel was written at first in Greek, or if it is the translation of a Hebrew or Aramaic original. This question brings us face to face with one of the strangest conflicts between tradition and internal criticism. From Papias (about 120), in effect, to Jerome (about 400), the Fathers unanimously affirm that Matthew wrote in Hebrew; see p. 50 and article v. of this chapter. On the other hand, the majority of critics affirm, after internal criteria, the Greek origin of our gospel. I here name some of them: Erasmus, Calvin, Beza, Hug, Credner, Harless, Thiersch (see below), de Wette, Bleek, Tischendorf, Anger, Ritschl, Ewald, Holtzmann, Zahn, Weiss, Keil, Jülicher, Morison, Salmon, etc.; while the following remain faithful to the opinion of the Fathers: Grotius, Mill, Storr, Eichhorn, Olshausen (see below), Sieffert, Guericke, Thiersch (see below), Tholuck, Luthardt, Güder, Meyer (see below), Westcott, etc. The most apparent reason advanced by the former is the character of the style, which is at once firm, precise, and perfectly flowing, which indicates rather an original writing than a translation. Keim calls it *lapidary,* and even goes so far as to say that one often finds in it "the fine Greek turn."—Besides, they allege certain compounded words like βαττολογεῖν (vi. 7), πολυλογία

(*ibid.*), and some paronomasia, as ὄψονται . . . καὶ κόψονται (xxiv. 30), ἀφανίζουσι ὅπως φανῶσι (vi. 16), κακοὺς κακῶς ἀπολέσει (xxi. 41), forms that only suit the Greek language. In fine, they insist on the fact that in the account of the birth of Jesus the Holy Spirit is designated as the paternal principle, which would not agree with a Hebrew narrative, in which language the word *ruach*, spirit, is of the feminine gender. This remark is confirmed by passages in certain Judæo-Christian apocrypha, where Jesus calls the Spirit "His mother" or "His sister."

Of these reasons the first, derived from the general character of the style, is certainly the strongest. It is not, however, decisive; for a writer, even a Jew, who, as Keim says, often possesses "the fine Greek turn," might well, even in translating a Semitic text, be led of himself to those turns that rendered in a piquant manner the heaviest forms of the Aramaic. B. Weiss himself owns that these compounds and plays of words may be reconciled with the liberty of style of a translator (*Einl.* p. 537). An example of it is seen in the expression *fel cum melle misceri*, by which the translator of Muratori's Fragment has rendered we know not what expression of the Greek original. And then, on the other hand, we must take account of the Aramaic terms that are found from time to time in our first gospel, and which seem to be the remains of a Semitic original, as *raca* (v. 22), δικαιοσύνη, *righteousness* (vi. 1), taken, quite like the Hebrew *tsedaka*, in the sense of beneficence, *mamonas* (vi. 24), *gehenna* (v. 22), to which should be added the Hebrew plural οἱ οὐρανοί (the heavens), in the whole course of the book.—As regards the argument derived from the feminine gender of the Hebrew word *ruach*, even if one does not grow tired of repeating it (see again Holtzmann, Jülicher, etc.), it does not seem to me serious. The word πνεῦμα, the Spirit, is no more masculine than feminine; it is neuter, that is to say, devoid of gender; moreover, in Luke's account, though derived from an evidently Semitic text, the part attributed to the Spirit in the birth of

Jesus is that of the father, not of the mother; comp. the expressions used (Luke i. 35). By reason of this parallel passage, the argument in question should, it seems to me, disappear from criticism. In general, the sublime biblical conception of the Holy Spirit, a conception to the height of which Jesus and the apostles constantly kept themselves, forbids us to attribute a sex to this divine being. Let us bear in mind (Gen. i. 2) the Spirit hovering over chaos and co-operating with Elohim in the creative act, and the formula of baptism (Matt. xxviii. 19).

Since the brilliant demonstration of Hug in his *Introduction to the New Testament*, it is universally recognised that in the time of Christ the use of the Greek language was much diffused in Palestine. In consequence of the conquests of Alexander, then of the Roman dominion, and specially by the influence of the family of the Herods, Greek had become the ruling language in the higher classes; it was the judicial and commercial language which all had naturally to know who did business with foreign countries. Numerous cities, Cæsarea, Ptolemais, Scythopolis, Pella, Dora, etc., had a population in large measure Greek.[1] And this circumstance has been made use of to maintain that the first gospel may very well have been written in Greek. Still the mass of the people in the country, and even at Jerusalem, appears to have preserved the use of Aramaic as the language of ordinary life. This appears clearly from the account (Acts xxii. 2), according to which, when they had heard that Paul was speaking in the Hebrew language, they kept silence to hear. It is remarkable that, according to Acts xxvi. 14, Paul, relating his conversion to Festus and Agrippa, declares that it was in the Hebrew language that Jesus spoke the word to him on the way to Damascus.

To be convinced that Jesus usually spoke in this language, one must remember the Aramaic surnames Cephas and Boanerges, given by Him to the first three of the apostles; then the Aramaic terms preserved by Mark:

[1] See Gloag, *Introd. to the Syn. Gospels*, p. 126.

*Ephphatha*, *Talitha kumi*, *Abba* (in the prayer at Gethsemane), and, above all, the supreme cry of anguish on the cross: *Eloi, Eloi, lema sabachthani.* The book of Acts (i. 19) positively calls Aramaic the language of the inhabitants of Jerusalem (*ἡ ἰδία διάλεκτος αὐτῶν*). How can we doubt after that, that the habitual language of Jesus was Aramaic? When Josephus was called by the Emperor Titus, whose prisoner he was, to speak for him to his fellow-citizens, he relates that he did it in the Hebrew language.[1]

We can certainly conclude from this with Schürer (*Gesch. des jüd. Volks im Zeitalter Jesu Christi*, ii. p. 43), that the lower classes in Palestine did not know Greek, or only knew it imperfectly.[2] As regards the subject we have in hand, nothing is to be inferred from this great diffusion of the Greek language in Palestine at this epoch. For, as H. W. Meyer rightly observes, even if this diffusion had been more complete than it really was, it would only prove that the first gospel *could* have been composed in that language, but not that it was so.

To conclude, it seems to me that if a great many critics who formerly maintained with energy the Greek origin of our first gospel had as their principal motive the fear of shaking the authority of this book by making it a mere translation, the reason that now exerts the most influence on the partisans of this position is rather the desire to find in the Greek text of Matthew a means of explaining the relation of mutual dependence existing, according to them, between the Synoptics. Thus Holtzmann says (*Einl.* p. 388): "Every supposition of a translation falls before the fact that the first evangelist has done nothing but work over either a writing that is at the foundation of Mark and Luke, or Mark itself." Jülicher (*Einl.* p. 191) enumerates without hesitation among the arguments against the authenticity of our Matthew the fact

[1] *Jewish War*, vi. 2. 1.

[2] Despite these reasons, the contrary position has been maintained by Roberts in the treatise, *Greek, the Language of Christ and His Apostles.* This question has been handled with much care by Arnold Meyer in the treatise, *Jesu Muttersprache*, 1896.

"that one apostle would hardly have copied another, and still less a disciple of apostles" (Mark).

These quotations prove that the question of the original language of our first gospel is not at present handled for itself, but that in the view of many critics it is complicated with the solution of quite a different question, that of the relation between the Synoptics.—But what if we were led to this result, that the two opinions are each partly true, and that our first gospel is partly a Hebrew writing and partly an original Greek writing? In any case, is it not evident that if Jesus spoke in Aramaic, every *Greek* reproduction of His words is consequently a translation either of His *spoken* words, or of His words committed to *writing*? But how can we pronounce with certainty on such an alternative?

We should mention yet a hypothesis that seems to have been advanced for the first time by Bengel (*Gnomon*, p. 2),[1] namely, that Matthew after having, as the Fathers say, written his gospel in Hebrew, published it anew in Greek. One can quote as an instance of a like procedure what Josephus tells us of himself,[2] "that he had first written his book in Hebrew, his mother-tongue (τῇ πατρίῳ γλώσσῃ), for the barbarians (τοῖς ἄνω βαρβάροις),—thus does he designate his own people,—and that then he translated it into the Greek language (ἑλλάδι γλώσσῃ) for those who are under the Roman dominion." Gloag cites further the procedure of the historian Ihne, who published an excellent Roman history in German, and then in English, while the English work was not precisely a translation of the German. Bengel's hypothesis has been admitted by Olshausen, Thiersch, Guericke, and by Schaff, who explains the disappearance of the primitive Aramaic writing thus: "When the Greek Matthew was diffused in the Church, it naturally prevailed over the Hebrew." But, as we have already observed, this supposition

[1] He expresses himself thus: "According to them (the most ancient Fathers) Matthew must have written in Hebrew; but what is to hinder him from having written thereafter the same book in Greek, without however translating it literally?"

[2] *Jewish War*, Preface, i.

of an apostle repeating himself in a second work is by no means natural.

2. A second question has been raised in connection with a difference that has been remarked between the numerous quotations of the Old Testament contained in our gospel. Bleek (*Einl.* § 106) has instanced a fact already noticed by Jerome, namely, the existence of a difference between the quotations belonging to the evangelist, who had borrowed them directly from the Hebrew text, that is those in which he states the fulfilment of certain prophecies by the formula: *that it might be fulfilled* . . ., and the quotations which occur in the discourses of Jesus which were rather derived from the text of the LXX. This would be the indication of a duality in our gospel, not in the sense of Baur, but in a purely literary sense. Is it the exact fact? The examination of the quotations of Matthew has been made several times, in particular by Anger [1] and by Massebieau.[2] The result of these labours is that the distinction established by Bleek is only partially true. The result that I have myself obtained agrees pretty much with this.

We reckon about forty-five quotations of the Old Testament in the first gospel. It is difficult to make this reckoning in a rigorously exact way, so different are the forms of allusion or quotation: "Have you not seen that . . ., it is written . . ., that it might be fulfilled . . ., you have heard that it has been said," or other forms that indicate a mere allusion. On the whole, I take my stand with Massebieau on the number forty-four or forty-five, omitting ii. 23, which appears to me to be a quotation entirely general (p. 127).

These forty-five quotations divide themselves into two groups:

Those whose author is the evangelist himself and which bring together an event of the life of Jesus and a prophecy, by a common formula: *that it might be fulfilled*, or, *then was*

[1] *Ratio quâ loci V. T. in evangelio Matthei laudantur*, 1861.

[2] *Examen des citations de l'A. T. dans l'évangile selon saint Matthieu*, 1885.

*fulfilled* . . .; one may call them apologetic quotations; they are eleven in number. Of these eleven, eight can only have been written out by using or at least consulting the Hebrew text. These are i. 22, ii. 15, iv. 14–16, viii. 17, xii. 17–21, xiii. 35$^{b}$, xxi. 4, xiii. 14, xxvii. 9, 10. The quotation xi. 10 properly belongs to the following group.

The second group comprises all the quotations that are found in the discourses of Jesus Himself. They are thirty-four in number, and may be called contextual quotations.

Fifteen seem to me to proceed purely from the LXX; in six or seven the text of the LXX is combined with the Hebrew text.

Twelve seem uncertain, whether because the translation could not be formulated in two different ways, because the relation of the texts is not clear, or because the editor may have quoted from memory.

However this may be, we see that Bleek's distinction, while true to a certain extent, is not decided enough to establish the critical conclusion of a double origin of our gospel that he has drawn from it.

3. But if the dualism admitted by this scholar cannot be maintained, it is not less true that one can show a certain very real dualism in our gospel, so real that, if I am not mistaken, the author has intentionally notified it himself. We have remarked, in effect, at certain points of the narrative, some great discourses (or rather bodies of discourses) placed as a sort of conclusion at the end of each of the groups that the account contains: 1st, *the Sermon on the Mount*, crowning the picture of the beginning of the preaching of Jesus in Galilee (chaps. v.–vii.); 2nd, *the instructions given to the apostles* in view of their first mission, ending the collection of the acts of Messianic power (chap. x.); 3rd, *the collection of the parables of the Kingdom*, which closes the collection of the words of Messianic wisdom (chap. xiii.); 4th, *the discourse instructing on the relations that ought to unite the members of the new society*, ending the picture of the ministry in Galilee (chap. xviii.); 5th and last, *the great*

*eschatological discourse*, revealing the course of the dispensation that would open on the departure of Jesus, and announcing, with the destruction of Jerusalem, the end of the then present dispensation; this last discourse serving as a solemn full stop to the whole teaching of the Lord (chaps. xxiv. and xxv.). We have besides ascertained that the mode of composition of all these discourses is evidently the same: a historical basis, forming the beginning of the discourse and connected with a well-defined situation, a situation signalised in the same way in Mark and Luke; then the addition to this primitive nucleus of other materials, heterogeneous as regards the situation, but homogeneous as regards the matter. These five great groups of teachings are clearly distinguished from the anecdotic style that reigns in the narrative, and is common to it and the two other Synoptics, which is the more remarkable that the most part of the words thus grouped in Matthew is found dispersed in Luke's account. Finally, we have seen that the author himself has carefully marked the relation between these five great pieces by the nearly identical formula of transition with which he resumes, after each of them, the thread of his narrative: "And it came to pass, when Jesus had ended these sayings . . ." (vii. 28, xi. 1, xiii. 53, xix. 1, xxvi. 1). Is not one naturally led, by these analogies that connect together these five pieces, to see in them the parts of one whole, anterior to our gospel, which has been dismembered and distributed in the course of this gospel narrative? In effect, it only needs to bring them together to see in them the five chapters of a single and complete work, meant to instruct the young churches on the fundamental points of the teaching and will of Jesus. These five chapters may be entitled, as M. Réville has very happily proposed: **Περὶ τῆς δικαιοσύνης** (*Concerning righteousness*); **Περὶ τῆς ἀποστολῆς** (*Concerning the apostleship*); **Περὶ τῆς βασιλείας** (*Concerning the Kingdom*); **Περὶ τῆς ἐκκλησίας** (*Concerning the Church*); **Περὶ τῆς συντελείας τοῦ αἰῶνος** (*Concerning the consummation of all things*). The aim of such a work was evidently *didactic*, rather than historical; and this easily explains the procedure of the author, who has felt no scruple in combining in the same discourse words uttered in very different situations. In editing them he above all followed, in conformity with his aim of instruction and edification, an order of the matter, and only took account in the second place of the order of time. From these facts it seems to me natural to conclude that, as Reuss has said, "these discourses originally belonged to an earlier work from which the author of the gospel introduced them into his own."

The plan of this writing was simple and grand. The general idea was: the foundation by Jesus of the kingdom of heaven on the earth. It comprised the five following chapters forming one whole:—1st, Jesus the *legislator* (v.–vii.); 2nd, Jesus the *founder*, by means of His envoys the apostles (x.); 3rd, Jesus the *sovereign* (the parables) (xiii.); 4th, Jesus the *organiser* (of the Church, His instrument to prepare the kingdom here below) (xviii.); 5th, Jesus the *perfecter* (of the kingdom, as judge of Israel, of the Church and the world) (xxiv. and xxv.).

I have noticed the general agreement in which I find myself on the subject of the book of the Discourses with MM. Reuss and Réville, two authors with whom I do not often follow the same path. However, I should observe that this agreement is far from being complete. These two critics include in the pre-existing work other discourses than the five of which alone I have spoken; thus, according to Reuss, the preaching of John the Baptist (chap. iii.), the discourse of Jesus on the Forerunner (xi. 7–13), and others; according to Réville, the discourse (xii. 25–45) on the casting out of demons by the exorcists, and the discourse of chap. xxiii., where Jesus pronounces the condemnation of the scribes and Pharisees (in all, then, according to him, seven Logia). Others, as Holtzmann and Weizsaecker, include in this earlier book all the discourses of Jesus reported in our gospel. But is not that to ignore the very special description with which the author has himself marked the five great bodies of discourses? And is not this, besides, to break the beautiful whole that the book of the Discourses presents? Is not it, in fact, clear as day that the other discourses which are put in one and the same line with the five principal ones, differ completely from them by the *nature of the subjects* that are treated in them? They are allocutions referring to certain particular circumstances, but not teachings devoted to expounding the work of Jesus in its fundamental points. For example, is it not false to unite in one whole, as Reuss and Réville do, chap. xxiii. (the condemnation of the scribes and Pharisees, a special and temporary subject) with the great eschatological prophecy contained in the discourse of chaps. xxiv. and xxv.? The error on this last point is the more evident that the author himself has separated these pieces by the indication of a change of situation and by a new preamble (xxiv. 1–3).

In general, the other discourses contained in the first gospel do not seem to partake of this mode of composition by way of agglomeration of heterogeneous elements which we have noticed in the five of which we make a whole by itself. It is of course that the author of the gospel, in inserting in his Greek writing the translation of the earlier writing, did not mean to deprive himself of the right of reporting also, just like the two other Synoptics, the different discourses or conversations of Jesus on other matters, of which he had knowledge by tradition or otherwise. To distinguish in his writing these two species of materials, I think we must, if we would not risk falling into arbitrariness, adhere to the criterion that the author himself has given in the identical formula with which he has finished the five discourses that he borrowed from the collection of the Discourses.

There remains the opinion of Weiss, Salmon, and very many critics who apply the word Logia in the testimony of Papias to our first gospel altogether, or to an analogous narrative work more or less complete. We shall discuss immediately the sense of the word Logia in this ancient testimony.

Everything leads us to believe that the primitive work of Matthew, if it really existed, as I think it did, distinct from our gospel, was written in Hebrew or in Aramaic. This is the affirmation of Papias, and, from what we have said above of the language of the people in Palestine in the time of Jesus, the most natural supposition. One would not begin to write the teachings of Jesus in a different language from that which He Himself had used, and which was the usual language of the nearest readers. Besides, one finds some vestiges of the Semitic language in certain terms that have passed into our Greek text; for example, raca (v. 22); Mammon (vi. 24): δικαιοσύνη, *righteousness* (vi. 1), used in the sense of alms or liberality, as *tsedaka* sometimes is in the Old Testament; one may further quote in the sixth beatitude (v. 8) the expression *pure in heart* (καθαροὶ τῇ καρδίᾳ) substituted after the Hebrew term for the Greek term of the LXX (εὐθέσι τῇ καρδίᾳ, *upright in heart*), Ps. lxxiii. 1. It is to be observed that all these examples occur in the five great discourses.

My purpose has been in this work on the first gospel to seek above all in the data furnished by the writing itself the solution of the questions raised by its composition, and only subsidiarily to resort to the guidance of tradition. But as the result to which I have just been led by the series of internal indications does not, however, surpass the value of a hypothesis, I feel the need, by reason of its importance, immediately to inquire if it be not confirmed by any traditional datum. I will anticipate, then, on this point the subject treated in article vi. (Traditional Data).

### *The Meaning of the Word* Logia *in the Testimony of Papias*

We have studied in a general way (pp. 48–55) the testimony of Papias in its relation to the formation of the collection of the four gospels. In the part of this testimony specially concerning Matthew's writing, occurs a word directly referring to the subject we have in hand, and which has given rise to considerable discussion. Eusebius, after having said (*H. E.* iii. 39. 1) that Papias wrote five books that are entitled, *Explanations of the Discourses of the Lord* (λογίων Κυριακῶν ἐξηγήσεις), adds that this Father said this besides: "As to Matthew, he composed the discourses in the Hebrew language (Ματθαῖος μὲν οὖν Ἑβραΐδι διαλέκτῳ τὰ λόγια συνεγράψατο)." What work did Papias mean to designate in thus entitling the writing of Matthew? Was it a complete gospel, containing deeds and words, or only a collection of *discourses* properly so called? It is a strange thing that all the Eastern and Western Fathers declare, in agreement with Papias but not solely after him, that Matthew wrote his book in Hebrew, and that, however, they do not hesitate to apply this tradition to our first gospel written in Greek. Jerome first seems to have given attention to this inconsistency, and explains it by declaring that our first gospel was a translation from the Aramaic. He says (*De vir. ill.* c. 3): "Matthew first composed in Judea the gospel of Christ in Hebrew characters and words, with a view to those among the Jews who had believed. Who is it that later translated it into Greek? Nothing certain is known of this." At the time of the Reformation the contradiction was clearly seen of attributing to the Apostle Matthew a Greek writing that all the Fathers said had been composed by him in Hebrew; but in order not to deprive our gospel of its apostolic authority, it was thought prudent to deny the existence of the Hebrew original attested by all patristic tradition. Thus did Erasmus, Calvin, Beza, etc., and a host of others after them, especially in the Protestant Church. It needed Schleiermacher, not to see that Hebrew is not Greek and that a collection of discourses is not a gospel, but energetically to draw the conclusion from these two facts.[1] This conclusion, which inaugurated a new phase of criticism on this point, is simply: that the testimony of Papias, on which the Church till then had founded its belief in the composition of our first gospel by the Apostle Matthew, does not apply to our canonical gospel, which is written in a different language, and whose contents are quite other than the writing of which Papias spoke.

We shall have afterwards to give an account of the first of these two points (that of the language); we shall only here consider the second (the contents of the writing). The question is the meaning of the word *Logia*, used by Papias to denote the contents of Matthew's writing. The word λόγιον is a diminutive of λόγος (*word* or *discourse*), and denotes a short and sententious speech, such as the oracles usually were. Also, with the Greek writers (Herodotus, Thucydides, Euripides, Diodorus, Plutarch, etc.), this word always denotes a divine declaration. It appears, then, natural to apply the word of Papias to a writing containing the *discourses* of Jesus as so many divine sentences, and in some sort oracles, but not to an account of the facts of His life, such as a gospel. As Jülicher says: "It would have been

[1] In the journal *Studien und Kritiken*, 1832, 4tes Heft: *Ueber die Zeugnisse des Papias von unseren beiden ersten Evangelien*, S. 735-768.

a mode of expression singularly apt to mislead, to designate a complete gospel as *discourses*." However, a great number of authors do not think that this restricted sense of the word Logia can be admitted, and allege that this term does here denote a complete gospel containing facts and discourses; but granting, however, that if Papias designated this gospel writing by the name *discourses*, it is in virtue of the adage: *A potiori parte fit denominatio*; so Lücke, Hug, Luthardt, Zahn, Anger, Keim, Weiss, etc. These authors found on certain passages of the New Testament and the Fathers; so Rom. iii. 2, where Paul says that "the privilege of the Jews is to have received in trust τὰ λόγια τοῦ θεοῦ (the oracles of God)"—that is to say, the Old Testament,—then Heb. v. 12, where the author says to his readers that they have need to learn the first elements of the beginning of the oracles of God, τὰ στοιχεῖα τῆς ἀρχῆς τῶν λογίων τοῦ θεοῦ";—Acts vii. 38: "Moses received living oracles (λόγια ζῶντα) of God to give them to us";—1 Pet. iv. 11: "Let those that speak in the assembly speak as uttering the oracles of God (εἴ τις λαλεῖ ὡς λόγια θεοῦ)." Also a passage of Philo is adduced where that author quotes as λόγιον θεοῦ the account of the fact reported Gen. iv. 15, and a passage of Irenæus where that Father accuses the heretics "of misleading the minds of the simple by falsifying the oracles of the Lord (λόγια τοῦ Κυρίου)." (Compare Salmon, *Introd.* pp. 98 and 99.) Then it is affirmed that a series of discourses that were not accompanied with the mention of the circumstances in which they were delivered is a thing altogether improbable; Salmon even goes the length of saying "absurd." Lastly, the testimony of Papias himself on Mark is invoked, in which that Father defines the matter of a gospel by these two words: "The things *said* or *done* by the Lord," which clearly proves that in his view the deeds could not fail to be joined to the discourses.

These reasons do not seem to me valid. If the word *Logia* in Rom. iii. embraces the entire Old Testament, it is because from the point of view of inspiration, as the Jews understood it, that book was entirely a divine oracle. But in the time of Papias the gospels were not yet regarded in this manner. What proves it is the lack of order which he reports in Mark, and excuses by the circumstances of its composition. No doubt a word of Jesus might be quoted as a divine word, as the so-called Epistle of Barnabas does (4. 14); but this might be in consideration of the authority of Him who had spoken it.—In the passage of the Epistle to the Hebrews, the question is not of the first elements of the sacred *history*, but of the gospel *doctrine*.—The words of Stephen (Acts vii.) apply not to narratives, but to the commandments of Sinai.—The words of 1 Pet. iv. oppose the ministry of the doctors who *teach* to the active functions of those who administratively *labour* for the

Church, an opposition that clearly proves that the expression, the oracles of God, refers to teachings. When Philo calls the account in Gen. iv. an *oracle*, where God puts a sign on Cain's forehead that no one might kill him, it is because this fact is accompanied by a divine declaration, a λόγιον. And besides, this feature is related, according to Philo, under the guarantee of the same inspiration as all the rest of the Old Testament.—As regards the passage of Irenæus, that Father evidently means by the Logia that the heretics falsified the *teachings* of Jesus, and not the facts of His life, as the following words prove, where he says of these same heretics, that "they show themselves bad interpreters *of things well said*."—A year ago I would have believed it necessary to refute the assertion of Salmon, who regards as an impossibility a collection of discourses destitute of all historical circumstances. A fragment recently found in Egypt, where the words are mentioned following each other without any other transition than *Jesus said*, exempts me from proving to this author that the idea of such a writing is not "a mere dream."—Lastly, the passage of Papias on Mark says precisely the contrary of what it is alleged to contain. After having described the Book of Matthew as "a collection of discourses" (σύνταξις λογίων), he *opposes* to this writing the Gospel of Mark, which, composed after the narrations of Peter, contains alike the things *done* by Jesus and the things *said* by Him (τὰ ὑπὸ τοῦ χριστοῦ ἢ λεχθέντα, ἢ πραχθέντα).

The true sense of the word *Logia* seems to me to appear, not only from the ordinary use that is made of it in classical Greek, but also from the passages of Clement and Polycarp, where the orthodox gospel teachings are designated by this term. The very title of the work of Papias: *Explanations of the Discourses of the Lord* (Explanatio *sermonum* Domini, as Jerome translates), would suffice, if necessary, to decide the question, and to prove the *didactic* nature of the writing of which Papias gave the explanation. One relates deeds, but *explains* words. Doubtless, Papias mentioned certain facts of the history of Jesus; but we have shown (p. 14) that he quoted them occasionally, as means of illustrating certain words.

We may conclude from all this, it seems to me, that by those Logia of which he endeavoured to give the true explanation, in opposition to the heretical falsifications, Papias just meant the *teachings* of Jesus edited by Matthew in Aramaic, and not a complete history of His ministry. And I believe, consequently, I have the right henceforth to quote his testimony as a confirmation of the hypothesis to which I have been led by the study of the book itself.

Resch has recently reached the same result as those whom we are here opposing, but by quite a different way. In a remarkable study, forming part of the *Theologische Studien* (collection of studies presented to Professor B. Weiss for his seventieth birthday), he assimilates the term Logia, used by Papias, to the Hebrew term *Debarim*, in the titles of several of the historical books of the Old Testament, where this word, translated by the LXX λόγοι (words), yet means *history*; for instance, *Diberé Schemouel*, history of Samuel; *Diberé David hammélech*, history of King David; and other similar cases (comp. 1 Kings xi. 41; 1 Chron. xxix. 29 and 30, etc.). Strictly speaking, the word λόγια might have had this wide sense in Papias (comp. Acts i. 1); but it is impossible, after the well-established usage of the Greek writers, thus to explain the word λόγια in a writer in whom is found no trace of acquaintance with Hebrew. Besides, in the Hebrew terms quoted by Resch, the sense is not words (and deeds) of Samuel, words (and deeds) of David, etc., but *narrations* concerning Samuel or David. How should the expression [λόγια Κυριακά], oracles of the Lord, be equivalent to *narrations* about the Lord? Resch seems to have let himself be dazzled, in this as in other cases, by a seductive appearance.

D. We have still to discuss more specially the *Greek style* of our gospel, and that compared with the style of the other Synoptics.[1]

In a general way it may be said that, if the Greek of the first gospel partakes in some measure of the Aramaic colouring that is characteristic of the three Synoptics, the style of this writing is, so to say, equidistant both from the often heavy and prolix simplicity of Mark and from the almost classical elegance of Luke (at least in the parts where the latter does not reproduce, intentionally and almost literally, an Aramaic text).

To come to detail: the style of the first gospel presents, both as regards the vocabulary and the grammatical forms, numerous peculiarities that it is important to notice. The most characteristic term is *kingdom of heaven* (βασιλεία τῶν οὐρανῶν), which occurs thirty-seven times in this gospel, and not once in the two other Synoptics; the term used in these latter, *kingdom of God* (βασιλεία τοῦ θεοῦ), is only found five times

[1] See Gersdorf, *Beiträge zur Sprachcharakteristik der Schriftsteller des N. T.* Holtzmann, *Die drei synopt. Evangelien.* B. Weiss, *Einleit. in das N. T.* § 37; *das Evang. Matthaei und seine Lukas-Parallelen*, pp. 44–47.

in Matthew (once in the form *kingdom of the Father*, βασιλεία τοῦ πατρός). There is no difference in this respect between the various parts of the book (see chaps. iii., iv., v., vii., xi., xiii., xvi., xviii., xix., xx., xxii., xxiii., xxv., *passim*).[1] — The expression *heavenly Father* (ὁ πατὴρ ὁ ἐπουράνιος or ὁ ἐν τοῖς οὐρανοῖς) occurs twenty times, and is found in the various parts of the book, while it is only found once in Mark (xi. 25), and never in Luke, not even in the Lord's Prayer (xi. 2); —*Consummation of the age* (συντέλεια τοῦ αἰῶνος), five times (xiii. 39, 40, 49, xxiv. 3, xxviii. 20); this term is not found in the other Synoptics;—Ἱεροσόλυμα (always except xxiii. 37, where Ἱερουσαλήμ occurs); in thirty instances Luke only uses the form Ἱεροσόλυμα four times (Tischendorf's text);—*son of David* (υἱὸς Δαυίδ, seven times); this term only occurs once in each of the two others.

Certain expressions frequent in Matthew are foreign or almost foreign to the two others: ἀναχωρεῖν, *to retire*, ten times (once in Mark, never in Luke);—μαθητεύειν, *to make disciples*, three times, and only in Matthew; — συμβούλιον λαμβάνειν, *to take counsel*, five times (Mark, twice: συμβούλιον ποιεῖν);—διστάζειν, *to doubt*, twice;—τάφος, *sepulchre*, six times (the others: μνημεῖον or μνῆμα);—σφόδρα, *extremely*, seven times, and always with verbs (Mark and Luke each once, and only with adjectives). Schaff quotes yet seven terms used by Matthew which occur neither in the other Synoptics nor in the rest of the New Testament. We find, lastly, in Matthew peculiar forms: προσκυνεῖν, *to prostrate oneself*, eleven times with the dative of the person (Mark twice and Luke always with the accusative); — ῥηθείς, ἐῤῥέθη, eighteen times, not elsewhere in the gospels;—ἐγείρεσθαι ἀπὸ, instead of ἐκ;—λέγων used like the Hebrew *lemor*;—τότε, as a transition, ninety times (Mark six times, Luke fourteen times).

"These favourite constructions," M. Réville concludes, "entwine the whole book in a net evidently stretched by one and the same hand." Credner, in finishing his study of the

[1] We remit to the following Appendix the study of this fundamental idea of our gospel.

style of Matthew, says to the same effect (§ 37): "These peculiar modes of expression, which uniformly recur in the whole course of the writing, show the unity of the author," and, I will add, render far from probable the use by the evangelist of a plurality of sources, at least of Greek sources.

I here add two Appendices on two particular points that require an explanation.

*The Conception of the Kingdom of Heaven in the First Gospel*

As the idea of the kingdom of heaven is the central conception of this writing, this term is also the one that most particularly characterises the style of it. The Greek expression βασιλεία τῶν οὐρανῶν may be explained in two ways. One may make of the genitive τῶν οὐρανῶν a complement of the subject: "The royalty that the heavens exercise," or a complement of origin: "The kingdom which, pre-existing in the heavens, should descend thence to the earth, to take the place here below of the reign of evil, and to make the earth a province of heaven." In this latter sense this kingdom denotes the heavenly state of obedience, order, and peace which should result from the salvation brought to the world by Jesus Christ. The first of these two meanings is connected with the frequent use, in the rabbinic language, of the paraphrase, *the heavens*, to designate God, as when we say familiarly: "Heaven preserve me!" or, "Heaven helps those that help themselves." This meaning has been defended with much ability and erudition by Schürer in a very remarkable article (*Jahrbücher für protest. Theologie*, 1876). But on reflection it seems to me difficult to believe that so abstract a mode of designating God could have been that of Jesus, who lived in so intimate and personal a relation with Him. It would be a mistake to quote Luke xv. 21 in favour of this mode of speaking: "I have sinned against Heaven and before thee." The difference of the prepositions itself proves that the two governed words are not synonymous.

The term *kingdom of God*, which the two other Synoptics often make use of, hardly differs as regards meaning from Matthew's one. It opposes the state of things thus denoted to the heathen kingdoms, while Matthew's term opposes it to every political organisation of earthly origin. The predilection of the apostle for this expression is easily explained. In following Jesus he found himself at every moment in presence of a degenerate state of things that had become almost entirely earthly, consequently ready to fall, and his whole heart was transported towards a new order of things, heavenly in nature and origin, which would come in the person of his glorified

Master to take the place of all that he had before his eyes. Thus Jesus, on the evening of Palm Sunday, after having taken a last and long look of the visible sanctuary (Mark xi. 11), beheld in spirit the new sanctuary not made with hands, but spiritual and imperishable, which was to take the place of the old (John ii. 19).

The question has of late been much discussed whether, when Jesus speaks of the kingdom of heaven, He is thinking of something *actual* or *solely future*. It is quite evident from the predominant part that the expectation of the Messianic kingdom played at this epoch in Jewish thought, an expectation that is found set forth in all the Jewish Apocalypses of the time, that when Jesus spoke to the people of the kingdom of heaven, the thoughts of His hearers were at once carried towards the great renewal that men hoped from the Messiah. The world was seen suddenly transformed by a stroke of divine power, the Jewish people exalted, and the heathen powers abased before it and forced to yield to it the empire of the world. Philo himself, with all his spirituality, is not altogether devoid of these carnal hopes of his people. In certain passages he also sees in the Messiah a great warrior victorious over the nations (see Schürer, *Geschichte des jüd. Volks im Zeitalter J. C.* ii. p. 435); and here we can measure the elevation of the thought of Jesus above the religious conceptions of the best thinkers of His time and people. He is, no doubt, very far from denying the great catastrophe, proceeding from heaven, which will shake the world to determine the coming of the divine kingdom. But his view of the course of things is so profoundly moral and spiritual that he cannot but take account of the co-operation of human action in this final transformation. He perfectly understands that a merely external act would be powerless to produce the kingdom, as he conceives and describes it in the third petition of the Lord's Prayer. For that there will be needed a moral preparation carried on for a long time in the midst of mankind, which He represents by the images of the grain of mustard seed, growing little by little till it become a real tree, or of the leaven gradually transforming the whole mass of dough. To lay the foundation of this preparation is the task of His sojourn here below. The Church of His redeemed will have to continue it after Him, and this preparation He certainly regards as a labour that *already belongs* to the kingdom itself. It is in this sense that He says: "the kingdom of heaven is at hand" (iv. 17), that He declares to His adversaries that the casting out of the demons, performed by Him with the power of the divine Spirit, should prove to them that the reign of God has already come upon them (ἔφθασεν ἐφ' ὑμᾶς), a word as threatening for them as it was encouraging for His disciples.

He even utters this saying, Luke xvii. 21: "The kingdom of God *is* within you." It seems to me indeed difficult, despite the opinion of most exegetes, to admit that the ἐντός, *within*, is simply the synonym of ἐν, *in*, not only because the sense of the two prepositions is *in itself* different, but even in virtue of the context, which they oppose to the proper sense of the preposition *within*. In reply to the question of the Pharisees, Jesus would show that the coming of the kingdom of God cannot be the object of sensible observation, and He proves it by the very nature of that kingdom, which is an *internal* fact and consequently inaccessible to the senses. For the precise sense of ἐντός, comp. Ps. xxxix. 3: "My heart was hot *within me*," a passage in which, as in several others, the proper meaning of ἐντός is strongly accentuated. The kingdom then is, in the view of Jesus, *future* and yet *already present*, first in His person and His work, then in believers, the first-fruits of that work. It is a troublesome error committed by the excellent Meyer and those that follow him, invariably to give to this term an eschatological sense, and that even in a passage such as Rom. xiv. 17: "The kingdom of God is righteousness, peace, and joy in the Holy Spirit."

### *The Second Coming of the Lord*

The whole period preparatory to the establishment of the reign of God in *the old covenant* is summed up in this word of the prophets: "The Eternal cometh." Comp. Zach. ii. 10 and ix. 9: "Daughter of Zion, rejoice, saith the Eternal, thy King cometh to thee"; Mal. iii. 1: "Behold He cometh"; and finally this threat, the last word of the Old Testament: "Lest I come and smite the earth with a curse" (iv. 6). As a promise, it is equally *the coming of the Eternal* that is presented to Israel as the meaning and the aim of its national history. From the moment that man drove God from him by wilfully sinning, God has sought to draw near to him and to find entrance again to his heart. He also immediately opens to him the prospect of final victory over the enemy who had just mortally wounded him (Gen. iii. 15), and soon gives him two pledges of that final salvation: the removal of Enoch and the deliverance of Noah.

With Abraham begins the series of measures destined to effect this return of the Eternal, and to produce here below the re-establishment of His reign. The first act of this long work is the personal relation that God establishes between Himself and Abraham, and the solemn promise that He makes him to bless in him and his posterity all the families of the earth (Gen. xii. 3). That is, as it were, the first step of the advent of the Eternal into the midst of mankind. The glorious deliverance from Egypt, the putting Israel under the tutelage of the law, the settlement of the people in Canaan, the laborious career of David and his elevation to the sovereignty, the serious recalls to order addressed under his successors by the prophets to the fallen people, the Messianic visions like lightning suddenly illuminating the darkness of an idolatrous and corrupt present, the frightful stroke of the Exile, the resettlement of the people, the beginning of its diffusion among the heathen nations, into the midst of which it brings its monotheism, its sacred books, its superior morality, and its expectation of a glorious future which a divine messenger should realise; finally, the appearance of a forerunner proclaiming the presence of the expected Christ: these are the links of a chain of divine manifestations, constituting, in the language of the Old Testament, the coming of Jehovah, the gradual approach of His *advent* in the person of the Messiah. This term being announced, Malachi thus described it in the vision that ends his book and the prophecies of the Old Testament (iii. 1): "And the Lord whom ye seek, the Angel of the covenant whom ye desire, shall suddenly come to His temple; behold He cometh, saith the Lord of hosts." It was four hundred years before the Christian era that this *He cometh* was pronounced. For each moment was hastening His advent. From the fall of the first man till John the Baptist all history is summed up in this word: *The Eternal cometh.*

But Israel refused to receive Him. "He came unto His own, and they that were His own received Him not" (John i. 11). They even banished Him from the midst of them and from the land of the living. Here begins on the side of God a new *I come.* The departure of Jesus by His death and ascension is the time from which is dated this new divine advent. Jesus declares this with asseveration in the midst of the Sanhedrin: "Thou hast said it," He responds to the high priest when he adjures Him by the living God; and even "I say unto you that *henceforth* (ἀπ' ἄρτι) ye shall see the Son of Man sitting at the right hand of power, *and coming* on the clouds of heaven" (Matt. xxvi. 64). The word *henceforth* shows that Jesus regards all the time which is henceforth to elapse till the end of things as the period at once of His heavenly sovereignty and of His invisible return hither. As the history of the old covenant had no other meaning than this word, *He cometh*, that of the new, after men have banished God from this earth a second time, is entirely summed up in this: *He comes again.*

The manifold applications of this idea of the coming of Christ which we find in Scripture are thus explained.

1. Jesus calls the gift of the Holy Spirit His coming, because it is He who by His Holy Spirit comes to dwell in the

heart of the believer: "I will not leave you orphans; I will come to you . . . Ye shall know in that day that I am in the Father, and ye in Me, and I in you . . . If a man love Me . . . My Father will love him, and we will come to him, and make our abode with him" (John xiv. 18, 20, and 23). We ought consequently to regard as the constant coming of Jesus, the always renewed action of His Holy Spirit in the hearts that He awakens and converts, as well as within the churches which He causes to feel His presence by the spiritual movements by which He draws them from their languor and ever anew confounds the already triumphant unbelief. "I stand at the door and knock; if any man open to Me, I will come in to him, and will sup with him, and he with Me" (Rev. iii. 20). This word is the revelation of the presence and incessant action of Christ daily effecting His merciful advent in the Church and in the hearts of individuals.

2. The death of each believer is equally represented as a coming of Jesus. From on high where He hovers sovereignly over the course of the ages, His hand is lowered to pluck the ears that have reached maturity: "When I shall have prepared the place for you, I will come and receive you to Myself; that where I am, there ye may be also" (John xiv. 3). "If I will that he tarry till I come, what is that to thee?" (John xxi. 22). "And be ye ready, because ye know not the hour when the Son of Man will come; blessed is that servant whom his lord when he cometh shall find watching; he will appoint him over all his goods . . .; let your loins be girded and your lamps burning" (Luke xii. 36–40). In all these words Jesus is thinking of the death of His people and of the reception that He is preparing for them beside Him.

3. The ruin of Jerusalem and the judgment of the Jewish people are equally designated by the Lord as facts that are included in His coming: "Ye shall not have gone through the cities of Israel, till the Son of Man be come." "This generation shall not pass away, till all these things be accomplished" (Matt. x. 23, xxiv. 34).

4. The judgment of the Lord on the unfaithful and degenerate churches is announced in the Apocalypse in this form: "Repent . . .; or else *I will come to thee,* and will move thy candlestick out of its place (ii. 5) . . . Repent, or else *I will come to thee quickly,* and will make war against the unfaithful with the sword of My mouth (ii. 16) . . . Repent; if thou dost not watch, *I will come as a thief,* and thou shalt not know what hour *I will come upon thee*" (iii. 3); comp. again xvi. 15, the general warning addressed to all the faithful.

We see from all these examples how elastic is the idea of the coming of Christ. He comes when He touches a heart to repentance to draw it to Him; He comes when He awakens a church that is gradually dying; He comes when He removes the candlestick of a church obstinately unfaithful; He comes when He takes to Himself the servants whose fidelity He would reward. His coming has taken a gigantic stride in the last century, when He awoke zeal in the whole Church for the evangelisation of the heathen world and set on foot the work of missions, till then neglected but since so flourishing. Had not the preaching of the gospel to all the nations been committed by Him to the Church as the condition of His return? And if this return has been so long delayed, is it not herself and not Him that the Church ought to blame, who has so long neglected to clear His way and to push on the wheel of His chariot? There is another condition regarding which the Church has doubtless to make the same reproach to herself. Deprived, like the widow of the parable, of the visible presence of her husband, the Church had to do what Jesus relates of that desolate woman who claimed with perseverance, and even with entreaty amounting to importunity, to be put in possession of the inheritance that rightly belonged to her. The Church has the right to possess the earth (Matt. v. 5), for her task is to realise there the blessed state of the kingdom of God. Does she sufficiently beset the throne of Him who alone can accomplish this work? Does not she leave, without suffering and groaning enough for it, her property in the hands of the adverse party, so much that Jesus, foreseeing this negligence of His people, has Himself asked beforehand whether, on His return, He would still find faith on the earth (Luke xviii. 1–8)?

It is important, regarding the return of the Lord, to distinguish two things that are usually confounded, namely, His *coming* and His *arrival*. The Greek word (ἔρχεσθαι) combines the two ideas. The coming embraces the whole interval between the Ascension and the last day. It is the time of the journey, the time of which Jesus said, *henceforth*, and of which He Himself declared that He knew not the duration (Matt. xxiv. 34; Mark xiii. 32), perhaps because it depended partly on the fidelity of the Church in fulfilling the two conditions of which we were just speaking. The arrival is the end of the coming, the sensible manifestation of His presence. The apostles, urged by a feeling of impatience that Jesus had well foreseen, when He said to them: "The days will come when ye shall desire to see one of the days of the Son of Man," abridged in their thought the interval that had to separate the departure from the arrival. Another thing that may have influenced them in this direction is that Jesus, regarding them as the representatives of the faithful of all times, had urged them to expect and watch continually, as if they had to be present personally at that supreme moment of

His return. They applied to themselves, as indeed each Christian ought to do from a purely moral point of view, words of Jesus such as this (Luke xxi. 34 and 35): "Take heed to yourselves, lest your hearts be overcharged, and that day *come suddenly upon you*; for it shall come as a snare upon all the inhabitants of the earth"; and many other similar exhortations.

On the one hand, the *duration of the coming* was uncertain in the eyes of Jesus, and the apostles seem in their thought to have too much abridged it; but, on the other, the *fact of the arrival* was certain in the eyes of Jesus and in theirs, and they have faithfully attested it. The first point, like questions of time in general, was of secondary rank; what proves it is the ignorance of Jesus Himself in this respect. The second alone belonged to the very essence of salvation, which, without the return of Christ, would remain an unfinished edifice. On this second point there was no hesitation in the thought either of Jesus or of His apostles.

When in the night we perceive before us a luminous point approaching, we cannot measure the distance that still separates us from it, and the time it will need to reach us; so the apostles contemplated in the future the arrival of the Master announced by Him, and believed it nearer than it really was. This was the more natural that the idea of the arrival of Jesus was more or less confounded for them with that of His constant coming, as we have set it forth above. When James said: "The Judge is at the door"; when Paul said: "The Lord is at hand"; when the Church said: "Maranatha, the Lord cometh!" it was because in the hearts of all the feeling of His continual actual coming was partly confounded with that of the future arrival, which might take place from one moment to another.

These ideas of the coming and the arrival of the Lord together constitute that of His *return*, which is the great, I might say the only, subject of the last book of the New Testament, the Apocalypse. Jesus is there called from the opening of the book: "He who is, who was, and *who is coming* (ὁ ἐρχόμενος, i. 4)." And the apostle immediately adds, i. 7: "Behold, *He cometh* with the clouds, and every eye shall see Him." That is the opening of the book, and here is the conclusion of it: "Yea, *I come* quickly (ἔρχομαι ταχύ)." Our versions say *soon* instead of *quickly*, as if the term *come* referred to the arrival, and the sense were: "I shall soon be there!" But in its true sense, this promise bears, not on the arrival, but on the coming: "I am coming swiftly; I do not delay, I do not relax My pace (however it may seem)." And the Church in responding to Him: "Amen, come, Lord Jesus!" does not prescribe to Him the moment of His arrival, but rather undertakes herself to do all that is in her power to clear the way, and hasten the progress of the retinue that brings Him back. All that the book contains between that beginning and that end is, it seems to me, the picture of the *progress of Jesus coming*, that is to say, of the ever-repeated alternation of the increasing graces diffused by Him on the Church, and of the more and more severe judgments by which the rebellious world is smitten; such is, in two words, if I do not mistake, the sense and the unity of the apocalyptic drama.

As regards the epoch of the arrival of the Lord, it is as vain as it is rash to pretend to determine a thing that Jesus had to consent to be ignorant of Himself.

## IV

### The Composition of the Book

A. The first question that here presents itself is of the *aim* that the author proposed to himself.

This question is twofold: it bears, on the one hand, on the Greek gospel in its totality, and, on the other, on the older Aramaic writing, which, as I think, has been inserted as a translation in the gospel.

(*a*) The older of the two works, that which is called, after the famous passage of Papias, the *Logia*, and which merely comprised, as I suppose, the five great discourses, had a *didactic* and not a historical aim. The author sought to fix the exact tenor of the instructions of the Lord, in order to engrave on the mind of the Church the principles that should direct her progress and determine the line of conduct of each of her members, if she would accord with the will of the Lord and continue His work here below. As Weizsaecker has rightly said: "The *great discourses of Matthew* themselves show clearly that they have their origin in the needs of the community."[1] The book of Acts (ii. 42) mentions, among the essential factors of the life of the primitive Church, *the doctrine of the apostles* (ἡ διδαχὴ τῶν ἀποστόλων). This apostolic teaching did not merely comprehend the account of the salient facts of the history of Jesus. The term *doctrine* especially denotes the reproduction

[1] *Apostol. Zeitalter*, p. 392.

of His teachings. The necessity must early have been felt of giving day after day sound nourishment to the new belief of the faithful who formed the church of Jerusalem. And besides, there was a great number of evangelists who, like Philip in Samaria, or the refugee disciples at Antioch, wrought to found churches in the surrounding countries; and if they could be allowed, without too much danger, liberty to reproduce, without a precise text, the account of the facts that they had often gathered from the lips of the first narrators, it was not the same with the words, precepts, threatenings, and promises of the Lord. So important a subject could not be long abandoned to free oral transmission. "The words of Jesus," says Weizsaecker again, "did not circulate in the Church in an entirely free manner; they were for her a permanent teaching; they had then to be constantly engraved and renewed in the memory; and precisely because they had obligatory force they were fixed and ascertained by the co-operation of witnesses."[1] This mode of viewing the matter agrees with what Muratori's Fragment relates on the mode of composition of the fourth gospel: "John, it is said, edited his account, *recognoscentibus cunctis*," that is to say, submitting it to the control of all the other apostles and old disciples who were beside him at that time.

The writing thus composed had to serve as basis for the primitive teaching of the Church, and it is doubtless its contents that James has in view when he speaks of the *royal law*, of the *perfect law of liberty* as well as of the *word implanted in you, that can save your souls*, expressions by which he characterises the new teaching and distinguishes it from the commandments of the old covenant (i. 21, 25, ii. 8). If there already existed a writing containing the formula of this new life, it was very certainly that of which we are speaking. It is these Logia of Jesus which have impressed so firm a bearing on the moral life of primitive Christendom.

[1] *Ibid.* p. 384.

(*b*) Our *first gospel* has sought first to preserve this primitive document, while putting it within the reach of the Greek-speaking churches; but its author had in view at the same time another aim of quite a different nature. He has embodied the Logia, translated into Greek, in a narrative of the life of Jesus, designed not to edify believers, but, above all, to convince the unbelieving Jews, and to make them comprehend the great fault they had committed, as well as their heads, in rejecting Jesus, their divine King. The aim of this book was not didactic but *apologetic*, or even, according to a more energetic term used by Hofmann, *elenchtic* (severely convincing). Not only, indeed, does the author condemn Jewish unbelief by giving, at each step of the history, by means of the prophecies, the proof of the Messianic dignity of Jesus; but at the same time he reduces to nothing the most widely diffused objections by which the Jews sought to justify their hostile attitude towards Him. "If He were the Messiah, said they, He would have come, not from the obscure Nazareth, but from Bethlehem, the royal city; He would not have been a Sabbath breaker; He would not have refused to perform miracles in the sky, a refusal that well proves that He only cast out demons with the complicity of Satan. He even openly blasphemed in calling Himself the Son of God. Finally, the shame of the cross, which He was unable to escape, has unanswerably shown the falsity of His pretensions. The disappearance of His corpse from the tomb where it had been laid is explained quite otherwise than by His pretended resurrection." The narrative of our gospel contains the solution of all these objections. Nay more, it takes the offensive, and while refuting these arguments, it shows the true motives that impelled the authorities of the nation to reject Jesus. Their hatred was caused by jealousy, ambition, the obstinate wish to maintain their usurped power in the midst of the people of God. Pilate himself very well discerned these interested motives of the Sanhedrin; his judgment on the person of Jesus was more upright than that of this supreme council. If the work of Jesus in Israel failed, if that people is thenceforth rejected and the kingdom of God passes to the Gentiles, it is not God that was unfaithful to His covenant, but Israel that rejected God by putting to death His Envoy, His own Son. As Weiss says (*Einl.* p. 537): "the intention of this gospel is to show how it could come about that the Messiah, who came to fulfil the law and the prophets, did not realise the national hopes of Israel, and that in order to strengthen in presence of this ruin the faithful, afflicted and shaken in their faith." I am far from denying this last motive, but can only regard it as secondary. The first gospel is at once the justification of the Messianic sovereignty of Jesus, and the sentence of condemnation of the people of the old covenant. It is a supreme appeal to the conscience of that rebellious people, and in some sort the ultimatum that God addresses to it before definitively smiting it.

Thus the aim of the book of Discourses addressed to the part of the people that formed the nucleus of the Church, and the aim of the evangelic narrative designed to open the eyes of the unbelieving portion of the same people, are totally different.

But despite this difference, the two aims are yet in full harmony, and mutually confirm each other. The five discourses, by tracing the ideal of the true righteousness which contrasts so radically with the formal righteousness of the ruling pharisaism (chaps. v.–vii.), by substituting for the great theatrical incidents which were expected from heaven for the foundation of the divine kingdom, the modest mission of twelve men of the common people, ignorant and without a name, having as a weapon only the peaceful and slow power of the Word publicly preached (chap. x. and chap. xiii.), by organising a new society solely bound by love, brotherhood, mutual pardon, and common prayer (chap. xviii.), by opening finally the glorious prospect of the return of the Master, which should wash away the stain of His ignominious punishment, and consummate the work begun by His first advent (chaps. xxiv. and xxv.),—these five discourses strongly supported the apologetic aim of the gospel, just as the gospel, on the other hand, by the prophetic demonstration with which it was filled, gave all their weight to the solemn declarations contained in these discourses. Thus, despite its duality, our first gospel preserves none the less an imposing unity, which explains the incomparable part it has filled from the beginning and that it fills still in the world.

B. Second question: Who are the *readers* with a view to whom the book of the Logia and the first gospel were composed?

(*a*) The *Logia* were certainly designed for readers of Jewish origin, speaking Aramaic, dwelling in Palestine, and already converted to the gospel. All this appears from the following facts: the readers respect the Mosaic law, believe in the prophecies, and expect the return of the Messiah and the coming of His kingdom as the end of history. The author, for the rest, does not deem it necessary to explain to them certain Jewish usages of which Mark and Luke give an account to their readers of Gentile origin; thus with regard to Jewish ablutions (comp. Matt. xv. 1, 2 with Mark vii. 3 and 4), and touching the so-called day of unleavened bread (comp. Matt. xxvi. 17 with Mark xiv. 12 and Luke xxii. 7). What proves finally that the author regards his readers as believers is the manner in which he addresses them in the five discourses: "Ye are the salt of the earth . . ., the light of the world (v. 13 and 14) . . . The Spirit of your Father shall speak by you (x. 20) . . . He that receiveth you receiveth Me (x. 40) . . . To *you* it is given to know the mysteries of the kingdom; but *to the others* it is not given (xiii. 11) . . . Whatsoever ye shall bind . . . loose on the earth, shall be bound . . . loosed in heaven . . . If he will not hear thee, tell it to the Church . . . If two of you shall agree on earth to ask anything, it shall be done for them of My Father who is in heaven (xviii. 15–20) . . . When *ye shall see* in the holy place the abomination of desolation . . ., then let them that are *in Judea* flee to the mountains" (xxiv. 15 and 16).—All these words had doubtless been addressed by Jesus to His disciples; but if the apostles recall them to the churches founded by them, it is evidently because, in their intention, they had to become the permanent rule of conduct of those to whom they recalled them. When we read these words, Acts ix. 31: "And the Church in all Judea and Galilee and Samaria had peace . . . and was multiplied by the comfort of the Holy Spirit," we may be assured that those Judæo-Christian communities, already so numerous in Palestine at that remote epoch, were the circle with a view to which the book of the *Logia* was composed. Also that writing was drawn up in the language generally spoken by the people, Aramaic, as is proved by the words of the Semitic dialect that have passed into the Greek translation (see above, p. 185).

(*b*) The circle of readers for which *the gospel* was designed was different in several respects, as is even proved by the language in which it is written. It still, indeed, concerns Jews, for these readers also believe in the prophecies and expect the Messiah; but they are Hellenist Jews, ignorant of Hebrew; otherwise it would not have been necessary to translate for them the terms Emmanuel (i. 23), Golgotha (xxvii. 33), Eloï, Eloï . . . (xxvii. 46); besides, these Hellenistic Jews may well have been partly Palestinians, but it is natural to seek the greatest number of them in the Greek-speaking synagogues of the countries surrounding Palestine, for instance, in Syria (Antioch), in Mesopotamia (Babylon), and Egypt (Alexandria). These Jewish populations came every year to Jerusalem to the great feasts (Acts i.); they had contracted on those occasions the prejudices hostile to the gospel that had determined the condemnation of Jesus. Their minds had been filled with the arguments and objections of all sorts enumerated above, by which the national unbelief was justified. How important it was for the Church to remind them that Jesus was born in Bethlehem, though He had grown up at Nazareth; that if He had taught, not at Jerusalem but in Galilee, this was in accordance with prophecy; that He had not broken the Sabbath by His cures, nor in general opposed the law, but only the false application that the rabbis made of it; that, if He had called Himself the Son of God, the holiness of His life, His wisdom, and His miracles proved that He had said the truth; that Pilate himself had only with repugnance consented to confirm His condemnation; that even in His execution He had been signalised as a second David; that the precautions taken by the Jewish authorities proved that He had issued from the tomb resuscitated, and not taken away by His disciples; in a word, that from His birth to His death, the prophecies had found in Him their full accomplishment. Thus, while the book of the Logia laboured to direct and confirm the progress of the believing Jews, forming the nucleus of the Church, the author of the gospel sought to convince the not yet believing Jews within and beyond Palestine, and to bring them to recognise in Jesus the Messiah whom they were expecting.

The ambition of the evangelist probably went still further. If he makes prominent with evident complacency the words of Jesus on the place reserved at the table of the patriarchs for believers coming from the four corners of the earth (viii. 10 and fol.); if he recalls the striking word: "The field is the world"; if he brings out with emphasis (xxi. 41 and 43) the words in which Jesus declares that the vineyard will pass to new vine-dressers; if he commands the apostles to administer baptism to all nations, while teaching them to observe *all that he has commanded*,—it is clear that a circle of countless readers was revealed to his view, especially by reason of the book of the Logia, where those chief instructions of Jesus were recorded, which had, according to His orders, to be preached to the whole world. Transmitted by the congregations in Palestine to the Hellenist Jews, that book was to pass from the hands of the latter to all the nations among whom the believing or unbelieving Jews were already dispersed.

C. The third question is regarding the *time* when this gospel was composed. Opinions are still divided on this point. Some place the composition *before* the destruction of Jerusalem in the year 70: especially Hug, as well as the other Catholic writers, in this following Irenæus and Eusebius; then Meyer, Holtzmann (*Die syn. Evang.* and *Einl.*), Keim (*Leben Jesu*), Keil, and many others. On the other hand, a great number of authors place it *after* the year 70; Weiss and Harnack *immediately* after (from 70 to 75); others after a longer or shorter interval: for example, Réville, in the time of the Flavians (69–96); Jülicher, in the reign of Domitian (81–96); Volkmar comes down to the year 110, for the reason that Matthew uses Luke; and Baur comes even as far as 130–134, in the reign of Adrian. The arguments of Weiss and Harnack are chiefly drawn from the passages xxiv. 29 and xxii. 7, which we will examine immediately. What decides Jülicher is the great work of the Church for the evangelisation of the world, which, according to him, the words xxviii. 18–20 already imply, as well as the announcement of the persecutions by the heathen world (x. 18 and fol.), indications that lead to the time of Domitian. But these reasons would assume that Jesus could not know beforehand the great extension that His work would assume in the heathen world, nor the violent enmity it would there encounter. It will be understood that, for us, these reasons fall to the ground. As regards the date received by Baur, it is now universally rejected. How should the second destruction of Jerusalem under Adrian be so expressly mentioned in this discourse, while the first, in the year 70, was passed in entire silence?

We come to Weiss and Harnack's date and to the two passages on which these critics base it.

The words *immediately after* (εὐθέως μετά), with which Matthew begins the announcement of the Parousia (xxiv. 29 and fol.), according to these scholars, closely connect, but erroneously, that event with the destruction of Jerusalem. On the other hand, these words have very often also been used to prove the composition of this gospel *before* the year 70, a date that would alone explain such an error. The two writers of whom we speak say, *after*, but *immediately* after, that is to say, when men had not yet had time to convince themselves of the error contained in these words. These two contrary conclusions seem to me to be both alike erroneous. I believe, indeed I have shown from the passage of that discourse (vers. 23–28), and from a number of other words of the Lord, that in His thought, between the ruin of Jerusalem and the Parousia a great interval occurred, which is even an indispensable period of history, that which Luke calls *the times of the Gentiles,* in which must take place the successive call of the nations to salvation, a period that Jesus Himself had announced as the time during which the vineyard of the kingdom of God should be committed to *new* workers. And indeed what would become of Christian universalism, which all the theocratic particularism had in view, if there were not a place in history for that indispensable work! Jesus could less than anyone be ignorant of that necessity, and everything proves that He was not ignorant of it. Consequently, as we have shown (p. 154 and fol.), either the *immediately* (εὐθέως) of ver. 29 has been wrongly added in Matthew's account, under the influence of the same preoccupation that determined the form of the question addressed to Jesus in ver. 3 (comp. the omission of this word in Mark); or else it only remains to extend, as we have proposed, the meaning of the expression "*after the tribulation of those days*" to the whole state of things that resulted from the ruin of Jerusalem, and to give consequently to the word εὐθέως the sense of *suddenly* or *rapidly*, in opposition to the security in which the world will be plunged at that moment. As regards the passage xxii. 7, where Jesus represents the king whose banquet has been slighted sending an army to punish this act of rebellion by burning the revolted city, such words, it is said, too evidently suppose the deed already done, not to have been written after it. But admitting that Jesus Himself had not prophetic knowledge, He at least knew the prophecies of the Old

Testament; and how could He have been ignorant of this threatening of the prophet Daniel, from whom He quoted another saying: "Until the complete ruin that shall be poured out on the desolate" (ix. 27), or this terrible word that ends the entire Old Testament: "Lest I come and smite the earth with a ban" (Mal. iv. 6), a word that threatens Israel, in case of unbelief, with subjection at the hand of God to the same destruction to which Israel by His command had subjected the Canaanites! Jesus, who saw in spirit His kingdom extending over the whole earth,—let us recall the undoubtedly authentic words that He uttered upon the anointing by Mary: "The act of this woman shall be related wherever this gospel shall be preached, in the whole world (ἐν ὅλῳ τῷ κόσμῳ),"—Jesus could not fail to foresee the fate reserved for the people, who, by their unbelief, put themselves athwart this irresistible current. Keim himself says (*Leben Jesu*, i. p. 49): "It has been said that Jesus could not have foreseen the ruin of Jerusalem. But the contrary appears from the details furnished about His trial and that of Stephen (comp. Matt. xxvi. 61; Mark xiv. 58; John ii. 19; Acts vi. 14). Even among the Jews this tragic end was foreseen, and already under Cumanus, in 52, men thought of the destruction of the temple (Josephus, *Jewish War*, ii. 125, and *Antiq.* xx. 6. 1)."[1]

Let us notice lastly the terms of the declaration of Jesus on the destruction of the temple, Matt. xxiv. 2: "I say unto you, there shall not be left here one stone upon another that shall not be thrown down." If the prophecy had been made after the event, he who put it in the mouth of Jesus would have done so in a way more conformable to history; for the temple was not pulled down but burnt.

The passages we have just examined, then, are insufficient to prove the composition of our gospel after the year 70.

[1] The numerous emigrations of Jews of noble family from before the beginning of the war are attested by Josephus (*Jewish War*, ii. 14. 2). The state of things was compared to a vessel ready to suffer shipwreck, and from which men are hastening to escape by swimming (ii. 20. 1).

On the other hand, there is one that seems to me decisive in favour of the opposite opinion. We speak here of the date of the gospel, and return afterwards to that of the book of the Logia. The passage that seems to me positively to prove the composition of the gospel before the year 70 is xxiv. 15, 16. After having reported the warning given to the Church by Jesus Himself to flee from Judea at the moment when the devastating profanation should invade the sacred soil, the evangelist suddenly interrupts his account to underline this warning and introduce this exhortation into the discourse: "Let him that readeth give attention (ὁ ἀναγινώσκων νοείτω)." This parenthesis, due to the evangelist, seems to me to prove three things: 1st, that the discourse was already *edited*, and edited in Greek, at the time when this notification was inserted in it; 2nd, that it was *read*, either privately or in the assembly by the official reader (ὁ ἀναγινώσκων, Apoc. i. 3); 3rd, that the author would persuade the Church *seriously to realise* the direction given by Jesus for that time, and to draw from it the practical conclusion by preparing to emigrate. The moment was approaching of which Jesus had spoken when He said: "Pray that your flight be not on the Sabbath nor in winter." It seems to me contrary to all probability to suppose that this species of *nota bene*, whereby the author gives prominence to this exhortation of Jesus to flee from Judea is later than the ruin of Jerusalem, and even than the time of that flight itself, which took place about the year 66. That would be as if, at the moment when Paris was invested by the German army, an official proclamation had requested the inhabitants of the city to pass beyond the Channel. The warning of Jesus in itself would perhaps prove nothing certain as regards the date of the writing where it is recorded; but the energy with which the evangelist insists on the attention to be given to it clearly proves that the fulfilment was still to come, and was even becoming urgent in his view.

It follows from this that the writing in which this notification occurs must be a little earlier than the year 66, when the war commenced and the migration of the Church to the other side of Jordan took place. I believe consequently that one may fix as the date of the composition of the first gospel the period of 60–66.

When we proceed from the gospel to the *Book of Discourses*, we are led to place its composition in the years that preceded that of the gospel. But it is precisely to this period that we are also led by the time of the dispersion of the apostles, which, as we have inferred from Acts xxi. 17 and fol., must have taken place before the year 59, and when the necessity must have been more keenly felt of such a book for the churches of Palestine. This period is also that when the ascendency of James over the Judæo-Christian Church attained its height, and which for this reason best corresponds with the despatch of His encyclical letter addressed to the Judæo - Christian churches of the East, a letter whose affinities with the first gospel are so remarkable. Hilgenfeld too assigns to this date the composition of the Aramaic gospel, which he identifies with the Gospel of the Hebrews, which he makes the first link of the synoptic literature.

We shall deal in the following Appendix with the question of the relation between the book of the discourses and other books of the New Testament. Perhaps there will result from this a confirmation of the date that we have just assigned to this writing, and consequently also to the gospel that contains it.

### *Relation of the Book of the Logia to other Writings of the New Testament*

1st. *With the Apocalypse.*

B. Weiss believes he has found a proof of the composition of Matthew after the year 70 in the use made by the evangelist of the Book of Revelation, composed according to him in the year 68. This is not the place to examine the truth of this date, which is not now so generally admitted as previously (see, for example, Harnack, *Chronologie*). Apart from this question, I do not believe, indeed, that one can deny a relation of dependence between the two writings; but I think the relation is the reverse of that held by Weiss; for it seems to me that the apocalyptic vision rests on the eschatological discourse contained in Matt. xxiv. and xxv. The proof is not difficult:

The vision of the seals in Revelation (chap. vi.) begins with the appearing of a horseman traversing the earth on a white horse with a bow in his hand as a symbol of victory (ver. 2): this vision agrees with the command given to the apostles in Matt. xxiv. to go and preach the gospel "to all nations and through all the earth" (ver. 14); for the emblem of the white horse comp. Rev. xix. 11 and fol.—The following vision of the Apocalypse, that of the second seal (ver. 3), shows a horseman mounted on a red horse, holding a sword and unchaining war: the first of the calamities mentioned in the prophecy (Matt. xxiv. 6) as having to afflict the earth are *wars* (πόλεμοι).[1]—The third seal in the Apocalypse (ver. 5) shows a horseman mounted on a black horse with a balance in his hand, symbol of the dearth of victuals: the wars in Matthew are succeeded (ver. 7) by *famines* (λιμοί).—With the fourth seal appears in the Apocalypse a horseman mounted on a horse of pale hue with death and the grave behind: this is the symbol of contagious disease. It is the same in Matthew; the famines in the discourse of Jesus are succeeded by *pestilences* (λοιμοί).[2]—The opening of the sixth seal[3] (Rev. vi. 12 and fol.) produces a violent earthquake that shakes the universe and gives men a presentiment of the end: in Matthew the expression following is: *earthquakes in divers places* (σεισμοὶ κατὰ τόπους).—The fifth seal (Rev. vi. 9) represents the souls of the martyrs, victims of persecutions, longing for the promised glory: ver. 9 in Matthew contains the announcement of persecutions. — This parallelism continues in the sequel of the apocalyptic picture. In Rev. xiv. 6 there is mention of an angel bearing the eternal gospel to all the inhabitants of the earth: ver. 14 in Matthew announces the preaching of the gospel to all nations before the end.—In Rev. xiii. are described the appearing and the power of the Anti-christ, with the help that the False Prophet will lend him by every sort of false prodigies: vers. 11 and 24 of the discourse in Matthew intimate the appearing of false Christs (ψευδό-

[1] These plurals (*wars*, *famines*) in the discourse in Matthew are remarkable, proving that it is not a question of some particular fact, but of a whole category of calamities of the same kind that will continue to desolate humanity from epoch to epoch after the departure of Christ and until the end of things.

[2] The authenticity of this word is not certain. No doubt it were possible that a copier had wished to complete the text of the gospel in accordance with that of the Apocalypse. But is it probable that this assimilation had been made, and would they have thus arbitrarily amplified the discourse of Jesus?

[3] I pass from the fourth seal to the sixth, as the fifth belongs to another category.

χριστοι) and false prophets (ψευδοπροφῆται), doing great wonders, so as to seduce, were it possible, even the elect.—The Apocalypse (xix. 11 and fol.) describes, as the supreme fact of history, the appearing on a white horse of Him who is called the Word of God (κέκληται τὸ ὄνομα αὐτοῦ ὁ λόγος τοῦ θεοῦ): Matt. (ver. 30) describes likewise, as the last act of the eschatological drama, the glorious appearing of the Son of Man.—Lastly, in chap. xx. 11 and fol., the Apocalypse describes the judgment of the living and the dead by Christ, after their works: Matt. xxv. 31 and fol. announces the judgment of all the nations, exercised by Christ according to the works of charity done or omitted by each one.

Can this parallel, so faithfully pursued, leave us in doubt about the literary affinity between the apocalyptic picture and the eschatological discourse contained in chaps. xxiv. and xxv. of Matthew? The only question is which of the two writings possesses the priority. The answer does not seem to me doubtful. The literary movement goes from the simple to the composite, but not from the composite to the simple. It is not the rich apocalyptic pictures that have been condensed into some dry and prosaic terms such as we find in the discourse of Jesus (Matt. xxiv.); it is rather those terms of the discourse of Jesus (wars, famines, earthquakes, antichrists, false prophets) that served as themes to the Seer of the Apocalypse and were amplified by him into complete pictures. We believe then we can draw from the relation between the two writings the inverse conclusion of that drawn by Weiss, and hold that the author of the Apocalypse had before him, about the year 95 when he wrote, the great eschatological discourse of Jesus.

2nd. *The Epistle of James.*

Does not this writing offer us a second example of the influence exerted in the domain of the New Testament by the book of the Logia? I have already remarked that the expressions of James: *the royal law* (ii. 8), *the law of liberty* (ii. 12), and *the word planted in your hearts that regenerates them* (i. 21) are naturally applicable to the new rule of moral life formulated for the first time in the book of the Logia. The prohibition of swearing (v. 12), which almost literally reproduces the words of Jesus (Matt. v. 34), may, it is true, have been borrowed from oral tradition. But we better understand the extraordinary importance given by James to this prohibition in the words: *Above all things*, if it concerns an express command proceeding from the mouth of the Lord Himself, and recorded in the book containing His precepts. The earnestness with which James brings out the divine predilection for the poor and the riches of the heritage that awaits them (ii. 5 and 6), as well as the consideration that he claims for them

(ii. 1–4), recall the beatitudes of the Sermon on the Mount. Lastly, and above all, the terrible ruin with which he threatens the rich in Israel who live in luxury and carnal pleasures, who madly lay up treasure for the last days, and who, in fine, to crown all have "condemned and put to death the just One who did not resist them" (v. 1–6), is not this threatening, uttered in the tone of the ancient prophets, the echo of the announcement of the near ruin of the Jewish State and its capital (Matt. xxiv. 15 and fol.)?[1]

3rd. *Epistles of St. Paul.*

These writings, at least the oldest of them (according to a chronology which I do not at all think I ought to exchange for that now adopted by Harnack), date from the period 53 to 59. The Epistles to the Thess., Gal., Cor., Rom., would be, according to Harnack, five years earlier, from 48 to 55.

These letters present several remarkable points of contact with the book of the Logia, and there is nothing against the admission of this if that book dates, as I believe, from the period 50 to 60. No doubt it may be thought that Paul borrowed from oral tradition the passages we are about to cite. The reader will judge for himself if this explanation can suffice. In any case, if it be believed sufficient, one will have to infer, from the striking similarities that we are about to state, the complete analogy that existed between the apostolic tradition collected by Paul and the contents of the Logia. The passages in the five discourses of which Paul seems to me to have made use are these:

1. *In the Sermon on the Mount* (Matt. v.–vii.).—Jesus forbids divorce and a new marriage after divorce if it has taken place (Matt. v. 31 and 32.) The apostle not only does the same, but appeals on this point to an ordinance of the Lord: "To those who are married I ordain, yet not I but the Lord . . ." (1 Cor. vii. 10 and 11.) The same prohibition

[1] Harnack, in his *Chronologie*, believes he can place the Epistle of James in the second century, between 130 and 140, as forming a transition to the subsequent catholic legalism. But the Epistle of James seems to me to represent apostolic Christianity issuing in its primitive freshness from the Sermon on the Mount, far rather than an enfeebled and degenerate Paulinism. The warnings relating to the punishment of the rich would no longer have in this case the appropriateness we have just indicated, they would have but a vague and common application, and one cannot well conceive what could have provoked language so threatening and solemn addressed to the Jewish synagogues towards the middle of the second century. The Epistle of James was addressed by that head of the first Judæo-Christian Church a little before his death, in 62, to the communities of Judæo-Christians dispersed in the East and still more or less mingled with the synagogues. James doubtless desired by this writing to introduce Christianity into the midst of these last.

occurs anew Matt. xix. 3–9, but it is found there in the *gospel*, which is doubtless of later date than the Epistle to the Corinthians. The apostle quotes then rather after the Logia.—Regarding lawsuits that occurred at Corinth on questions of property, the apostle writes these words: "Why do ye not endure wrong? Why do not ye suffer yourself to be defrauded?" Would the apostle have expressed himself thus had he not felt himself supported by the words of the Master (Matt. v. 39–41): "I say to you not to resist the wicked; if any one strike thee on the right cheek . . ., if any one would take thy cloak . . ., force thee to go a mile with him . . ., etc."—We read, Rom. xii. 14: "Bless them that persecute you (τοὺς διώκοντας ὑμᾶς); bless and curse not." Is not that an echo of Matt. v. 44: "Love your enemies; pray for them that persecute you (ὑπὲρ τῶν διωκόντων ὑμᾶς)."—Lastly, it would seem to me very difficult not to see in the passage 2 Cor. i. 19, 20 an allusion to the words of Jesus (Matt. v. 37): "Let your yea be yea, and your nay, nay (ναὶ ναί, οὒ οὔ)."

2. *In the discourse instructing the apostles* (chap. x.).—The order given by Jesus (ver. 10): "The workman is worthy of his food," is recalled by Paul (1 Cor. ix. 14) in these words: "The Lord hath ordained that they that preach the gospel should live of the gospel." The word *live* is very closely connected with *food* according to the evidently entirely primitive tenor of the text of Matthew. In the passage Luke x. 7, where that evangelist also recalls this order, he does so in a form already more remote from the first form, by substituting the term *hire* for food. The quotation of this same rule (1 Tim. v. 18) is naturally conformed to Luke's.—What Paul says 1 Thess. iv. 8 of the punishment that will follow contempt of his apostolic words is based no doubt on the words (Matt. x. 40): "He that receiveth you receiveth Me, and he that receiveth Me receiveth Him that sent Me"; comp. Luke x. 16.

3. *In the discourse in parables and the conversation that followed* (chap. xiii.).—Just as Jesus (vers. 10–15) denounces the judgment of hardening that lies heavy on the greater part of the people, while He excepts believers and says: "*To you* it is given . . ., but *to them* it is not given . . .," so Paul (Rom. xi. 7) notifies the existence and continuance of this judgment on the Jews of his time, while he also notifies a minority among them, a chosen remnant (the ἐκλογή), to which he opposes—just as Jesus does—the mass of the people (οἱ δὲ λοιποί), "who have eyes and see not, and ears and hear not."

4. *In the discourse on the relations between brethren* (chap. xviii.).—The brotherly arbitration that Paul requires for disputes between the members of the Church (1 Cor. vi. 1–6), and which was already in use among the Jews, is the method that the Lord also prescribes to His disciples (chap. xviii. 15

and fol.).—In the passage 1 Cor. v. 3–5 Paul pronounces a mysterious judgment regarding the incestuous man in the name of the church of Corinth, which ought to have begun, according to him, by acting itself. The conduct of the apostle in these exceedingly grave circumstances recalls in a striking way the declaration of Jesus (Matt. xviii. 18–20): "Whatsoever ye shall bind . . . loose on earth, shall be bound . . . loosed in heaven." The incestuous man is thenceforth bound by the sentence that the apostle has pronounced on him, and by it in consequence delivered to Satan. And how is he so? Jesus had declared in the same passage that: "Where two or three are assembled in My name (δύο ἢ τρεῖς συνηγμένοι εἰς τὸ ἐμὸν ὄνομα), and shall agree to ask anything, it shall be done to them; for He will Himself be in the midst of them." And this is how Paul describes the way in which he proceeded in judging the culprit. He did not act alone, for he expresses himself thus: "Although absent in body, but present in spirit, you and my spirit being assembled in the name of the Lord Jesus, I have judged to deliver this man to Satan by the power of our Lord Jesus (ἐν τῷ ὀνόματι τοῦ Κυρίου ἡμῶν Ἰησοῦ συναχθέντων ὑμῶν καὶ τοῦ ἐμοῦ πνεύματος, σὺν τῇ δυνάμει τοῦ Κυρίου ἡμῶν Ἰησοῦ κέκρικα παραδοῦναι . . .)." One cannot fail to recognise in this description of the extraordinary act performed by Paul in spiritual communion with the church of Corinth, the execution of the direction given by Jesus, at least so far as that execution was possible at the distance that separated him at the time from this church. Such an act of judgment would be difficult to understand without the disciplinary power given by Jesus to his Church.

5. *In the eschatological discourse* (xxiv. and xxv.).—In chap. ii. 14–16 of 1 Thess. Paul gives vent to his indignation against the Jews who, instead of favouring the Christian mission in heathen lands, everywhere excite hatred against the gospel, but says, in closing this piece, the measure is full, "and the wrath is coming on them *to put an end to them* (εἰς τέλος)." This very positive threatening no doubt is based on the express threatening of Jesus, Matt. xxiv. 15 and fol., and especially ver. 34: "This generation shall not pass away till . . ."—The apostle gives the description of the Parousia (1 Thess. iv. 15–17 and v. 1–3), reproducing the principal features of the picture traced by Jesus (Matt. xxiv. 30 and fol.). I shall mention three of them: 1st, The state of things at the moment of the Parousia; this state will be such as that of the world before the Flood, a state of carnal security and complete worldliness (xxiv. 37–39). It is described in the same manner by Paul (1 Thess. v. 1–3): "When they shall say, Peace and safety . . ., sudden destruction shall come upon them." 2nd, The glorious appearing of Jesus (Matt. xxiv. 30): "The Son of

Man coming in the clouds with great power and glory"; Paul says the same (1 Thess. iv. 16): "The Lord shall descend from heaven at the signal given by the voice of the archangel and by the trump of God." 3rd, The effect produced by this heavenly manifestation. That effect is twofold both in Matthew and Paul; Matt. xxiv. 30: "All the tribes of the earth shall mourn, smiting the breast"; so 1 Thess. v. 3: "Sudden destruction shall come upon them, and they shall not escape." And, on the other hand, after Matt. xxiv. 31 and fol., at the sound of the trumpet the elect are assembled by the angels from one end of heaven to the other; so 1 Thess. iv. 16 and 17 the faithful are caught up to meet the Lord who reappears on the clouds; the faithful already dead in virtue of a resurrection; the faithful still living by the fact of a glorious transmutation. This same teaching occurs again 1 Cor. xv. 51 and 52. Paul himself gives it as a *word of the Lord*, 1 Thess. iv. 15 (ἐν λόγῳ Κυρίου). It is difficult to know whether this term denotes a special revelation, or refers to the word of Jesus in Matthew. But in 1 Cor. xv. 50 this teaching is designated by Paul as a μυστήριον (a revealed fact), which would rather suggest the former sense.

Did all the coincidences between Paul and Matthew we have just mentioned result solely from the knowledge Paul possessed of the oral tradition? It is a remarkable fact that each of the five discourses of which the book of the Logia is composed contains one or more of these passages the echo of which we find in the first epistles of Paul, while, of all the conversations and discourses contained in the rest of the first gospel, and which the author, as well as the two other Synoptics, doubtless borrowed from the oral tradition, there is not a single word that Paul made use of in those same epistles. That appears to me to confirm the view that the quotations mentioned above were derived from the Logia rather than from tradition.

To sum up: The use the author of the Apocalypse made of the book of the Logia shows that it existed before the reign of Domitian; the use that James made of it, that it existed before 61–62; the use that Paul made of it, that it was used between 53 and 59, and must consequently go back to the first years of the period 50 to 60.

With the question of the date of the gospel is connected that of the *place* where it was composed. If the book of the Logia was written in Aramean, as that language scarcely any longer prevailed over Greek except in Palestine, it seems certain that it was published in that country. Besides, we are led to that primitive centre of the Church by its contents. As Weizsaecker says, "it belongs by its spirit to the apostolic Palestinian circle." That scholar has well developed this fine observation that, as the discourses delivered by Jesus and preserved in the Logia served to explain to His hearers His breach with the medium where He taught, they were also, for the same reason, for the churches of Palestine a constant support in the pains of their own rupture with the old Judaism. For no Christian, indeed, can the pain of separation from the past have been so cruel as it must have been for the believing Jews (*Apost. Zeitalter*, p. 382).

As the Logia could only be understood in the Aramean form in Palestine, in proportion as the Church extended into the surrounding *Greek* countries, it became necessary to reproduce them in that language then universally spoken; and as the words of Jesus could not be understood by those who did not inhabit the primitive centre and had not themselves enjoyed the apostolic tradition, without the knowledge of the ministry of Jesus in its totality, the Greek translation of the Logia cannot have been long of being embodied in a complete Greek gospel. Renan thinks that it was in Batanea, to the east of the Jordan, where the Palestinian church had sought a refuge before the destruction of Jerusalem, that this very important work was done. But it is doubtful whether it could have been done at the time of the emigration or immediately after the catastrophe. Besides, we think we have above set aside both these suppositions. Moreover, despite the tint that the Greek style of our gospel has preserved of its Semitic origin, this writing, so flowing and firm in language, seems to me to have issued from the midst of a Greek population rather than from an entirely Aramean society. Renan's idea is also that of Resch in the *Nachträge zu den Paralleltexten von Matthæus und Marcus*, 2tes Heft, pp. 449–456. This author makes the presbyter Ariston of Pella (the town in Batanea, where the church of Jerusalem had taken refuge) here play a considerable part. This Ariston, whom a henceforth famous note, found in an

Armenian manuscript of the gospels, designates as the author of the unauthentic conclusion of Mark (xvi. 9–20), and to whom Resch attributes in addition the formation of the Canon of the four gospels about 140, would also be, according to him, the man who had constituted the text of the first gospel as it is preserved in Cod. D, in several Codd. of the Itala, and in the Syriac translation called the Curetonian. This whole most ingenious construction seems very hypothetical, all the more that it is not entirely certain that the Ariston mentioned in the copy of the Armenian version is not rather the Aristion of Asia Minor of whom Papias spoke, as Zahn and Harnack think.

B. Weiss believes it can be concluded from some passages where mention is made of faulty believers, such as vii. 22, xiii. 41, xxiv. 12, that this book was written in a country where the Church had already degenerated, such as Asia Minor. But are the words that the evangelist puts into the mouth of Jesus invented then by him? And could not He who had penetrated the infidelity of Judas have already discerned germs of infidelity in several among the disciples that accompanied Him as well as He showed them in Judas (John vi. 70 and 71)? Weiss further relies on the expression, *in all that land* (ix. 26 and 31), to prove that the gospel was written outside Palestine; but the context shows that by this expression the author opposes, not Palestine to a foreign land, but the district where the fact related had just occurred, to the rest of Palestine itself.—After all, the most natural supposition appears to be that of a country bordering on Palestine, like Syria, in the capital of which there was so numerous a Greek Christendom.

Fourth question: Who was *the author* of the first gospel?

(*a*) As regards the *book of the Logia* I think that, properly speaking, the author was not a single individual. There was no single man, or even single apostle, to whose memory and intellect the composition of such a document could have been exclusively confided. The business was to collect for the

Church the essential declarations of the Lord on the nature and progress of the kingdom of God which He had come to found here below, to formulate in some sort the charter of the new covenant in a manner conformable to His will. Such a work could not be accomplished by a single one of the several witnesses who had accompanied Jesus and collected His thoughts. As Weizsaecker has well said (*Apost. Zeitalt.* p. 384), "there was needed here the *co-operation* of several witnesses." The true author of the book of the Logia, as we conceive him, was then, not *an* apostle, but the apostolate.

It is clear, however, that the task of drawing it up must have been intrusted to one of them. Even if the title, *According to Matthew*, attached from the beginning to the first gospel, did not point out a name to us, we would suppose with probability that, among the apostles, he to whom this task was confided was the former toll-collector Levi, bearing in the Church as an apostle the name of Matthew. The others had learned to handle the net or hold the plough; the profession of Matthew, as secretary at the custom-house, had accustomed him to the use of the pen. And even though *According to Matthew* is the title of the whole gospel, and not specially of the collection of the Logia, it remains no less the case that the name of this author applies specially to the discourses that form the essential part of the book.

(*b*) Can we regard this author as being also the author of *the Greek gospel*? In this case it would have to be admitted that the apostle, after having composed the Logia in Aramean, had resumed the pen to reproduce the discourses in Greek and insert them in a complete gospel. But it is hardly natural, it seems to me, to suppose in an apostle the very rare case of an author translating and reproducing himself. Besides, many indications are opposed to this view. We shall say a word later on the small differences between his account and that of the two other Synoptics, such as the mention of *two* demoniacs cured at Gadara, or *two* blind men healed at Jericho, or the fact of the death of the daughter of Jairus, placed too soon by Matthew, differences for which, strictly speaking, explanations more or less plausible can be found. I wish to speak of graver facts, such as the confusion of the first two returns into Galilee (iv. 12) that Matthew and Mark (i. 14) make, or the close connection of the two accounts of the entrance into Jerusalem and the expulsion of the dealers that Matthew places in the same day (xxi. 12–17), while we clearly see from Mark (xi. 11 and 15) that the second of these acts only took place on the morrow of the day when the first occurred; or the conversation on the withering of the fig-tree, which Matthew places immediately after the curse pronounced by Jesus (xxi. 20), but which only took place on the morrow after the more circumstantial account of Mark (xi. 12 and fol.). Leaving these questions of detail, I pause at a fact that seems to me decisive, namely, the close relation that unites the narrative of the first gospel to those of the second and third. These three writings evidently belong to the same kind of composition: have the same anecdotical and fragmentary character; the same choice of discourses and miracles; a host of identical phrases and clauses; especially the same considerable omissions, such as of the first sojourn in Judea and all the subsequent journeys to Jerusalem; then, lastly, the same lack of clearness on the very important point of the day of the death of Jesus.

These are so many proofs of the close relationship existing between the composition of the first gospel and that of the two other Synoptics. We have not, then, to see in it, in contrast to them, a work of one mould, the product of the immediate and personal remembrance of a witness; it is rather a branch issuing from the same trunk as the two other Synoptics; and if the apostolic tradition formed the foundation of the last two, it must equally be at the base of the first. What a difference with the fourth gospel! That is a writing of one mould, having quite a particular style resembling no other, containing new and original materials unknown to the tradition! This common tradition the author knows, dominates, and completes; he sovereignly corrects it, as one who not only knows better, but who is sure of being recognised as such. There is no trace of a previous elaboration of the subject treated, that would interpose between the facts and the account, whether as regards the substance of things or the manner of relating them. The independent, personal remembrance shines through in the smallest details of the narration (comp., for example, i. 35–43, or xx. 1–10), and that very individual style remains perfectly like itself from the beginning to the end of the writing. The difference between the really apostolic writing and the first gospel is sensible.

And, nevertheless, beside all these indications contrary to its being drawn up by the hand of the Apostle Matthew, there are others not less telling that attest his personal intervention in this narration; thus, as we have seen, the use of his apostolic name in the account of his call (ix. 9), and the express addition of his title publican to his name Matthew in the list of the apostles (x. 3). A symptom, insignificant in appearance and yet significant, is again the place he occupies in the fourth pair of apostles; his name is here placed after that of Thomas, while in Mark and Luke Matthew occupies the first place. The apostle could not displace the pairs, but he could displace himself in his pair. Again, there are in this gospel two very special words of Jesus, which did not find entrance into the tradition, and which only a witness can have preserved. The first is the commission Jesus gives to two of His disciples for the man at whose house they had to prepare the Passover supper at Jerusalem: "The Master saith, My time is at hand; let Me keep the Passover at thy house with My disciples" (xxvi. 18). These words, which are only found in Matthew, are the more striking that they *declare* and *explain* that Jesus is obliged to anticipate the Passover supper by keeping it a day before that prescribed by the law and observed by all the people. It was, if I mistake not, the evening of the 13th Nisan at the time when the 14th was about to begin (the day when they prepared themselves for the feast by removing all leaven from the houses) that Jesus expressed Himself thus, as if to say:

"To-morrow evening it would be too late for Me; for the time of My death is quite near. Let me keep now (ποιῶ, the present) the Passover at thy house with My disciples." That is the only possible logical connection between the two propositions that these words contain. The disciples were thinking of the feast on the morrow; but Jesus, who knew the betrayal by Judas, and well understood that His enemies were hastening to profit by so unexpected an opportunity, had in view the evening of the very day on which He gave this command. For that evening there was no competition to be feared as regards the room; and, as regards the Paschal Lamb, there was no other needed on this occasion than Jesus Himself, devoting Himself for His people, and giving Himself to them in the *Holy Supper*.

This saying, preserved by Matthew and by him alone, contains, then, implicitly the justification of the whole Johannine narrative, and that is the more remarkable that it contrasts with the lack of precision of the synoptic narrative. Its authenticity results precisely from this apparent disagreement with the three synoptical accounts; only a witness can have thus preserved and reproduced it despite this disagreement. The other remarkable saying that Matthew has alone in like manner preserved, and the memory of which is easily explained by the impression it must have made on the former publican, is this (xi. 28–30): "Come unto Me, all ye that labour and are heavy laden, and I will give you rest. Take My yoke upon you, and learn of Me; for I am meek and lowly in heart." Who could appropriate this saying and engrave it for ever in his heart better than the publican, who had, no doubt, been very often hurt by the haughtiness of the Pharisees, and could so well compare with their factitious holiness the real holiness which was at the same time full of sweetness and charity, of the new teacher that spoke thus!

What above all shows the apostolic origin of the first gospel is the way in which it gives us the impression of the power of the word of Christ. The author himself describes that power in these words (vii. 28): "And the multitudes were astonished at His teaching, for He taught them as having authority, and not as their scribes." With these, there were subtle discussions on the texts of the Old Testament, in which each teacher sought to surpass the other in knowledge and perspicacity; but in Jesus, divine truth directly viewed, humanly lived and expressed, flowing from the fountain and revealing itself to upright consciences in language absolutely destitute of circumlocution and subtilty! If we can still form an idea of the power exercised by Jesus as a popular orator, we certainly owe it to the first gospel. The best means to appreciate the unique beauty of the words of Jesus, as the first gospel has transmitted them to us, is to compare them with the lucubrations of the writers who a little later, sometimes with good intention, tried to make Jesus speak after their fancy. Among this mass of words attributed to Jesus, of which Resch has succeeded in collecting so many examples, one is immediately struck with the style, at once trivial and studied, as well as the pretentious and too refined contents. With some one or two exceptions, all those words might relapse into oblivion without the world thereby losing the least particle of truth, while not a word of the discourses of Jesus preserved in the Logia of Matthew is common or without moral bearing. "The greatest part of these words," says Jülicher—he could have said more without fear of exaggeration—"may very well have been recorded by an apostle nearly as we read them in Matthew" (p. 191). The elevation, whether of matter or of form, remains constantly like itself, and he who thus reproduced these discourses can hardly have done so save under the same impression with which the officers of the Sanhedrin were struck when they cried: "Never man spake like this man."

How are we equitably to take account of these indications, in some sort opposed, that we have just remarked in the first gospel, those that do not allow us to attribute the drawing up of this writing to the pen of the apostle, and those that prove his intervention in its composition? There is only, it seems to me, one sole means of reconciling these contradictory internal criteria. Just as Peter had with him as companion in labour and secretary the evangelist Mark, and the latter has given us the apostolic tradition as he heard it issue from the mouth of that apostle, as Paul was accompanied by Timothy and Silas in his journeys, so the Apostle Matthew, on quitting Palestine to devote himself to the evangelisation of the surrounding Greek nations, did not undertake that new task alone. He procured the company of a devoted disciple, who had served him till then as collaborator. Only the name of that disciple has remained unknown. It was to him that Matthew committed the task of reproducing the book of the Logia in Greek. That was a trust that he alone could transfer to another. At the same time he confided to his disciple the task of joining to the Logia a narrative of the life of Jesus as it had been formulated at Jerusalem (not without the co-operation of Matthew himself), a narrative that was an indispensable frame for the discourses. This explains the lack of local colour and of descriptive details that strikes us in the accounts of the first gospel; the more or less considerable inaccuracies that one remarks in it, on comparing them with the accounts of the two others, and especially with John's, are thus also more easily explained. And, on the other hand, one gets a clear idea of the reasons why the personal stamp of Matthew is so deeply imprinted on it.

Jerome tells us that in his time the name of him who translated the Aramean writing of Matthew was unknown; it will certainly always be unknown. Perhaps the most beautiful picture of the Salon Carré of the Louvre, the Unknown Young Man plunged in Meditation, is by an artist who has remained unknown. So the book to which mankind is perhaps the most indebted, which has opened and still daily opens the kingdom of heaven to the world, has for its author a writer whose name history has not preserved. One can understand that that name was lost between the name of Him who was the subject of his book and the name of the apostle who was indirectly its author.

As regards the *sources* from which this author drew his account, we have only hitherto, it seems to me, ascertained four:

1. The information, oral or written, that lies at the base of the accounts of the infancy (chaps. i. and ii.);

2. The Logia of Matthew;

3. The apostolic tradition, especially in the form in which Matthew reproduced it;

4. Some accounts that did not belong to the apostolic tradition, and which the author must have privately collected at Jerusalem (the resurrection of some of the dead at the moment of the death of Christ; their appearance after the resurrection to different inhabitants of the city; the angel sitting on the stone rolled away from the sepulchre, and the flight of the keepers on seeing this; the report spread by the Jews of the removal of the body by the disciples, etc.). But we must take good care not to confound with these particular facts the final scene (xxviii. 16–20), which took place in presence of the Eleven, and probably of the whole gathering of the Galilean believers, the five hundred of whom Paul speaks (1 Cor. xv. 6); for it would be difficult to assign another place for this appearance in presence of so numerous an assembly.

Among the sources of the first gospel hitherto ascertained, I do not cite the Gospel of Mark, regarded as such by so great a number of critics. This is a question to be examined later; see Chapter V. of the present volume.

## V

## The Truth of the Accounts contained in the First Gospel

No one now doubts that there existed in Judea in the time of the first Roman emperors a man called Jesus, who was distinguished for His holiness, His teaching, and by a multitude of acts held as miraculous by those who were witnesses of them and by Himself; it is further admitted that this man, condemned as a blasphemer and crucified at the instance of the heads of His people, nevertheless succeeded in assembling around Him a group of believers who became the nucleus of the existing Christendom.

These facts do not rest merely on the account in our gospels, but also on the reports of Jewish or heathen writers (Josephus, Tacitus, Suetonius); they are now scarcely any longer disputed. But what is denied is the truth of certain features characterising this history that absolutely surpass the course of ordinary life, namely, the miracles with which it is filled. As almost all the particular objections that are raised against the truth of the gospel narrative are connected with this principal objection, I will in the first place take in hand the question of miracle. It goes without saying that I do not pretend here to present a complete discussion on this subject. I wish here to consider above all two facts: 1st, that which is the foundation of all history, the creation; 2nd, that which is its culminating point, the appearance, in the midst of our fallen humanity, of a holy and sinless being.

1. The fact of the *creation* can only be denied by those who deny the existence of God. It is necessary in this case to affirm the eternity of the world; but the world is in daily progress, and the notion of an eternal progress is self-contradictory; for a progress eternally begun would also be eternally achieved. But if the universe, as well as time itself, has had a beginning, this can be only by an act of the divine will, and that is the miracle of miracles, that surpasses and embraces beforehand all particular miracles. Or will it perhaps be said that in this initial miracle the Creator exhausted at one stroke all the fulness of His power, and thenceforth abdicated in favour of the laws He has given to nature? No; for an incessant continuance of the creative will is needed in order that the universe may not relapse into the nothingness whence it was drawn. Then, creation is not an achieved and definitive fact; it is incessantly progressing by the appearance of new beings. It has only

gradually attained its actual state and its desired end, the appearance of the free being. And just in presence of this privileged creature who, in virtue of his liberty, could become at one time or another an adversary to God, by making himself the enemy of goodness, God behoved to reserve to Himself the means of maintaining His sovereignty and of restoring man in any case into the way that must lead him to the end for which He has taken him from nothingness. It is on the *inexhaustible* treasure of the divine power that the possibility of miracle rests.

What is a miracle? It is not, as was formerly said, a suspension of the law that God has established in nature; nor yet is it, as some now suppose, a combination of the divine power with that law, or the setting agoing a natural force as yet unknown to science. Miracle, in the biblical sense of the word, has been exactly defined by Scherer as "the product of a *different force* from those that together constitute the system of nature; it is a direct and creative act of God" (article on *Apologetics in England*). It goes without saying that for him this is a mere logical definition in no way implying the reality of the fact thus defined. I only quote it because, as a pure idea, it seems to me very exactly formulated. It was even thus that Jesus Himself regarded miracle, when, to explain the healing of the impotent man, He said (John v. 17): "My Father worketh even until now, and I work." In presence of the world He has created, God is not like the maker of a musical box, remaining inactive before the rotation of the roller adjusted by him, and passively enjoying its harmony. He rather resembles, if one may venture to make such a comparison, the organist whose thought pierces all the parts of his instrument and makes them vibrate with the emotion with which he is penetrated himself, so as to communicate it to those that hear him, and, that he may more surely attain this end, using means to increase the sound that the maker of the instrument adjusted beforehand. In God, says St. Paul, "we live and move and have our being." And Jesus declares: "Not a bird falls to the ground without the will of your Father." There is nothing in this that violates the regularity of the laws of nature. God has established these laws as the indispensable condition of the free and intelligent labour of man; but He did not mean to make of them a chain for Himself. Nature is not a wheel destined to turn uniformly on itself; it is a soil prepared in view of a superior end, in some sort a building ground on which has to be accomplished a second entirely different work of the moral order, the education of the free being for his high and eternal destination: the realisation of the kingdom of God. Now the miracles belong to this new work which is superior to nature and yet is accomplished on the soil of nature, and it can consequently require the use of means which, while acting in nature, proceed from other forces than those that are inherent in nature.

It is with the distinct feeling of His participation in the divine action in view of the supreme end of which we speak that Jesus did the works that bear the name of miracles and that He Himself calls *signs*, the signs of the power of God acting by Him and designed to qualify Himself as being in reality what He claims to be. "I have a better witness than that of John (the Baptist). The works that My Father hath given Me the power to do, these works that I do bear witness of Me that the Father hath sent Me." In these words is revealed the inward consciousness that Jesus had of the divine force by which He wrought His miracles. On the one hand, God gives Him the power to do them, and on the other He performs them Himself, the power of God passing through His human will: "Father, I thank Thee that Thou hast heard Me. And I know that Thou hearest Me always" (John xi. 41). It is God that raises Lazarus; but, on the other hand, Jesus explains this miracle by calling Himself almost at the same moment, "the resurrection and the life." It is then He also that raises. Could the sentiment of *the divine power exerting itself through Him* be expressed more clearly?[1]

It has often been alleged that Jesus never put forth His miracles as means of producing faith. It is very true that He sometimes appealed to means of a higher order, at least for those possessing a more cultivated spiritual sense. But this sense does not exist in all; it sometimes fails even in His apostles. In John xiv. 11 Jesus says to them: "Believe *Me* that I am in the Father, and the Father in Me; or else believe Me *for the works' sake*"; that is to say: If you do not believe *Me* (on My word), believe Me because of these works that the Father gives Me the power to do. The true way, after Him, would then be to believe in *His person* on His word, but those who cannot immediately discern the divine character of this revelation in word ought at least to have eyes, and supply by sight the lack of moral sense. The miracles were then in the eyes of Jesus a means of believing, although not the highest. They might dispose the heart to believe. The same conclusion appears from the words (John x. 37, 38): "If I do not the works of My Father, believe *Me* not, but if I do them, though ye believe not *Me*, believe *the works*." The day after the multiplication of the loaves Jesus said to the crowds that had followed Him (John vi. 36): "You have seen Me (multiplying the loaves), and (yet) ye believe not!" According to Him, faith, a certain faith at least, ought to have resulted from what they saw. The same thought results also from this threatening of Jesus (Matt. xi. 20 and fol.): Chorazin and Bethsaida will be more severely treated than Tyre and Sidon, because, *despite the miracles they had witnessed*, they did not repent, as the inhabitants of those heathen cities would have done; and Capernaum, that the presence of Jesus and the sight of His

[1] In the face of those words, and of so many like them, M. Sabatier alleges that "the explanation that refers the miracles directly to God is not in accordance with the gospel accounts, and is only an expedient of *modern theology*" (*Encyc. d. Sc. relig.* art. "Jesus Christ," vol. vii. p. 368).

miracles had raised to heaven, will descend to Hades, because Sodom would have better used such favours, and would still remain had it been the object of them.

Jesus could not more clearly affirm at once the divine causality of His miracles, and the influence that they ought to exert to lead to faith those that witnessed them. The inward feeling of Jesus in performing these extraordinary works was that it was the Father *dwelling in Him* (John xiv. 10: ἐν ἐμοὶ μένων) who performed them by Him. To deny the supernatural character of His works, then, is to pretend to give a lesson to the religious consciousness of Jesus. We have seen above how some theologians of our days treat His *moral* consciousness; we see here that they no more respect His *religious* consciousness. We Christians of the nineteenth century have the mission to teach Jesus what His own works were!

Doubtless the omnipotent action of God is habitually enveloped in the natural concatination of causes and effects; but when, by the fault of man, the chariot of history gets stuck in the mud, there must remain in God the force and the means to set it agoing again. This means is the miracle.

2. The second fact on which it is important here to insist, since it is in some measure parallel to the fact of creation, is the perfect holiness of Jesus. If this be really the case, it surpasses all the particular miracles Jesus could have wrought. But this miracle is closely related to another, the exceptional birth of Him who accomplished it. We possess two accounts of the birth of Jesus. It is very evident that neither the one nor the other belongs to the great current of the apostolic tradition. This is proved by the omission of them from Mark, the gospel that seems to be the edition of that tradition in its simplest and most primitive form. These two accounts, then, are derived from private information, and the differences one notices between them and which seem to go the length of contradiction, prove that they proceed from two different sources. What is chiefly made prominent in Matthew are the impressions

of Joseph, his inward struggle, his anxieties, and the appearance of the angel that ends them. In Luke's account the impressions of Mary chiefly come out, her surrender to the will of God and her sentiment of adoration. Allusion is even twice expressly made to her inner experiences (ii. 19 and 51), and that in terms that betray an absolutely personal remembrance. One may, then, naturally enough suppose that the account of the first gospel reached its author from the side of Joseph, and that doubtless through James as intermediary, who was after Jesus the head of the family; and that the very striking details of Luke's account came to him from the side of Mary, perhaps through John as intermediary, with whose gospel Luke's presents very remarkable affinities.

If, then, these accounts do not offer the same guarantee as those that belong to the general apostolic tradition, they are not less worthy of credence. The differences existing between them attest their reciprocal independence, and confirm the reality of the fact that is the basis of them, and which alone explains this essential condition of the Christian salvation: the perfect holiness of Jesus. But is this perfect holiness real? It seems at the first glance impossible to be assured of it; for here the question is of what is most private in the person of a man who lived twenty centuries ago, and of a fact on which His own contemporaries could not have formed a certain judgment. Can we for our part now pierce into the depth of the heart of Jesus to ascertain the perfect purity of His most secret sentiments? I think we can, and that in this way:

The moral delicacy with which He was in any case endowed leaves no doubt of the vigilance He exercised over Himself. But He never spoke of sin as having to accuse Himself of it, but only as having authority to pardon it *on the earth* (ἐπὶ τῆς γῆς), as God pardons it in heaven (Matt. ix. 6). Of all the true human feelings, the only one of which we find no trace in Him is repentance. He formally establishes a moral opposition between Him and His hearers when He says to them: "If *you, being evil* know how to give good things to your children . . ." If Jesus had wished by this to oppose them to God and not to Himself, He would certainly have said, as we would all do: If *we* who are evil . . . The same is the case with His words addressed to Nicodemus, "*Ye must be born* anew." Nowhere in His life do we discover the indication of a crisis like what we name conversion. When He addresses this challenge to His adversaries: "Which of you convinceth Me of sin?" if He had not had, according to Keim's expression, "a conscience without a cicatrice," He must have blushed for the shameful reticence that such a question would imply. Lastly, if He felt Himself under the burden of any fault, how could He believe that He had come to give Himself *as a ransom* for the sins of others (Matt. xx. 28; Mark x. 45)?

This consciousness of His innocence not only implies the absence of all knowledge of any external sin. Jesus feels Himself pure within as without. Could He, who charges as adultery a look of desire, as murder a word inspired by anger or hatred, had He ever observed such feelings in Himself, have addressed such words to His hearers without a downcast look, while saying, as from the elevation of a judgment-seat: "But I say unto you."

It is not denied that the conscience of Jesus was pure from every stain; but it is alleged that that still does not prove His real and absolute holiness. M. Sabatier says (*Encyc. d. Sc. relig.* art. "Jesus Christ," vii. p. 368): "There can be no question of the objective holiness of Christ, but only of a subjective holiness, conceived as *an upright state of conscience*" (the italics are mine). For my part, I believe it is possible to ascend from the subjective consciousness that Jesus had of His holiness, to the absolute objectivity of that moral state. It is an experience that the facts daily establish, that the more a man progresses in holiness, the more prompt is he to detect the least symptom of sin, the slightest impure feeling that comes to defile his heart the more humbled and painfully affected is he by such a thing. The clearest mirror is also the one that is most quickly obscured by contact with vapour; the more delicate the sense of smell, it is the more certainly offended by the odour of a decayed object. If Jesus had not been objectively holy, He would have been the most humbled and repentant of men. Otherwise He must be denied not only the subjective holiness that is allowed Him, but the simple degree of moral perspicacity or sincerity that is found in the saints that endeavour to walk in His steps.

If, then, Jesus was not only subjectively, but also, and by reason of that very fact, absolutely holy, one has to recognise in that the most extraordinary phenomenon of the history of mankind, and agree that a fact so absolutely exceptional must have had an equally exceptional cause. To this postulate the gospel account of the miraculous birth answers. It will perhaps be said that that is to make of it an explanatory legend, derived from the very fact of which we are speaking. Be it so. But in that case the birth of this legend is itself the proof of the reality of the fact to which it owes its origin.

The philosopher Charles Secrétan wrote the following lines in *La Raison et le Christianisme*: "If it is certain that humanity is corrupted in its first organs and first acts, that the impulse to evil has become one of the elements of our nature, it is clear that the appearance of a man without sin is absolutely contrary to the accidental order introduced by the Fall, and that it forms the beginning of a new order. Between the idea of an excellent man, of the first religious genius, of the best of men, and that of a pure man, of the living *ideal*, there is an infinite difference. To recognise the purity of Jesus Christ is to take the decisive step, is to admit the reality of the divine economy, to grant all. After that, the immaculate conception of the Saviour will no longer astonish us . . . Jesus is the second Adam, the beginning of a new humanity engrafted on the first to transform it. Jesus is a new creation of God. A new creation of God is not more incredible than the first, which is the miracle of miracles, the universal, the absolute miracle. . . . Why do the gospels assure us that Jesus was born of a woman without having had a human father? Assuredly we would not have imagined it, any more than the rest. But the fact being given, it seems to me that we can understand it. Does not the man represent individual initiative, progress, the particular, in human society; and the woman, tradition, continuity, the general, the species? The Saviour could not be the son of this or that man in particular; He had to be the son of humanity."

And is not that, I will ask in passing, and despite the recently advanced hypotheses, the true explanation of the name *Son of Man* that Jesus gave Himself with a sort of predilection? Not the son of a particular individual, but the son of the race itself, its definitive, perfect fruit, eternally foreseen and willed.

But it is objected that, even on the supposition of a supernatural conception, the heredity of sin remains none the less by the intermediary of the mother. The answer to this objection is found in a very remarkable saying of the Apostle Paul (Rom. viii. 3): "God sending His Son in *flesh like the flesh of sin* (ἐν ὁμοιώματι σαρκὸς ἁμαρτίας), condemned sin *in the flesh*." The flesh, in the scriptural sense of the word, denotes properly the organ of sensation of pleasure and pain. From this purely physical sense, the term flesh often passes to a moral one, and denotes the active desire of pleasure and the fear that induces to escape from pain. So far there is no sin in what is called the flesh. Sin only begins at the moment when the attraction of pleasure and the fear of suffering master the will and lead it to obey personal satisfaction, by treading under foot the sense of good, the consciousness of duty, the law of the spirit. Jesus did not sin in being hungry and thirsty, and in thanking God for the satisfaction of these needs; He did not sin in yielding to the need of rest and sleep after fatigue. He did not even sin by feeling beforehand, as painfully as we ourselves would have done, the strokes of the rod tearing His back, the nails trans-piercing His flesh, the burning thirst and other tortures that form the train of the punishment of the cross. He did not sin when experiencing at Gethsemane a mortal terror at the thought of that bloody drama that He saw approaching Him. This anguish was a thing of *the flesh,* but not of the flesh *of sin*; the latter would only have begun with murmuring against the cup that God gave Him to drink, and refusing to raise it to His lips or to drain it to the dregs. The flesh *in itself* deserves no moral qualification; it only takes the character of good or bad by its relation to the spirit, whether it dominates or is subdued by it. As a master, it may lead to the greatest crimes, as is seen every day. As a servant, it becomes the occasion of the most touching and heroic sacrifices, as is seen at Gethsemane. The means of breaking its dominion will not then be to weaken it in itself, to change or destroy it; it will rather be to strengthen the spirit to such a degree that it may be able to recover its dominion over it.

Thus, then, the flesh may well have been transmitted to Jesus by His mother without being accompanied by sin, the latter only consisting in the abnormal relation between the flesh and the spirit. Now in Jesus the dominion of the spirit over the will was freely and constantly maintained, in spite of all thė solicitations and claims of the flesh. But whence comes it that it was thus with Him and Him alone? He Himself says: "That which is born of the flesh is flesh" (John iii. 6). That is the state of the matter created in man by the fact of the Fall; all that is born has sprung from carnal inclination, and brings with it into life this feature of the preponderance of the flesh over the spirit. The illicit connection that the human will has contracted with the flesh by the free act of the Fall has been communicated to all the race by the heredity of birth. The egoist self, eager for personal enjoyment, the enemy of self-sacrifice, has reigned in the heart of man and has drawn him to the very opposite of his real destination. It was necessary to break the chain and make a new beginning, as Jesus Himself declares in that antithesis that completes the saying I have just recalled: "That which is born of the Spirit is spirit." Here is the remedy: the Spirit breaking in Jesus the connection contracted by the Fall between carnal inclination and the human will, and restoring to the latter its first liberty to subjugate the flesh and even lead it, if the divine will should require it, to the bloody altar of sacrifice! This means was certainly more worthy of God and of man than that which would have consisted in causing Jesus to descend directly from heaven to Capernaum without His incarnation in the womb of a mother where He could take possession of human nature. That would not have been a victory over the enemy, but a flight. God caused the Restorer of fallen humanity to be born *in* the flesh, but not *of* the flesh; in the flesh, that He might conquer sin in the very domain whence sin had derived its victory, but not of the flesh; for there was nothing carnal in the action of the breath from above that determined the development of the predestined germ in the womb of Mary, and brought to birth the new prototypical Adam, from whom was to proceed the new humanity answering the divine end. For this was needed that creator Spirit who at the beginning raised from chaos a world of light and at length a free and sovereign personality. He alone could replace Jesus in that liberty that man had voluntarily alienated, and by this liberty restored *in Him*, offer and communicate it to all those who freely attached themselves to Him. Those also, the regenerate, are included by Jesus in the expression, "All that is born of the Spirit is spirit." It is even to them, according to the context, that this saying applies first of all. But if Jesus there properly describes the regeneration of believers, the exceptional mode of His own birth is none the less implicitly affirmed by the principle contained in this declaration. If in the course of His own life a new birth did not take place, it is because His birth, properly so called, did not permit any such renewal; for it was it that had to serve as the point of departure and principle for every subsequent act of regeneration.

We end these observations on the miraculous birth with these striking words of Charles Secrétan: "Whence comes it that a holy one is born to us? It is not a chance, a happy accident of nature; there would be at least two, I imagine. No, it is a miracle."

We have still to speak of some facts specially assailed:

And first, of *the Temptation.*—The belief of Jesus in the existence of Satan, that so-called superstition of the Middle Ages, is not doubtful; it specially appears from the didactic and prosaic statement He gives on this subject (John viii. 44); and the proof that His initial victory over the old prince of this world was in His view a real fact, is found in the very striking words that Matthew has preserved to us (xii. 29) and Luke (xi. 21 and 22), where Jesus represents Himself under the image of a leader, who, before penetrating into the stronghold of a hostile chief and giving up his dwelling to pillage, must have conquered him in single combat; only after that can he take possession of his goods, an expression comprehending his treasures, slaves, and captives. Such is the comparison whereby Jesus explains His cures of the possessed, attributed by His adversaries to complicity with Satan. Quite the contrary, it was because He began by conquering him in a personal moral combat, that He can now snatch his victims from him. What can that initial struggle and victory be but the fact of the Temptation, placed by our three Synoptics at the threshold of the ministry of Jesus? Keim has plainly recognised this application (i. p. 570).

*The multiplication of loaves.*—After what has been said on miracles in general, I have only a word to add on this one: In creating the grain of wheat and bestowing on it the power to multiply itself each year, God did not deprive Himself in its favour of the power of multiplying matter ten and a hundred fold, nor of the right to use this power Himself, if He ever found it well to do so. The same thing may be said of the changing of water into wine. In creating the vine-stock and giving it the power to transform each year the water of the sky into wine, God did not Himself abdicate this power, nor the right to exercise it when needful.

The account of *the second multiplication of loaves* (Matt. xv. 32 and fol.; Mark viii. 1 and fol.) requires our attention a little longer. It is usual at present in criticism to regard this account as a duplicate of the account of the first multiplication. Jülicher calls it *eine Vergröberung* (how shall we translate this word: thickening? materialisation?) of the first, and declares every other supposition unworthy of discussion (p. 288). What! the *four thousand* men of the second multiplication an exaggeration of the *five thousand* of the first! The satiety wrought by means of the *seven* loaves in the second, an amplification of the miracle accomplished by means of *five* in the first! The *seven* baskets of fragments remaining after the second, an amplification of the *twelve* collected after the first! On all points there is diminution, not enlargement; it would be then a gradation *a majori ad minus*! Then, I ask, since the invention of the second fact evidently did not design to strengthen the first, what end must it have served? Would it perhaps be to furnish a better reason for the very severe and humiliating reproach that Jesus a little later addresses to the apostles: "When I divided the five loaves among five thousand men, how many baskets full of fragments took ye up? *When I divided the seven loaves among the four thousand, how many baskets full of fragments took ye up?* Do not ye hear and understand? Is your heart hardened? Having eyes, see ye not, and ears, hear ye not? And do ye not remember?" Would it be the apostles themselves that had invented a second multiplication with the view of being able to put in their Master's mouth a reprimand the like of which, to our knowledge, He never addressed to them! But a truce to so absurd a supposition! And yet that is what one would be forced to admit. It is simpler, it seems to me, to believe that Jesus saw fit to do a second time what He had done before, if the same case recurred and required recourse to the same procedure.

*The walking on the water.*—This miracle recalls the saying of Charles Secrétan: "The will is substance." In this miracle there doubtless co-operated both the power that the will of man possesses over his own body and that which the divine will exercises over the whole of nature.

*Fishing for the stater.*—Here is one of the accounts most generally treated as legendary. The fact is in itself, however, not unexampled; we know the history of the tyrant of Samos. If there is a miracle, it is found in the coincidence between the find and the need that Jesus had of it. Such coincidences are met with elsewhere than in romances, and the very original and lofty words that Jesus spoke on this occasion, and that no one else would have invented (Matt. xvii. 26 and 27), are the guarantee of the reality of the fact that gave rise to them.

*The extraordinary circumstances that signalised the moment of the death of Jesus.*—The obscuring of the sun at noonday, reported in the three accounts, is a fact that is not unexampled (see my *Comment. on Luke*, 5th ed. vol. iii. p. 336). As regards the earthquake (in Matthew), that phenomenon is frequent in the East. The miracle is not then in these facts, but in their coincidence with the death of Christ; and whoever could not understand that nature herself may have uttered a note of terror in the course of that event, the centre of history, would incur the risk of not having grasped the supreme range of it.—The rending of the veil of the temple, related by the three Synoptics, is a symbolic divine act, partaking in the highest degree with all the miracles the character of a *sign*, for it proclaims the abolition of the special consecration of the most Holy Place as the abode of the Eternal, and consequently also that of the holiness of the Holy Place, of the court and the temple altogether. In killing their Messiah, Israel had destroyed their own temple, as Jesus had foretold (John ii. 19). This fact corresponds in some sort with that of the high priest tearing his priestly garment on hearing a blasphemous word; it is the abolition of the profaned Levitical worship, which gives place to the only and permanent sacrifice. The gospel of the Hebrews spoke of the breaking of a beam "of immense size," from which the veil of the most Holy Place was suspended. That Judæo-Christian writing no doubt endeavoured thereby to make the rending of the veil a purely material fact consequent on the earthquake, and thus to deprive it of its humiliating and tragically symbolical character.—The resurrection of many saints at the time of Jesus' death, and their appearance to certain inhabitants of Jerusalem after the resurrection, are only related in the first gospel, and did not form part of the general tradition. But if the death of Jesus, in removing the condemnation of sin, sapped the foundation of the kingdom of death, might not a sign of that victory of life have been given by a sensible commotion in the domain of the dead? Doubtless the appearance of believers restored to life as the train of the first raised One, and pledge of the universal action of that victory, is a fact the reality of which baffles every estimate; but the whole event with which it is connected belongs to an order of things that surpasses the limits of our rational conception; lastly, let us not forget that this is the account of an apostolic disciple, and not of the apostle himself.

*The resurrection of Jesus.*—This fact belongs to a category differing entirely from that of the resurrections reported by the gospels and wrought by Jesus. This is a miracle accomplished not by but on Him, and consequently, if it is real, directly by God Himself. "God raised Jesus," said Peter (Acts ii. 24). Besides, there is not here merely a body that the spirit that previously animated it comes to inhabit anew, and which has soon to quit it again. It concerns a transformation of the body itself, destined to serve as an abode for a personal being raised to a mode of existence superior to that of the earth. From the body of flesh that has succumbed is mysteriously disengaged a body of a superior nature, that still remains in organic relation with the first. For this new body proceeds from a principle of life inherent in the old body, as one sees in the vegetable organism the imperceptible germ of life contained in the grain of seed expand in the new organism designed to replace the old. In Jesus also the development of this new body is effected by degrees, and that the more that it has not to be a mere repetition of the old, but the appearance of an organ appropriate to a new life. This is what explains the apparently opposite characteristics presented by the body of the risen Jesus. On the one hand, He eats and drinks, not because He feels the need of it, as men more than once have thought fit to say, but to convince the disciples of the full reality of this body, and even by inviting them to touch Him; and, on the other hand, He appears and disappears suddenly, as if He now obeyed only the law of the will. One can understand from this the strange expression used by Jesus when, surrounded by the disciples, He says to them (Luke xxiv. 44): "This is what I said to you *when I was yet with you.*" He is in the midst of them and speaks to them, and already He is no more with them! In His body that is being transformed He inhabits another sphere than that in which He visibly moves. Would it be permitted to compare this transitory state to that of the butterfly whose new body is being disengaged by degrees from the old in the tomb of silk where the latter is contained? The Ascension marks for Jesus the term and achievement of the transformation of the earthly body into the *spiritual body* (1 Cor. xv. 46). This term used by Paul is apparently contradictory, but it denotes not a body of spiritual *nature*, but a body designed to serve as organ to a (quickening) *spirit*, and no longer merely to a (living) *soul*, as the apostle says.

The first gospel does not speak of the different appearances by which the apostles were brought personally to believe in the resurrection. Its bearing is more objective than that of the third. The manner in which the apostles were subjectively brought to their personal faith did not belong to the exposition of the Messianic dignity of Jesus. On the other hand, the first gospel has preserved to us the memory of the solemn appearance of the risen Jesus, in which He Himself proclaimed, in presence of all His Church of that time, His elevation to universal sovereignty, long before assured to the Messiah in Ps. ii.: "I will give Thee the nations for Thine inheritance, the ends of the earth for

Thy possession" (comp. also Ps. cx. 1, 2). This is the fact that was important for his subject, and formed the true culmination of this essentially Messianic account.

There may yet be alleged against the truth of the narrative of our gospel some historical errors not touching the question of the supernatural. There are chiefly two to which it is important that we should attend. These are, the *omission of the journeys to Jerusalem*, related by the fourth gospel; and then the *indication of the day of Christ's death*, in which our account differs from the account in that writing.

The first of these two facts is certainly the greatest and most important difficulty presented by Matthew's narrative, as well as by the two other Synoptics. But this very circumstance that it occurs in all the three proves that we have not here a gap due to a purely individual cause, and that the omission of which we speak must go back to the common source whence the three accounts proceeded.

First of all, let us show that these journeys to Jerusalem, to the number of four and even five (comp. John ii. 13, v. 1, vii. 10, x. 22, xi. 17 [Bethany]), are not free arrangements of the fourth evangelist, but occupied a real place in the ministry of Jesus. From the age of twelve years, when He had made His first pilgrimage to Jerusalem, Jesus had doubtless often reappeared in that city; and during the three years of His ministry, in particular, why should He have made no attempt there to fulfil, or at least prepare, His work? That prolonged absence would have sufficed to render Him a suspected person (John vii. 2–4). It was considered a sacred duty for every Israelite to celebrate, at least once a year, one of the three great feasts at Jerusalem; and the proof that Jesus had not failed in this duty is found in a saying of Jesus Himself preserved by Matthew (xxiii. 37) and by Luke (xiii. 34): "Jerusalem, Jerusalem, how often would I have gathered thy children together, as a hen gathers her chickens under her wings, and ye would not!" These sojourns, to which Jesus here makes allusion, explain the pretty numerous relations with different inhabitants of the capital or neighbourhood, shown during His last sojourn at the feast of the Passover; above all, His intimate relation with the family of Bethany (Matt. xxvi. 6 and fol.); then the freedom with which He requires of an inhabitant of Bethphage, the riding-animal He has need of (xxi. 2 and fol.), or with which He sends word to an inhabitant of Jerusalem (xxvi. 18): "My time is at hand; let Me keep the Passover at thy house with My disciples." Jesus had then in Judea a whole circle of intimate acquaintances, in which He was commonly called "the Master" or "the Lord" (Matt. xxi. 3, xxvi. 18, 49; John xi. 28, xiii. 13; Luke xii. 13, xxi. 7, etc. etc.).

How can the omission from these three narratives of these journeys, of which we thus ascertain different traces in the Synoptics themselves, be explained? It seems to me that since that omission is common to all the three of them, the cause of it must be sought elsewhere than in the negligence or ignorance of one of them in particular, who had occasioned it in the two others; for, first of all, this strange gap in the first must be explained; then it must be shown how one at least of the two others, by means of his special information, Mark, the hearer of Peter's narratives, Luke, in possession of very abundant and exact sources, quite peculiar to him, had not repaired that omission.—To explain then this common, very grave omission, we are obliged to go back to the origin of the three narratives, to the apostolic tradition, the trunk from whence sprung our three Synoptics like three branches. Perhaps, by going back to that, we shall more easily find the explanation of the mystery.

Three reasons appear to me to have prevented the primitive tradition from retracing the sojourns of Jesus at Jerusalem: a reason of *prudence*, a reason derived from *the difficulty* of the subject, and a third from its lack *of utility* at the time when the tradition was formed.

1. The oral tradition, formulated at Jerusalem under

the eyes and with the participation of the apostles, had to have regard to the persons still living, who had played a part, and especially a part favourable to Jesus, during His sojourns in that city. The Sanhedrin was still reigning despotically, and that a long while after Pentecost. John relates (xii. 10) that that body was deliberating not only to put Jesus to death, but also to get rid of Lazarus, because many were believing on Jesus because of him. We can understand then how important it was for the security of Martha and Mary, who, at Bethany, were immediately under the power of the rulers, to be as much as possible left in obscurity by the oral tradition. They are also not named in the account of the anointing at Bethany (Matt. xxvi. 6–13 and Mark xiv. 3–9), where both accounts only mention the house of Simon the leper; and when Luke speaks of them (x. 38 and fol.), he no doubt names them, but omits the name of the place where they dwelt, and says vaguely: "in a certain village (*εἰς κώμην τινά*)," while it could not be guessed from his account whether it was in Judea or in Galilee. The same is the case with the name of the disciple who had struck with the sword at Gethsemane. It is omitted in the three synoptic accounts, no doubt because they took care not to name Peter in the oral tradition, in order not to expose that apostle to a judicial inquiry. But when John, writing much later, after the destruction of Jerusalem and far from Palestine, composed his account, he could speak more openly than the primitive narrative had done, and relate in detail all that concerned the family of Bethany, the armed intervention of the apostle, and many other events besides that had occurred at Jerusalem, like the healing of the impotent man at Bethesda and the man born blind. Thus is explained in particular the most surprising omission, that of the resurrection of Lazarus, on which it was especially important to keep silence, so long as the omnipotence of the Sanhedrin threatened the persons directly concerned in this miracle, who could bear witness to it in the most convincing manner.

2. Yet another reason must have co-operated towards the omission of the sojourns at Jerusalem from the tradition, namely, the great difficulty there was in reproducing discourses so lofty as those that Jesus had held in presence of the doctors at Jerusalem, for instance that reported in the fifth chapter of John, or discussions so animated as those related in chaps. vii. and viii., x. and xii. of the same gospel. There was perhaps only one apostle, and certainly not one evangelist, who could have conscientiously sought to reproduce before the people such struggles and discourses. This remark even applies to mere historical narratives, like the lively scene of the appearing of the man born blind before the Sanhedrin, or the conversations with the two sisters of Lazarus before the latter was raised from the dead. How great the difficulty to include these things, without alteration, in a public narrative destined to be a hundred times repeated! But above all, how could such a task be undertaken, when it concerned the intimate conversations of Jesus with the disciples in the last evening of His life (John xiv.–xvii.)!

3. Lastly, supposing the attempt had been made, despite the feeling of insufficiency that behoved to stop each one, can one imagine how such accounts could have been understood and appreciated by believers hardly clear of a legal Judaism or a gross paganism? The contents of the fourth gospel suppose Christians already arrived at a certain degree of personal maturity, and partaking in some measure of the state to which the apostles were found raised after the two or three years that they had spent in intimacy with Jesus. To throw words like those of the fourteenth and fifteenth chapters of John, or the prayer of chap. xvii., into the oral tradition of the first times would have been not only useless but dangerous. In place of attracting the crowds, they would have been thereby fatigued and wearied. We have, it seems to me, the proof of it in the fact that the Synoptics, after having all three related the multiplication of the loaves, pass over also all three in silence the great discourse re-

ported in John vi., that Jesus held on the morrow at Capernaum. The sight of the preceding miracle, and the personal presence of Jesus, could alone give to that discourse a sufficient authority with that multitude; and yet many even among the ordinary hearers of Jesus could not hear it to the end. What would it have been with those to whom the first evangelisation was addressed! With the least reflection one can easily understand that the popular evangelisation of the first days of the Church had rather to be fed with the varied, touching, interesting, easily grasped scenes of the Galilean life that fill the Synoptics, than with the scenes of ardent struggle and violent discussion that had filled the sojourns at Jerusalem.—There is in this common omission, it seems to me, a fact of the highest importance for the explanation of the origin of the Synoptics.

The second not less grave error with which our gospel is charged is the contradiction that must exist between its account and John's regarding the *day of Christ's death*. After John, in effect (comp. xiii. 1, 29, xviii. 28, xix. 31), Jesus was crucified on the 14th of Nisan, the day on which the lamb was slain in the afternoon, and when the paschal meal was celebrated in the evening. After Matthew and the two other Synoptics, as we have already said, one is, on the contrary, led to admit that the death of Jesus only took place on the morrow, in the afternoon of the 15th Nisan, the great Sabbatic day that opened the paschal week.

I have briefly set forth (p. 220) what seems to me to have been the real course of things as regards the last supper of Jesus; I may, I think, refer for fuller details to my *Commentaries on John and Luke* (John, 3rd ed. vol. iii. pp. 287–307; Luke, 3rd ed. vol. ii. pp. 344–346), where the causes are developed that, if there really was a discrepancy, would decide the question in favour of John's account. What remains for me to explain here is the lack of clearness that strikes one in the synoptic accounts. These accounts by no means affirm, as is usually believed, that the conversation of Jesus with the disciples on the place where the repast had to be prepared took place only on the morning of the 14th Nisan, which would, it is true, render our explanation impossible. And, on the other hand, no more do they expressly affirm, I admit, that this conversation and the repast that followed it took place on the evening of the previous day, which would remove the discord with John. But the circumstances of the time require this supposition. For Clement of Alexandria informs us in a piece preserved by the *Chronicon paschale*, that everyone took steps to make sure of a place *from the 13th*, a day that had for this reason received the name of *προετοιμασία*, that is to say, *pre-preparation* (the day of the *preparation properly so called* being the 14th, when the removal of the leaven took place). When the three writers then say: "on the first day of unleavened bread," or, as Luke says: "the day of unleavened bread came," nothing prevents us from applying these expressions to the evening of the 13th, and even when Luke adds: "when the Passover must be slain," the sense is forced, for if he had wished to speak of the evening of the 14th, he ought to have said: "when *they ate* the lamb (slain in the afternoon)." What can be charged against the synoptic account is not having expressed itself positively enough on this point. Perhaps it must even be allowed that a certain confusion took place in the tradition, and may have influenced this account. As, in celebrating His last supper on the evening of the 13th, Jesus had conformed to several rites of the paschal supper that the people kept on the evening of the 14th, and for which He would substitute the new repast of the Lord's Supper, perhaps there was introduced a confusion between these two so similar repasts, and that the more easily as of both it could be said that they had taken place on the evening of the 14th, that is to say, the evening of the 13–14 according to Jewish speech (as regards the repast of Jesus), and the evening of the 14–15 according to our Western speech (as regards the national repast of the Passover).[1] From this may have arisen a confusion of ideas that has influenced the form of the tradition recorded in our Synoptics.

There remain *certain details* contained in the account of the burial and the resurrection of Jesus, which are sometimes turned into ridicule; thus the guard placed at the tomb by the Jews, who on the evening of the execution had allowed the body to be laid in Joseph's tomb, and only on the morrow, perceiving the danger to which they were exposed, request Pilate to set a guard on the tomb. He consents to it, saying to them with a touch of irony: "Go, keep it safely, as you know how to do." For my part, I see nothing in all that but what is very natural. At the moment of the death, quite intoxicated with their triumph, they had not thought of taking any precaution; they only think of it on the morrow. "We have remembered (ἐμνήσθημεν)," they say themselves, to explain this tardy demand. For his part Pilate, who had performed for them so great an act of compliance as regards the main point, could not refuse them this insignificant service that they came yet to ask of him. As regards the attempt to corrupt the keepers, when once the resurrection had occurred, and the precaution taken had turned to the contrary effect, it is certain that the Jews must have sought at any price to neutralise the consequences of this overwhelming result; and the more absurd the means are they employ for this end, the alleged sleep of the keepers, since, if real, it would only aggravate their fault, the better does it prove the desperate state to which the Jewish cause found itself reduced by the unforeseen course of things. That is all the author wished to say, and there is nothing here but what is very sensible. The promise made to the soldiers to exempt them from punishment by gaining over

[1] The expressions *érev hasschabbath*, evening of the Sabbath, and *érev happésach*, evening of the Passover, mean in Hebrew the evening of *the day before* the Sabbath or the Passover, but in our Western speech, the evening of the very day of the Sabbath or the Passover.

Pilate is not incompatible with what we know of the character of his administration. The account of the appearance of the angel descending from heaven to roll away the stone, and then sitting on it as on a throne, has something a little theatrical, and differs from the simplicity of the appearances of angels in the other gospels. Meyer calls this feature legendary: the epithet poetic might have sufficed. Here is one of the points where one perhaps recognises the hand of the disciple of the apostle.

Altogether, with the exception of this feature and perhaps some inaccuracies of detail, which I have instanced, in the course of this gospel narrative, and if we set aside facts that are only assailed by reason of their supernatural character, I do not think one meets in this gospel anything at all that could render doubtful the truth of its account. The style is, on the whole, without a shade of emphasis, absolutely simple and precise, of a constantly sustained dignity, whether as regards the substance or the form; and as regards the words put in the mouth of the Lord, their sanctity remains without the least default, on the level of Him who behoved to have pronounced them.

What ought to be chiefly admired is the absence of any obtrusion of the personality of the author in his account, his complete annihilation, if I may so say, in presence of Him whose activity he retraces. Those are features of sincerity which science may sometimes ignore, but in which plain common sense will always be interested and will confide without reserve. It is in consequence of this uprightness of the plain natural conscience that the gospel has been believed in the world, not in consequence of scientific demonstrations. The apologetic of the Apostle Philip: *Come and see!* will remain good to the end, and in presence of this gospel picture every serious reader will always feel himself constrained to subscribe to this famous saying: "Here is a history the inventor of which would be greater than the hero."

## VI

### Traditional Data

In the first chapter I have set forth the manner in which the collection of our four gospels was formed, and to this end have indicated the traces of the progressive use of these writings, as they are contained in the patristic declarations. In the present chapter, which specially concerns the first gospel, I began by treating the questions relative to the composition of this writing, setting out from the indications contained in the book itself, before consulting the data of tradition. But it is important, before closing, still to state rapidly the declarations of the Fathers on this subject.

In formulating the result of the period that elapsed till the appearance of the entirely formed gospel collection in Justin and Tatian, I have avoided the use of the term *canonisation*, because, as I have explained pp. 93–100, this word seems to me to suggest the false idea of an ecclesiastical decision that had conferred on these four books the special authority they enjoy in the Church. If a decision of this importance had taken place, history would have preserved some trace of it. But neither Irenæus, nor Clement of Alexandria, nor Origen, nor Eusebius insists on any other source of authority for these writings than the tradition that transmitted them to the Church as proceeding from the apostolic circle. The very decided distinction between these four writings and the numerous analogous writings was not then the effect of an official act; it naturally resulted from the growing consideration that the Church accorded to these writings, as much by reason of their known and traditionally attested apostolic origin as by the immediate perception of their own value. This perception was powerfully strengthened by the comparison made of these writings with the rival accounts, proceeding from sources generally unknown and so little worthy of their subject. What has been called the canonisation of our gospels, their admission to the exclusive authority that has been conferred on them in the Church, was less a real elevation than their maintenance at the height of their primitive dignity, while all the others more and more lost the credit they had momentarily enjoyed in some churches, till they were at last almost totally forgotten.

We shall only here mention a certain number of traditional data specially concerning the first gospel.

The first trace of the use of the *Book of the Logia* seems to me to occur in the Epistles of Paul, and that in one of the epistles of the first group (1 Thess.), as well as in two of the second (1 Cor., Rom.); all written, in my view, from the year 52 to the year 59 (according to Harnack's *Chronologie*, from the year 48 to the year 53).

We have found, in the second place, this writing used in the Epistle of James, about 62 (according to Harnack, between 120 and 130 or 140).

In the third place, in the Apocalypse, about 95 (according to Harnack, from 93 to 96).

Our *first canonical gospel* seems to me to be quoted for the first time (conjointly with Luke) in the Epistle of Clement of Rome, about 95 (Harnack, from 93 to 97).—See p. 28.

It is quoted as well in the so-called *Epistle of Barnabas*, written probably at Alexandria (about 95 according to Hilgenfeld; from 130 to 131 after Harnack).—See pp. 28 and 29.

Matthew is quoted a great number of times in the *Didaché*, composed about the year 100 at the eastern extremity of the Church, if I am not mistaken (Harnack, 131 to 160).—See pp. 38–45.

A gospel similar to our Matthew was that exclusively made use of by the ancient *Judæo-Christian communities*, who possessed it under the title of the Gospel *according to the Hebrews.* According to Epiphanius, the Judæo-Christian gnostic *Cerinthus* (*Hær.* xxviii.) was their principal representative. An adversary of the Apostle Peter at Jerusalem, he must have lived and wrought later in Asia (*ibid.* c. 1), as adversary of the Apostle John at Ephesus. He availed himself of the beginning of our gospel to prove, by means of the genealogy, that Jesus was naturally born of Joseph and Mary. This opinion Epiphanius attributes as well to the Egyptian Judæo-Christian *Carpocrates*, who lived a little later. Other members of the same party, however, appear to have used a simpler means of getting rid of the miraculous birth of Jesus. This was to make the gospel begin with iii. 1 (the account of the coming of John the Baptist), and to suppress the first two chapters.

*Ignatius*, between 107 and 115 (Harnack, 110–117), several times quotes our gospels.—See pp. 41–45.

*Polycarp* as well; the passages of Matthew quoted by him are these: v. 3, 7, 10, vii. 1, 2, xxvi. 41.

All these quotations testify only to the existence and the general use of our gospel, as well as the authority it enjoyed in the churches from the first half of the second century; but they tell us nothing about its *origin*. It is otherwise with the following passage:

*Papias*, about the year 120 (Harnack says, between 145 and 160), relates, probably on the testimony of the presbyter John, that "Matthew composed the Logia in the Hebrew language (ἑβραΐδι διαλέκτῳ)." Did he mean by this expression Hebrew in the proper sense of the word, as Resch thinks, or the popular language of Palestine, Aramean, according to the more generally received opinion? Then, did the term Logia denote in his thought a complete gospel, as the Church has generally understood it, or only *the discourses* of Jesus, as many since Schleiermacher admit, and as I think? These questions are at present rather raised than determined.—See pp. 48–55 and pp. 185–189.

*Basilides*, at Alexandria, about 125, makes use of our gospel. He is the first to apply to our canonical writings the name of *gospels* (εὐαγγέλια). He quotes them with the formula: *That which is said* (τὸ λεγόμενον).—See pp. 45–48.

*Valentinus*, at Rome (according to Harnack, from 145 to 185), uses Matthew as well as the other gospels.—See pp. 55 and 56.

The Athenian philosopher *Aristides* (according to Harnack,

between 138 and 147), without expressly naming any of the gospels, speaks of these books as of a collection already formed and known.—See pp. 57 and 58.

Lastly, our canonical collection appears positively in *Justin*, who speaks of it as of a work known under the name of *Memoirs of the Apostles.* He does not, doubtless, use it exclusively; but the use he makes of it is such that it is impossible to mistake its identity with our four canonical gospels. Besides, Justin, so far from claiming to have himself formed this collection, declares that he had found it diffused and publicly read in the cities and the country, doubtless on repairing from Nablous, his native place, to Rome (about the year 140).—See pp. 62–72.

After him *Tatian*, his disciple, affixes in some sort the seal on the gospel collection, by combining the four accounts into a single and consecutive narrative. He calls his writing *Diatessaron*, a title that signifies "composed by means of four."—He wrote about 170.—See pp. 72–76.

The *Clementine Homilies*, a gnostico-Judaising romance, dating from nearly the same time, frequently quote Matthew, even though the heretical party whence this book proceeds was strongly opposed to the doctrine of the Church.—See p. 77.

*Muratori's Fragment*, which probably dates from the same epoch and contains the oldest known list of the writings of the New Testament, presents at the beginning a gap, which involves the omission of the indication of the Gospels of Matthew and Mark; but the mention of them is evidently supposed by all that follows.—See pp. 77–91.

Hitherto the tradition has only spoken to us of the *author* and the original *language* of our gospel; with Irenæus it takes a further step, and shows us approximately *the date* of its composition.

For *Irenæus* (about 185; Harnack, 181–189) the question of the quadruple gospel is definitively closed. This Father attests, like all his predecessors, the composition of our first gospel in the Hebrew language; then he fixes the composition of it at the epoch of the sojourn of Paul and Peter at Rome, which leads us to the year 64. This date coincides with that which has seemed to us to emerge from the gospel itself, in particular from the passage xxiv. 15.—See pp. 5–22 and 91, 92.

*Eusebius*, in mentioning (*H. E.* vi. 17) among the translators of the Old Testament a certain *Symmachus*, an Ebionite Judæo-Christian, attributes to him a work entitled *Memoirs*, in which he specially treated of the Gospel of Matthew. The expression that Eusebius uses (*ἀποτείνεσθαι πρός*) has sometimes been understood in this sense that Symmachus had opposed our gospel. But this explanation seems to me improbable enough, since the Gospel of Matthew was the only one admitted by the Judæo-Christians. And if that was the meaning, Jerome must have very ill understood the expression of Eusebius, as he says (*De Vir. ill.* c. 54) that Symmachus wrote *Commentaries on the Gospel of Matthew* by which (*de quo*) he seeks to confirm his own doctrine. This passage proves that our first gospel was peculiarly in honour at this epoch in the Judæo-Christian communities.[1]

About 190, *Serapion*, bishop of Antioch, interdicts in the parish of Rhossus the use of the pretended Gospel of Peter, for the reason "that it is not of the number of the gospels that have been transmitted to us"; and, about 200, *Clement of Alexandria* thinks that authority cannot be attributed to the Gospel of the Egyptians, "seeing it is not of the number of the four that have been transmitted to us."—See p. 92. These expressions of which the two Fathers make use seem to me to confirm what I said just now on the spontaneity of the mode of the canonisation of the Gospels.

About 230, *Origen* declares (Eus. *H. E.* vi. 25) that what he has learned from tradition is that "the former toll-collector Matthew, having become an apostle, published the first gospel in the Hebrew language (*γράμμασιν ἑβραϊκοῖς*) for those that had believed from the pale of Judaism."

[1] Comp. Resch, *Paralleltexte zu den Evangelien*, 2tes Heft, 1894, pp. 5 and 6.

We again find this same affirmation on the original language in which the first gospel was composed, in all the subsequent Fathers; and first in 325, in *Eusebius* (*H. E.* iii. 24), who says besides, as regards the *time* of composition, that it took place "when Matthew, after having preached to the Hebrews, prepared to go to preach to other peoples, in order to leave to those whom he was quitting a recompense for his absence." This indication would lead to the years preceding the year 59, when the dispersion of the apostles was, according to the Acts (chap. xxi.), an accomplished fact. This date would be a little anterior to that of Irenæus (in 64); it would relate rather to the book of the Logia, as well as the indication of Hebrew as the original language of Matthew's writing.

*Cyril* of Jerusalem, in 348, in his catechetic writing; *Epiphanius*, about 374 (*Hær.* xxx. 3); *Augustine*, in 400, in the *Consensus evangel.* c. 1–4, all agree in affirming the composition of the first gospel in the Hebrew language.

We come lastly to Jerome, who wrote before and after the year 400, and whose report is much the most important; for he does not merely repeat, like his predecessors, what has been transmitted to him, but claims to have had himself in his hands the Aramean original of our canonical Matthew, and even to have copied and translated it into Greek and Latin.

During a solitary sojourn that this Father made at Chalcis, in Cœle-Syria, or *Hollow Syria* (the name of the great valley that separates the two chains of Lebanon on the north of Palestine), in the years 374–379, he had knowledge of a copy of the Aramean gospel used by a community of Judæo-Christians called *Nazarenes*, and inhabiting Berœa, now Aleppo, a day's journey north from Chalcis. This name Nazarenes, that originally designated all the Christians, remained attached to the Judæo-Christian portion of the Church that came nearest to apostolic Christianity. "They differ," says Epiphanius (*Hær.* xxix. 1), "both from the Jews and the Christians;—from the Jews, in that they believe in Christ; from the Christians, in that they remain attached to the

Judaic rites, such as circumcision, the Sabbath, and the other ceremonies. Their principal seat is the city of Berœa; they also inhabit Decapolis, in the environs of Pella and Batanea and Chocab. Their origin dates from their departure from Jerusalem, when the believers left that city before the siege, in conformity with the warning of the Lord. Thus began their sojourn in Perea." What distinguished them from other more rigid Judæo-Christians was that, while observing the law, they did not claim, any more than the apostles, to impose it on the believing Gentiles. This is how Jerome expresses himself on the find that he made among them, in his writing *De Vir. ill.* 3 (in 392): "Matthew first composed in Judea a gospel in Hebrew letters and words (*litteris verbisque hebracis*) for those of the circumcision that had believed. It is not known who translated it into Greek. The Hebrew writing itself (*ipsum hebraïcum*) is preserved to this day in the library of Cæsarea, that the martyr Pamphilus formed with great care. With the permission of the Nazarenes that inhabit Berœa in Syria, and who make use of this writing, I have been able to take a copy of it (*mihi describendi facultas fuit*)." In his *Commentary on Matthew* (xii. 13), written in 398, he even speaks of the Greek and Latin translation that he has recently made of this writing, which, he says, "*is called by most* the authentic Matthew." Lastly, in his writing *against the Pelagians*, in 415, he expresses himself thus (iii. 1): "In the Gospel according to the Hebrews, which is written in the *Chaldee* and *Syriac* language, but in Hebrew characters (*chaldaïco quidem syroque sermone, sed hebraïcis litteris*), a gospel of which the Nazarenes make use down to the present day, [which is] the gospel *according to the apostles*, or, *as the most presume* (*sicut plerique autumant*), *according to Matthew*, which is still to be found in the library of Cæsarea, the history bears . . ." The fame of this important discovery soon spread and made a sensation. But the news was not favourably received by all, and some among them, particularly *Theodore of Mopsuestia*, accused Jerome of desiring to introduce a fifth gospel.

The question is to know what is the true relation between our first gospel and this gospel that Jerome sometimes says was written in Hebrew, sometimes that it was in the Chaldee and Syriac language, but in Hebrew characters. This problem is so obscure that Zahn only enters on it, saying that "some courage is needed for that" (p. 642), and that Harnack expresses himself thus: "I avow that I have nothing to say on this question, because everything in it is obscure to me" (*Chronol.* p. 694). The opinion of Jerome himself is anything but settled. In the early time after his find, his mode of view is not doubtful; he regards the writing that he has just discovered as the very work of Matthew, written in Aramean, whence it follows that our first gospel is in his view only a translation. He does not doubt this fact, while avowing that, like all the world, he is ignorant of the name of the translator. But, on the other hand, it seems that he himself contradicts this assertion by his mode of acting regarding this book. Why copy it? Why translate it into Greek and Latin, if it was really the Gospel of Matthew, which for at least two centuries was circulating, translated into these two languages, in all the churches? It appears that Jerome, on more closely studying this writing, had not been slow to discover in it greater differences from our Greek Matthew than he had recognised at first. Hence his desire to preserve the text of it, as fitted to interest the Church. In effect, when one peruses the numerous fragments of the Gospel of the Hebrews that are quoted by the Fathers and by Jerome himself, one is greatly struck by these differences. Also, as we have just seen, Jerome expresses himself later less resolutely: "which is called by most," he now says, or, "as most presume." It is possible, no doubt, that he meant thereby to appease a little the rumours at first raised by his too absolute assertion; but it is above all probable that, while continuing to maintain a certain identity between the two writings, he had more and more recognised the differences that distinguish them, and which no longer allowed him to see in them one and the same work.

Was the Gospel of the Hebrews really the original writing whence our canonical Matthew was derived? One may judge of it from the following examples: When His brothers invite Him to come and be baptized by John, Jesus answers: "In what have I sinned that I should go and be baptized by him, unless this word that I said be itself an affair [sin?] *of ignorance?*" After this ambiguous reply, He ends by joining them, at the instigation of His mother.—A fire is kindled in Jordan when Jesus issues from the water, and only at the end of the scene John asks Him to baptize him.—Jesus says, on the occasion of the Temptation (or of the Transfiguration): "My mother, the Holy Spirit, took Me by one of My hairs and transported Me to the great mountain called Tabor."—This is how the man with the withered hand healed by Jesus relates his history: "I was a mason, earning my living by my hands; I pray Thee to restore me my health that I may not shamefully beg my bread."—The rich young man who comes towards Jesus, on hearing what He asked of him, began, it is said, to scratch his head, because that did not please him; then Jesus reminds him: "that many of his brethren, sons of Abraham, are badly clothed and dying of hunger, while his own house is crowded with goods, and nothing goes out of it for them."—James, the brother of Jesus, who had, it seems, been present at the Lord's Supper with the disciples, had sworn that he would eat no more from the moment when he had drunk the cup of the Lord (it has been tried, but wrongly, to understand: "from the moment when the Lord had drunk the cup of death), until the moment when he should see Him raised up." After His resurrection, Jesus begins by placing the shroud in the hands of the priest's servant, and then goes straight to James. "After which Jesus took bread and blessed it and broke it, and gave it to James the Just, and said to him: My brother, eat thy bread, because the Son of Man is risen from the dead."—On reading such passages, can one really imagine, as Hilgenfeld and, to a certain extent, Zahn (*Gesch. des Kan.* ii. p. 707) and Harnack (*Chronol.* pp. 648–50) do, that the writing that contained them was the primary source of our canonical gospel? This would be to say, contrary to what history teaches, that the narrative has proceeded from the artificial to the simple, from the grotesque to the noble, from the magical supernatural to the truly moral supernatural, and that the more it has removed from its source, the more it has returned to a holy sobriety. No doubt one cannot dispute tastes; but can common sense really hesitate? Why not acquiesce in the judgment of Holtzmann: "The still existing fragments of this writing (the Gospel according to the Hebrews) bear an incontestably apocryphal character."

Hilgenfeld alleges, to prove the priority of the Gospel of the Hebrews, the two following passages. In the Lord's Prayer that gospel makes Jesus say: "Give us this day the bread *of to-morrow* (in Hebrew *machar*)"; and he thinks that is the true explanation of the Greek term ἐπιούσιος (wrongly translated in our versions by the word *daily*). This Greek word would be derived from ἡ ἐπιοῦσα (ἡμέρα), the day that follows, and would signify "the bread of the morrow." But this contrast between *to-day* and *to-morrow* in this prayer is somewhat strained, and, whatever may be said of it, this preoccupation with to-morrow's bread does not agree with the spirit of the injunction: "Take no thought for the morrow." It is more natural to make the opposite supposition, and to see in the *machar* of the Hebrew gospel an attempt to render the meaning of the Greek word ἐπιούσιος, which, being an unused term, might easily be misunderstood. As Zahn himself remarks, one does not understand, if the word *machar* was the original, how the Greek translator, in place of simply rendering it by τοῦ αὔριον, *of the morrow*, should have had to seek so obscure and unusual a term as ἐπιούσιος.—The other passage alleged by Hilgenfeld is that where our gospel by mistake designates Zachariah, killed in the court of the temple, as the son of Barachiah (Matt. xxiii. 35). The Gospel of the Hebrews, on the contrary, calls him more correctly *son of Jehoiada*; comp. 2 Chron. xxiv. 20–22. Hilgenfeld thinks that the author of our Greek

Matthew *wrongly* sought to correct his model, the Hebrew gospel, after Zechariah i. 1, where the prophet of this name, the post-exilic Zechariah, is designated the *son of Barachiah.* But where is mention made of the murder of this second Zechariah, and that "between the temple and the altar"? It is much more natural to think that it was the author of the Gospel of the Hebrews who corrected the mistake committed by Matthew or avoided it, if he did not know it.

The entirely opposite opinion, according to which the Gospel of the Hebrews would be a free reproduction or even a translation of our canonical Matthew, has been maintained by numerous and eminent critics, who defend the originality of our canonical gospel; so Hug, Reuss, Harless, Ritschl, etc. Only it is difficult in that case to explain the unanimous testimony of the Fathers, who all declare that Matthew wrote in Hebrew (Aramean). It is answered, indeed, that they only repeat the affirmation of Papias. But did that Father enjoy such credit that a line of his would have settled the general opinion, including the Alexandrians themselves, who were not likely to be disposed to much credulity towards a millenarian like Papias? It is, besides, far from probable that the teachings of Jesus had been drawn up in the first place in a different language from that in which He Himself had spoken them. And, besides, there occur in the later testimonies features going beyond the report of Papias; thus the date of the composition of Matthew in Irenæus and the account of the finding of this writing in Southern Asia by Pantænus (p. 119, note). Such facts are independent of the account of Papias.

But how, if the Gospel of the Hebrews is not the source of our Greek Matthew, and if, nevertheless, tradition affirms that the latter proceeded from an Aramean writing, how, I say, are we to explain the close relation which, after the testimony of Jerome, must have existed between the Gospel of the Hebrews and our canonical Matthew? Several critics have recourse to the hypothesis of a common source.

Thus Zahn thinks that, in conformity with the tradition,

the Apostle Matthew drew up a complete Aramean gospel (not merely a collection of Logia), and that this writing, after having undergone numerous transformations, became the Gospel of the Hebrews adopted by the Judæo-Christian communities, and found at Berœa by Jerome, while, on the other hand, the same apostolic writing had been maintained in a much more faithful manner in the Church, and has been preserved to us in the Greek translation presented by our canonical Matthew.

Meyer, who is of our opinion that the Aramean writing of Matthew was not a complete gospel, but a collection of Logia, allows that this writing, adopted by the Judæo-Christian communities, was there soon completed by an entire gospel narrative, written in the same Aramean language, that it underwent numerous alterations by curtailments or additions in conformity with the peculiar ideas of those churches, while, on the other hand, faithfully translated into Greek, it became our first canonical gospel.

On both these suppositions, it would always then be the Aramean gospel that, anterior to its subsequent alterations, had served as primary source for our Matthew.

Harnack declines to formulate a positive result; he confines himself to bringing out some points that appear to him the limits of the obscurity in which this subject is still enveloped (*Chronol.* p. 694): 1st, Antiquity does not know two Hebrew gospels, but one only; 2nd, our canonical Matthew, without being the translation of an Aramean original, proceeds from a source whose Hebrew origin can be demonstrated as probable; 3rd, our Greek Matthew touches much more nearly than the two other Synoptics the Gospel of the Hebrews, which, despite this resemblance, remains with reference to Matthew an independent writing, in no way secondary; 4th, the fragments of the Gospel of the Hebrews that we possess do not exclude the possibility that that writing is the source of our canonical gospel.—He dates the composition of the Gospel of the Hebrews in the period 70–100.

As Harnack admits that we have here in a great measure

a matter of impression, I shall boldly state the one that, in proportion as I have considered this question, has always grown stronger in me, namely, that the Gospel of the Hebrews, as we know it from the fragments quoted by the Fathers, must have been, not the source of our Matthew, but, on the contrary, an altering and a free reproduction, in the Aramean language and in Hebrew characters, of our canonical Matthew. The latter, we have seen, must have been composed between 60 and 66. That was nearly the time of the emigration of the Judæo-Christian Church to the east of the Jordan, into the regions of Batanea and Perea. The Christians of Jewish origin might very well bring with them either the collection of the Logia, composed before 60, or even the Greek Matthew dating from before 66. But this last writing, the language of which was more or less strange to them, could not long suffice them. They must soon, then, have reproduced it in Aramean, introducing into it the Logia already written in that language. This work must have been done, it seems to me, at the epoch indicated by Harnack, between 70 and 100. But it is in the nature of things that the ancient Judæo-Christian Church, the nucleus of primitive Christendom, would not wish to place itself in absolute and immediate dependence on a Greek writing like our first gospel. Those who undertook the task of reproducing it in Aramean sought then to show themselves independent of that model, and to insert in their work new features fitted to attest the originality of it. Besides, it concerned them to adapt the Greek writing to their peculiar ideas, and to remove from it several things that seemed shocking to them, and then to give to certain persons like the brothers of Jesus, who had a high position among them, in particular to James the Just, their venerated leader, more prominence than they had in our gospel, where they only played an obscure part. If one takes account of these natural intentions, one will easily understand the different peculiarities that distinguish the accounts of the Gospel of the Hebrews from those of Matthew, and which produce on some modern critics the deceptive impression of originality. Let us examine more closely some of the fragments quoted above.

And first the account of the *baptism*. Let us notice, 1st, the part attributed to the brothers of Jesus, who seek to draw their brother with them to John's baptism; then the equivocal reply of Jesus, which is a mere evasion, and does not at all resemble His true language, always frank and clear. The author dare not make Him openly affirm either His absolute holiness or His sin. Besides, who can believe that it was Mary that decided Jesus to a step so decisive as that of going to the baptism of John the Baptist? 2nd, The little lesson on biblical theology that God deems necessary to give to Jesus on the action of the Holy Spirit in all the prophets, at the moment when He reveals to Him what He is for Him, seems to me absolutely out of place. 3rd, The transposing after the baptism the conversation of John with Jesus, and his request to be baptized by Him, is evidently an attempt to solve the difficulty presented by John's request, placed as it is in Matthew before the divine manifestation. 4th, The last words in the gospel of the Hebrews: "Thus it is fitting that all be fulfilled" are certainly a free imitation of these words of Matthew's account: "Thus it becometh us to fulfil all righteousness."

Was it to the *Temptation* or to the *Transfiguration*, that the saying of Jesus referred: "My mother, the Holy Spirit, took Me by one of My hairs and transported Me to the mountain called *Tabor*"? However that may be, how can we ignore the fantastic and legendary character of this view: Jesus suspended in the air by a hair in the hand of the Holy Spirit, *His mother*! No doubt it has been sought thus to correct Matt. iv. 8: "The devil took Him to a high mountain . . ." Was it possible to do it in a more ridiculous manner?

We have already spoken of the form of the *fourth petition of the Lord's Prayer*: "Give us this day to-morrow's bread." Who does not feel that there is something affected in this opposition between the terms *to-day* and *to-morrow*, and how little conformable to the spirit and the words of Jesus is this preoccupation with the morrow!

The little speech put into the mouth of *the man with his right hand withered*, whose profession the author would give himself the air of having known, produces the effect of a silly enough paraphrase, introduced at little cost into the simple gospel narrative.

The reproach addressed by Jesus to the *rich young man* as if he had been a *bad* rich man after the fashion of the one in the parable, is without motive, and the homily on charity that He addresses to him is entirely out of place. How could Jesus affirm that nothing had ever proceeded from the house of that rich youth for the relief of the poor? He allows him, on the contrary, to have hitherto fulfilled all that the law prescribed, consequently also the duty of beneficence. According to Mark, after having heard the frank affirmation of the young man, He even views him with a look full of love; and He had only seen in him at the same time a vile egotist!

In the parable of the *talents*, the author, no doubt finding the penalty, inflicted according to Matthew on the servant who buried his talent, too severe, transforms him into a spendthrift who has squandered the sum intrusted to him by living in debauchery. He thinks thus to strengthen the application of the parable, and he weakens it. He does not understand that, for one man that sins by the abuse of his gifts there are ten who fail to utilise them very respectably and by mere indifference! And this the most numerous class was to be forgotten!

The account of the *appearance to James* is remarkable in several respects. First, in bringing in the priest's servant, to whom Jesus delivers the shroud with which He is covered on leaving the sepulchre, this account evidently supposes the presence of the keepers at the tomb, of which Matthew and Matthew alone speaks. Then the account implies something absolutely false, the presence of James at the last repast and his participation in the Lord's Supper, as if he were one of the apostles. Lastly, this appearance to James is placed before all the others, at the very moment of the resurrection, while Paul, who enumerates the appearances in their precise order, assigns to this one the fourth place (1 Cor. xv. 7), and the other Synoptics do not speak of it. One sees in all these features the very clear intention of the Gospel of the Hebrews to glorify James and to show that Jesus had accorded him a preponderating place; Jesus also recalls (certainly by anticipation) his surname of James *the Just*, and addresses him with the honourable appellation: "James, My brother!" It was very needful to give prominence to the recognised head of the Judæo-Christian Church, left in the background in the gospel.

We have spoken above of the breaking of the beam substituted for the rending of the veil, and think we have indicated the deliberate reason for this change (pp. 238, 239).

I omit other features that lead to the same result, and only add yet one important saying which, according to Hilgenfeld (*Adnotationes ad evang. secundum Hebræos*, p. 22),[1] was quoted in the tract *Schabbath* of the Talmud as a *saying of the gospel*, and which Hilgenfeld and others think had belonged to the Gospel of the Hebrews: "I am not come to take anything away from the law of Moses, but am come to add something to the law of Moses." This was just the opinion of the moderate Judæo-Christians who specially bore the name of Nazarenes. The gospel was for them a mere perfecting of the law by the addition of the gospel precepts to the commandments of Moses. They thus explained the expression used by Jesus (Matt. v. 17): to fulfil (πληρῶσαι) the law, taking this word in the sense of *to complete*. The form: "I am not come . . ., but I am come . . .," seems quite to prove that the Judæo-Christian gospel has appropriated this saying of Jesus after its manner.

I cannot help noticing here a curious enough circumstance: The word *but* (ἀλλά), in the passage of Matthew, recurs in the Aramean passage quoted in the Talmud in

[1] In his *Novum Testamentum extra canonem receptum.*

the form אִלָא (*ala*), which seems to be an imitation of the Greek term. I know neither Aramean nor Talmudic Hebrew, and cannot consequently judge of the value of this fact; I must confine myself to noticing it. In any case, if this passage is derived from the Nazarene gospel, it seems to me to leave no doubt of the secondary character of that writing.

This rapid review of the known fragments of that gospel renders completely impossible in my view the alleged priority of that writing with reference to our canonical Matthew. Men may speak of a certain relative independence of the former: that is conceivable, though with difficulty; but for my part, I only see in what is alleged as a reason for this judgment a certain cleverness in the author, who sought to give his writing an appearance of originality. So far from succeeding, he has done nothing, in all the instances quoted, but betray every time his part of amplifier, sometimes very silly, sometimes clever enough to serve the interests of his party.

The opinion I here express has been defended by de Wette, Delitzsch, Bleek, and many others; I have already quoted Holtzmann. Anger considers that "in the things in which the Gospel of the Hebrews differs from Matthew, it most frequently presents an undoubtedly derived form." Volkmar, in *Religion Jesu*, etc., p. 407, expresses himself thus: "All the fragments of the Gospel of the Hebrews that we possess betray their secondary origin in relation to the Gospel of Matthew." Strauss, in *Das Leben Jesu für das deutsche Volk*, 1864, gives this judgment: "It is evident from these passages, bearing to a great extent the imprint of a later tradition, that the Gospel of the Hebrews, so far from being the primitive Matthew, is rather a later adaptation of it." (See in Hilgenfeld himself, *op. cit.* p. 13.)

If this be really so, it is to the Gospel of the Hebrews, and not to that of Matthew, that the interesting chapters of Renan on the composition of the primitive Aramean gospel must be applied (*Les Evangiles*, chaps. iv., v., vi.).

Before quitting this subject, it is fitting to add a word on another Judæo-Christian gospel of which Epiphanius gives an account (*Hær.* xxx.), under the name of the Gospel of the *Ebionites*, and which also bore the name of the Gospel of Matthew. It must then have had some relation to the Gospel of the Nazarenes of which Jerome has spoken. It is easy to show that the latter did not know this writing, any more than Epiphanius knew Jerome's. These two gospels, despite some relation, were distinguished from each other by many features. The name Ebionites, by which Epiphanius denotes the party that used this latter one, was for him the name of a party of Jewish Christians very different from those that Jerome calls Nazarenes. They were not content with observing the law, circumcision, the Sabbath, etc., for themselves; they claimed also to impose them on the believing Gentiles. Their doctrine was partly gnostic, similar enough to that of the author of the *Clementine Homilies* at Rome. Their Christ was an archangel descending from heaven from time to time; it was he who had appeared in Adam, then anew in Jesus with the body of Adam in which He had been crucified. Besides the Gospel of Matthew, they used Luke's; for they spoke of the age of thirty years as the time when Jesus had begun His ministry; they regarded John the Baptist as being of the race of Aaron, having as parents Zacharias and Elisabeth (Epiph., xxx. 13). In several respects they came near to the Essenes, condemning like them bloody sacrifices and animal food, and requiring the frequent use of the bath. It was doubtless in consequence of their vegetarianism that in mentioning John the Baptist's food, their gospel substituted for the locusts of which Matthew speaks (ἀκρίδες) the wafers made with honey (ἐγκρίδες) of Ex. xvi. 31. Epiphanius quotes this saying put by their gospel into the mouth of Jesus: "I am come to abolish the sacrifices, and if you cease not to sacrifice, wrath will not remove." This gospel was written in Greek. The apostles, and in particular Matthew, in narrating spoke in it in the first person, like Peter in the *Clementine Homilies* and in the Gospel of Peter. It is doubtless from this circumstance that the name *Gospel of the Twelve Apostles* proceeds, given to it in some of the Fathers, and once applied by Jerome himself to the Gospel of the Nazarenes. This writing only appears to have been composed towards the end of the second century (see Harnack, *Chronologie*). It does not then play any part in the question of the origin of our first gospel.

## Conclusion

Everyone knows that the task of historical criticism regarding a biblical book is to throw as full light as possible on its origin. For this science possesses two kinds of means: 1st, the reports of writers nearest in time to the composition of the book, who have used and mentioned it in their writings; 2nd, the indications that the book itself contains, in which are betrayed the circumstances that controlled the composition of it. When the result of these two orders of indications harmonises, the solution is given, and the highest degree of scientific certainty is attained. But if the results differ, one must either abandon a scientific solution, or seek a hypothesis that reconciles the contradictory data.

The task of science regarding our first gospel is more complex than in the ordinary cases of which we have just spoken. Not only does discord exist in what concerns this book, between patristic information and the internal indications, since the former tell us almost unanimously of a writing composed in Aramean, and we have before us a Greek text. The discord goes still further, for it exists between the very data of each of the two orders. As regards the traditional data, the oldest witness, Papias, informs us, after a witness older still, that Matthew composed *a collection of the discourses* of Jesus, while all the other Fathers attribute to him a complete *gospel*. And, as regards the internal indications, we have seen that some suggest an apostolic origin, while the others are opposed to this view. What can we do in presence of these contradictory elements? It has seemed to me that the surest course in this state of things was to consult first of all the internal indications that are here present before our eyes as an actual fact, and to make use of them as a means of valuation, to judge the worth of the patristic information.

Following this method, we have been able to ascertain two facts positively affirmed by a unanimous tradition and confirmed by the study of the book itself: the one that the Apostle Matthew first composed a *gospel writing*; and the other that he composed it in the language that Jesus spoke, and that was then the language of the people in Palestine, the *Aramean dialect.* On these two points there is agreement between our different means of information.

On the other hand, there are two points regarding which we have had to raise doubts, in the name of internal criticism, on the assertions of tradition, namely: 1st, the affirmation, tacit indeed, but almost unanimously supposed, that the work of the Apostle Matthew is no other than our first canonical gospel, despite what is at the same time affirmed of the language in which Matthew wrote; and that till the fourth century, when Jerome at last rejects this view, and expressly makes our gospel a mere translation; 2nd, the other point, regarding which tradition must appear suspicious, is the opinion of most of the Fathers that Matthew's writing was a complete gospel, while, according to Papias, it was only a collection of discourses; we have seen that our gospel itself furnishes the counter-proof of the view of that Father.

Combining all these facts, so far from harmonious at the first glance, we have been led to the following conclusions that seem to us to reconcile them:

1. The gospel work first composed by Matthew was not a gospel, but a collection of the principal discourses of Jesus.

2. This writing, composed in a language far from accessible to believers not of Palestine, was without delay translated into Greek, and completed by a narrative of the ministry of Jesus, in which it was distributed and preserved for the use of the numerous Greek churches founded by Paul.

3. Nothing then obliges us to interpose any Aramean

gospel, like those supposed by Meyer and Zahn, between the collection of the Logia and our canonical gospel.

4. This last writing legitimately bears the name *Gospel of Matthew*, first by reason of the collection of the Logia of which it remains the depositary, and then in virtue of the influence that the Apostle Matthew personally exercised on the form of the apostolic narrative that is there recorded.

After all this, one may inquire how it comes that this writing so quickly acquired the preponderance in the Church that we find in the Fathers of the end of the first and beginning of the second century (Barnabas, Clemens Romanus, the Didaché, Ignatius, Polycarp, Papias), and that, as Jülicher says, "it is this writing to which is due the type according to which the image of the Christ is to-day engraved in all hearts." The reason of this peculiar influence is doubtless found above all in the presence of the five great discourses that form the nucleus of it, and contain the permanent basis of the teaching of Jesus; but it is found also in the special character of the gospel narrative in which these jewels have been set.

The distinctive character of this narrative seems to me to be the incomparable way in which it sets forth *the greatness* of Him who is the subject of it.

And first, *His personal greatness.* From His birth Jesus bears with Him two extraordinary titles of which His life was to prove the reality, that of *heir* of the throne of David, and that of *performer* of the promise of universal salvation confided to Abraham and his posterity (i. 1). Such are the two dignities with which He comes into the world. And when He leaves it, it is to exchange the earthly throne of David, to which He had the right, but which He renounced, for the divine throne, and to bear a name that, instead of figuring on the list of the kings of Judah, is placed in the formula of baptism between the names of the Father and of the Holy Spirit (chap. xxviii. 18–20). This greatness He was not afraid Himself to proclaim, although He constantly veiled it under an exterior of the deepest humility, saying: "More than Solomon is here" (a purer glory than that king's); and even: "More than the temple is here" (a consecration more real than that of that sacred edifice).

Greatness *in His word.* That voice resembles Ezekiel's resounding over the field where lie the thousands of dry bones, and recalling them to movement and life (John v. 25). This word bursts like a flash of lightning illuminating the darkened element of the religious and moral life of Israel, and for a moment dissipating the darkness diffused in the midst of that people of God by pharisaic formalism and Sadducean materialism. By it is seen all at once disengaged from the temporary and national form in which the moral law had provisionally been enclosed, the ideal of good in its adequate and permanent form, before which progressively all human tribes will bow. Strauss, while quite recognising the progress that the appearing of Jesus has caused the moral conscience of mankind to make, yet charges Him with a certain narrowness on some points: Jesus did not sufficiently understand the importance of commerce and the value of money. But the parable of the talents shows that Jesus did not ignore the useful function of the bank, and that of the unjust steward has no other aim than to explain the true value of money when it is used, not in the service of egoistic and momentary enjoyment or of self-interest, but in the service of the charity that endures for ever and extends its beneficent consequences even to the life to come.

In an unpublished course of lectures on the Bible, in 1866, Ewald spoke the following words, taken down by one of his hearers: "It is when one studies with care the *Logia* of Matthew that one can most vividly imagine the Christ just as He was and just as He spoke. It is there we see His holy figure stand out most clearly from the sombre background of the pharisaic medium in the midst of which He exercised His ministry, and that we can measure all the distance between the spiritual elevation in which He moved, and the moral mediocrity of His surroundings."

Lastly, greatness *in His work.* In creating the Church,

He planted on earth the germ of the divine kingdom. While firmly opposing His definitive work to the preparatory work of the old covenant, and strongly affirming the difference of principle that separates them, He has known how, by force of wisdom, to maintain the profound relation that unites them; and He has thus brought to light the admirable unity of the religious development of mankind. In acting in this way, He has become the centre of history, so that before Him all tends to Him, and after Him all proceeds from Him. In effect, from the Fall all tends to Israel, and in Israel all aspires to Him: the commandments that no one can fulfil without Him, the rites that prefigure Him, the prophecy that awakens the expectation of His advent. Thus, after Him all takes His imprint; every manifestation of human life receives from His Spirit a new impulse, and becomes like a ramification of His life; thought finds in Him an inexhaustible object of meditation and even of speculation; worship possesses in Him an object of adoration that brings the divinity within the range of man and permits him to unite with it; art in all its forms finds in Him an ideal to reproduce in ever new masterpieces; with Him, social economy does not despair of solving, by following His example and obeying His spirit, the grave problems that absorb it, and by the presence of this divine guest at the domestic hearth, family life obtains the union of hearts, the pardon of offences, the appeasement of conflicts and all the treasures of peace. With each believer, lastly, holiness of heart is substituted for merely formal obedience. Such is His work as it has developed in history; it was contained in germ in what the first gospel describes.

Renan has called this writing "the most important book of Christianity"; he has even added: "and the most important that was ever written" (*Les Evang.* pp. 212, 213). Holtzmann and Jülicher repeat this judgment, and associate themselves with it; I would do as much, if the fourth gospel did not exist.

At the time when Jesus was about to go to execution,

He said to His disciples: "The Spirit of truth . . . will glorify Me" (John xvi. 13 and 14). The Spirit of truth, on whom Jesus counted, has not failed in this mission. Under His impulse four writings have been produced, of which one has set forth all the greatness of Jesus, and which might be called His full-length portrait; the second has related His indefatigable activity; the third has described His beneficent compassion; the fourth has consummated the task by recalling and preserving for ever the testimony rendered by Jesus Himself to His essential divinity.

By these four writings, whose simple beauty defies all the fascinations of human art, the divine Agent has discharged His debt to the Crucified One. Even to this hour, in the whole world, as in the private tribunal of each heart that opens to Him, the divine Spirit, by this fourfold gospel, glorifies Jesus and rehabilitates that name that once figured on an instrument of punishment, but is destined gradually to make every human name grow pale.